D0379085

Also Available from Pantheon

READING THE NEWS
A Pantheon Guide to Popular Culture
Robert Karl Manoff and Michael Schudson, EDITORS

WATCHING

TELEVISION

WATCHING
TELEVISION

A PANTHEON GUIDE

TO

POPULAR CULTURE

Todd Gitlin
EDITOR

PANTHEON **B**OOKS
NEW YORK

Compilation, "Looking Through the Screen," and " 'We Build Excitement' "
Copyright © 1986 by Todd Gitlin
"We Keep America on Top of the World" Copyright © 1986 by Daniel C.
Hallin
"Search for Yesterday" Copyright © 1986 by Ruth Rosen
"The Shortcake Strategy" Copyright © 1986 by Tom Engelhardt
"The Look of the Sound" Copyright © 1986 by Pat Aufderheide
"Faking It" Copyright © 1986 by Michael Sorkin
"Deride and Conquer" Copyright © 1986 by Mark Crispin Miller

All rights reserved under International and Pan-American Copyright
Conventions. Published in the United States by Pantheon Books, a division of
Random House, Inc., New York, and simultaneously in Canada by Random
House of Canada Limited, Toronto.

Library of Congress Cataloging-in-Publication Data

Watching television.

    1. Television programs—United States.
I.   Gitlin, Todd.
PN1992.3.U5W38   1987   791.45' 75' 0973   86-12254
ISBN 0-394-54496-X
ISBN 0-394-74651-1

Designed by Robert Bull

Manufactured in the United States of America

98765432

Contents

WATCHING
TELEVISION

Looking Through the Screen

TODD GITLIN

Entertainer, painkiller, vast wasteland, companion to the lonely, white noise, thief of time. . . . What is this thing, this network of social relations, called television? The word, at roots, refers to seeing far. It does happen, at times, that television allows us to see far, bringing images of the unknown into the household, jarring our settled worlds, lifting curtains, letting fresh truths into otherwise closed rooms. Teenagers in the hinterlands discover rock 'n' roll dancing on *American Bandstand;* black Americans unearth their *Roots;* West Germans confront at least a soap-operatic version of the *Holocaust.* But these are singular moments. For the most part, television lets us see only close up: shows us only what the nation already presumes, focuses on what the culture already knows—or more precisely, enables us to gaze upon something the appointed seers think we need or want to know. Television may do private service as a time killer or a baby-sitter; but for the society as a whole, it is the principal circulator of the cultural mainstream.

Two and a half decades after the chairman of the Federal Communications Commission called American TV a "vast wasteland," one hesitates to resurrect a metaphor that instantly—deservedly—

became a cliché. But perhaps this time the cliché won't function to spare us the necessity of thought; rather it should clarify something that has been forgotten, or repressed, as television has made more promises, become more complicated and confusing. A wasteland that grows vaster and apparently more abundant by the year remains a wasteland. Like some primordial swamp, the image-making appliance and its attendant industries spawn new forms—cable, VCRs, big screens, stereo sound. As new channels and new gadgets spin variations on old themes, the newspapers and trade journals fill with booster talk about "revolutions." But even as television becomes television-plus, it remains the national dream factory, bulletin board, fun house mirror for distorted images of our national desires and fears. . . . And yet none of the metaphors seems quite right, because finally television is not quite anything else. It is just —television.

And therefore television bears special watching. It needs criticism and understanding which cut beneath annoyance or apologia. To be seen properly, it has to be seen as the place where force-fields intersect: economic imperatives, cultural traditions, political impositions. For television is not an apparatus invading us from without. Its very technology, like other technologies, emerges from a matrix of commercial interests, within a culture of privatized individuals. And it makes its home comfortably in American history. Alexis de Tocqueville, that most observant Frenchman of a century and a half ago, would have found TV familiar in many ways: American culture, he observed in the 1830s, already was given to comfortable, sensational, mass-produced amusements, "vehement and bold," "untutored and rude," aiming "to stir the passions more than to charm the taste." Television's spectacles have roots in centuries-old myths, just as they recycle and transform them. Television is a screen on which the absurdities and abominations of our politics and morals are displayed in living color.

Most people who watch television are amateur television critics, but few devote much energy to thinking their way into and through the wasteland with care. To do so is supposed to be the business of scholars. And indeed scholars and critics have been inspecting the electronic media for half a century now. The scholarly literature on the mass media in America began in the 1930s by analyzing the content of radio programs, counting words and themes, aiming to flush out hidden messages, subtexts, and mythic meanings in a presumably scientific fashion. The premise, at first, was that the media operated "hypodermically," injecting propaganda into the unsuspecting social bloodstream. But from the viewpoint of post-World War II social science, such suspicions amounted to primitive paranoia. More impressed with the bloodstream's powers of resistance, sociologists of the forties and fifties began to stress the ways in which readers, listeners, and viewers play an active part in deflecting or distorting messages from the press, radio, and later television, in effect "rewriting" the "texts" passed down to them. Overcorrecting a hitherto oversimple thesis, these analysts ended up underplaying the unifying styles and ideological homogeneities of the contemporary media: the ways in which they have agreed, for instance, on the pieties of the consumer society and the neat good/ bad polarities of the cold war. Each approach had, has, its virtues. Yet neither has paid much attention to the stultifying *forms* of popular culture, to the ways in which mass-circulation styles train their audiences to see accordingly and discourage practitioners from making unconventional statements. Moreover, neither has subjected the institutions of mass culture—the networks, studios, newsrooms, boardrooms, advertising agencies—to enough critical scrutiny. Television may fall into traditions and accumulate markets, but neither traditions nor markets automatically crank out the shows; institutions do that.

There have been other approaches to slippery television too. Some scholars, bothered by the refusal of English departments to take television seriously, have tried to equip television with genre pedigrees. Pressed too far, the impulse slips into pure apologia, as if once a program is located within a tradition, it is automatically sanctified, even seen as the repository of "emancipatory" yearnings. Against the belief that anything people watch is thereby in the public good—a belief these seekers after easy emancipation share with Ronald Reagan's FCC chairman—there are censoring campaigns: against TV's treatment of sex (usually from the right) and violence (usually from the left); both varieties of tunnel vision miss the way in which TV reproduces larger ideologies, registers grander fantasies. Meanwhile, the ever lengthening miles of everyday TV criticism—this show is bad, that one better—do not begin to address the relentless quality of television's presence in the nation's living rooms, or the ways in which it embodies the stratagems of broadcasting's proprietors. As long as television is among us, let us at least scrutinize it for what it reveals about our whole society, about the institutions where power is lodged, about the nature of life—including television watching—in the late twentieth century.

The seven original essays in this book were commissioned with a distinct purpose: to try to peer back at the screen and through it, to use it as a window into the industries that crank out the shows and ultimately into American culture as a whole. Their common stance is to take television seriously as a huge social fact without being wowed or neutered by it. Some of the essays are concerned principally with the themes and styles of particular genres (some of them not previously interpreted or even acknowledged); others devote more attention to how the shows are shaped behind the scenes. But several leitmotifs recur. (Having chosen the writers, and more or less the subjects, but having imposed precious few specifications on them, it was interesting to me to watch the same themes and approaches show up—like familiar faces taking shape in darkroom solution.) One fresh result is a common attention to the implications of form and style: pacing, sound, ambience, packaging, the voice in which the viewer is addressed. Second, each essay reveals traces of the ideological amalgam of the Reagan years (which of course predated 1980 and is likely to outlast 1988): Gilded Age attitudes toward business and money; the false populism which flatters the population for its good judgment and passes for democratic; certain ambiguities of freedom and authority; nostalgia aimed at elders, velocity and blankness at the young. Third, most of these pieces observe that the genres are blurring, even collapsing. The news turns to theme songs, coming attractions, rapid-fire cuts; children's shows become extended toy advertisements; one music video segues into what is apparently another—but turns out to be a car commercial. Television, with all its highly touted diversity, seems to be becoming more of a piece, more a set of permutations of a single cultural constant: television, our debased currency. Finally, most of the authors see television as the most popular instance of a distinctively more general "postmodern" attitude—authenticity is passé, criticism has been absorbed into television's "sophisticated" way of telling jokes on itself, and irony only binds the half-willing viewer closer.

Therefore, these essays cohere in a way which is unusual for a collection, especially one whose authors approach the territory from different backgrounds. (The five with university jobs teach in five different departments.) Daniel C. Hallin writes about the entertainment values of network news, and resolves the apparent contradiction that the network news criticizes White House policies yet bolsters the Reagan presidency as a whole. Ruth Rosen takes us beneath the coincidences and melodrama of the soap opera to its deep, stabilizing verities—the underlying ethic of Ronald Reagan's romantic small-town America. In the first substantial analysis of the business and mythos of children's television, Tom Engelhardt examines the new corporate-spawned look—programs as protracted commercials for violent and saccharine toys. Pat Aufderheide writes of the glitz and simulated dreaminess of music video, showing how MTV and its imitators mirror the commodity-mindedness and shifting identities of this shopping-mall age. In the slick images of high-tech car commercials and *Miami Vice,* I find the fast-track manager's attempt to reconcile images of freedom with realities of organization, as well as a blankness of tone, a sleek and otherworldly homelessness that haunts the larger America of manikins, postmodernism, and "Star Wars." Michael Sorkin unearths a new genre, "simulations," ranging from wrestling to Mr. T, lip-synching contests to *The People's Court,* all obscuring the boundaries between the real and the copy, the authentic and the put-on. Mark Crispin Miller discovers a logic in the decline of the sitcom Dad, and sees television's knowing ironies—from Pepsi commercials to *The Cosby Show,* from the evening news to *Knight Rider*—not as enlightenment, but as TV's stratagem for keeping its more "sophisticated" audience hooked.

In diverse ways, the essays show that criticism and analysis, cultural history and industrial dissection, belong to the same enterprise. Beyond simple apologia and jeremiad, each author tries to see

American culture steadily and to see it whole. As television's antennae scan the public's moods and demographics, we watch back, hoping to demonstrate that serious seeing is the highest form of disbelieving.

We Keep America on Top of the World

DANIEL C. HALLIN

*T*he *CBS Evening News* for June 20, 1985, began with the words and image of Allyn Conwell, an American held hostage in Beirut: "I am speaking on behalf of my fellow forty hostages, who have elected me as their spokesman to make a brief press conference to advise our families, friends, and loved ones of our welfare . . ." Dan Rather then cut in to introduce the day's events:

> "For the first time in a week, the first look at and word from some of the passenger hostages from TWA flight 847 in Beirut.
>
> "And in El Salvador, the bodies of six Americans gunned down by leftist rebels, a grim reminder that terrorism is not exclusive to the Middle East.
>
> "Good evening, this is the Western Edition of the *CBS Evening News,* Dan Rather reporting.
>
> "New assurances in Beirut today, assurances from one of the American hostages that all thirty-seven of the passengers still captive from that hijacked jetliner are still safe. This on the seventh day of the hijacking ordeal. Welcome news to the families of the hostages.

"But it was news of a different, more tragic kind from El Salvador, where thirteen people, four of them U.S. Marines, two of them U.S. civilians, were killed in a guerrilla attack."

The broadcast closed with a report on the funeral of the Navy diver killed by the hijackers in Beirut, and the reactions of the families of the Americans killed in El Salvador. Here is Rather's introduction to the closing report, and the close of Bruce Morton's narration.

Video	*Audio*
Still of sailor in uniform, in inset behind Rather.	"On this seventh day of the hijacking of the TWA plane, they buried the young hostage brutally beaten and then murdered by terrorists. But as the killing of Americans in El Salvador reminds us, that death proved to be preamble, the title page written in blood to a volume of terrorist violence against the United States."
Drawing of American flag at half staff, in inset.	
Bugler plays taps (sound continues under narration). *Still of American flag. Camera zooms out slowly to show huge flag hanging above flag-draped coffin and honor guard. Stills of Marines in uniform, alternating with stills of Arlington funeral.*	"The Marine Corps hymn says, 'We'll fight our country's battles, on the land and on the sea.' But these young men did not die fighting battles, fighting an enemy in a war they knew about. More and more American servicemen are going peacefully about their peaceful rounds and being murdered for it. *{Then a pause, while video continues}* Bruce Morton, CBS News, Arlington."

Putting a piece of the lead story before the anchor's introduction is television's equivalent of a banner headline—and this was, of course, no ordinary day for television news. But if not typical, the *CBS Evening News* on day seven of the TWA hijacking crisis was archetypical, and represents well the contradictory character of television news in the 1980s.

TV news, for one thing, is both journalism and show business, a key political institution as well as a seller of detergent and breakfast cereal. In the mid-1960s, television took its place alongside the wire services and the major daily newspapers and news magazines as an integral part of the fourth estate. Like the press, television news was accepted as a kind of quasi-constitutional branch of the American political system. The "press conferences"—whether Ronald Reagan's or Nabih Berri's—became a televised event; network journalists were granted their seats on Air Force One and in the front row of presidential briefings.

Network television journalists largely accepted the "professional" standards of news reporting that evolved in the print media. Yet TV news is also entertainment, carried on in an intensely competitive commercial environment. It is, as Rather's metaphor of the "title page written in blood" suggests, at least as much a teller of stories as a provider of political information and commentary. The combination of entertainment and journalism is not something television invented. It goes all the way back to the first commercial mass media, the penny papers of the 1830s. But television is its premier practitioner today. When an event like the hostage crisis comes along—full of characters that the audience can identify with, villains they can hate, a world political context that elevates the whole story to a realm larger than everyday life, and suspense over the outcome that keeps the audience coming back night after night—television can rarely resist making the news a melodrama. (Ratings at CBS, which profited most from the hostage crisis, jumped 11 percent during the early days of the crisis.)

The political consequences of this mix of journalism and show business are complex. Consider the issue of presidential authority. Conservatives have long argued that the media are hostile to established political authority, or at least serve unwittingly to undermine it. There are many versions of the argument: some, for example, focusing on the ideology of the "liberal intelligentsia"; some on the hunger of a dramatic medium for controversy and conflict. Most consider television the worst offender.

And, indeed, much of what appeared on CBS news on day seven

was potentially damaging to the Reagan administration. Hostage Conwell delivered an articulate statement calling on all the politicians involved to do what was necessary to "let innocent and free people go home," including those held by Israel—calling on the administration in effect to do precisely what it was refusing to do, to negotiate. The administration called the "parading of hostages before TV cameras" a "senseless exploitation," but the networks were not about to turn the cameras away from one of the best characters in the story. Nor were they about to ignore the relatives of seven Americans held in Beirut before the hijacking, who in interviews this same day criticized the administration, some of them bitterly, for lack of attention to the fate of their loved ones. White House correspondent Lesley Stahl, meanwhile, pointed out that the administration's actions did not fully match its rhetoric. "But as if to underscore the limitations involved," she reported, right after a tough statement by presidential press secretary Larry Speakes, "all Mr. Reagan was able to announce was a new study on terrorism and more military aid to El Salvador." The potential was there, then, for the administration to appear insensitive to the fate of the "little guy," or incompetent, or both. In any case, it was clear, at least, that the flow of information and the news agenda was in important ways out of its control.

There was, however, another side to television's presentation of presidential authority. Rather, for instance, introduced Stahl's White House report this way: "This has been one of the most turbulent weeks for our country in a long time. And, suddenly, President Reagan and his fellow Americans find themselves under attack from different sides in a war against faceless enemies." Stahl wrapped up in this fashion: "White House officials see a pattern of terrorism which they believe may be an attempt to test the will of President Reagan and the American people."

American journalists in the post-Watergate, post-Vietnam era are deeply ambivalent about political authority. They often treat the president as a self-serving politician, something which was extremely rare, particularly on television, fifteen or twenty years ago. Yet the president also appears in television's political dramas as the brave marshal who suffers with the town's citizens and rides out to defend the town from the bad men. In the end, for all the controversy over television's portrayal of the hostage crisis, the net effect on this president was about what it usually is in the immediate aftermath of an event that gets defined as an international crisis: Reagan's popularity jumped five points between the June and July Gallup polls.

There is, nonetheless, the question of television's power. TV news is widely believed to be the most powerful force in journalism, and often condemned for its political influence. The TWA hijacking was precisely the kind of event that has led to this perception. The whole episode seemed largely a performance staged for the media. Again, this is nothing television has invented. Politics has always been to a large degree a matter of orchestrating performances in order to project images to audiences of various sorts. Machiavelli's *The Prince* is in part a manual on image making. If television didn't invent image politics, however, it is the primary stage on which it takes place in the modern world.

Television is clearly in some sense an actor on the political stage as well. It doesn't merely transmit to the public information about what is going on. One of the things that is most distinctive about TV news is the extent to which it is an ideological medium, providing not just information or entertainment, but "packages for consciousness"—frameworks for interpreting and cues for reacting to social and political reality. If one looks closely at the CBS broadcast of June 20, 1985, it was clearly full of complexity and contradiction, but at another level it had a simplicity and unity, a single interpretation of the meaning of the news event. The broadcast returned again and again to a single simple theme: Americans under attack.

The network news was an active arbiter of political meaning during the Beirut hostage crisis, but the nature of the theme and the imagery it emphasized bring into focus the paradox of television's power. Here were the supposedly liberal media, indeed the notoriously liberal Dan Rather and CBS, emphasizing not the "Vietnam syndrome" or any such thing (the theme of the day's broadcast, after all, could have been "military intervention in civil wars doesn't pay"), but the nationalism and the military-oriented patriotism of Ronald Reagan. For all the hostage press conferences and live television interviews with their captors, viewers blamed the crisis on the same roster of enemies conservatives were urging television to assail. Respondents in one CBS poll, for instance, focused on Greek airport security (48 percent saying it was "a lot" to blame for the crisis), Iran (42 percent), and Nabih Berri, the man most often said to have manipulated television (46 percent). More than twice as many (24 percent) thought the Soviet Union bore "a lot" of blame as thought U.S. policy did (11 percent). Twenty percent named Israel.

News is pervasive in the modern television schedule, beginning with early morning news followed by two hours of morning news, continuing with the local news, also now two hours long in many areas, then the flagship network evening news shows (a rather small part of the news lineup), prime-time news magazines, "late fringe" local news, and finally *Nightline* and late-night news. For those who want something more or a little different, there are *The MacNeil-Lehrer Newshour,* CNN's *Primenews* and other cable news services, and occasionally network documentaries, although budget cuts have made these scarce in recent years. In San Diego, setting aside PBS, cable, independent stations, documentaries, and magazines, one can watch eight hours of news on any weekday.

Each of these forms of news is distinctive in certain ways, and it is impossible to do justice to all of them here. I shall focus on two forms which lie toward opposite ends of the continuum that connects TV news to the worlds of entertainment and journalism it often uncomfortably straddles: morning news, which is first of all entertainment, and network evening news, which is journalism set within an entertainment medium.

To grasp either form, it is important to grasp the complex implications of the *populism* of TV news. Populism is of course a central part of American political culture: at least since the age of Jackson, politicians, the press, and popular culture have paid obeisance to the wisdom of the People, often contrasting it with the corruption and selfishness of those who hold power. This strain in American culture, to be sure, coexists and interacts with other very different ones, including a reverence for "leadership" and order that was greatly strengthened by the development of the cold war doctrine of "national security." But its power is great enough to have left a distinctive mark on American journalism: in few countries, for example, would the news have focused on ordinary citizens caught up in political events the way American television focused on the Beirut hostages. The fact that CBS began its broadcast on day seven of the hostage crisis with Allyn Conwell rather than Ronald Reagan, the State Department, or Congress, is strong testimony to the populism of TV news. The populism of American culture affects journalism at all levels, but among the major media it affects television particularly strongly. This is so because of the intensely competitive nature of the television industry, in which the three networks compete head-to-head for a mass national audience. Television worries about pleasing and entertaining the ordinary citizen in a way that the *New York Times* does not.

The political consequences of television's populism are complex, and often, in fact, antidemocratic. At times, television's populism causes the news to spill beyond the bounds of official discourse, as it did in the reporting of Allyn Conwell's news conference. At other times, it causes the news to avoid controversies that seem likely to offend the mass audience, or to jump on the bandwagon of what seems a safe and appealing majority sentiment. Sometimes it manifests itself in "anti-establishment" themes; television loves nothing more than a story about a "little guy" who stands up to the "powers that be." Sometimes it serves as a resource to the power broker who knows how to play the populist hero. The success of Ronald Reagan in shaping the tone of television ironically owes much to television's populism, both because Reagan plays the populist hero particularly well, and because television has been fearful of crossing his popular appeal to restore American greatness and irresistibly tempted to adopt that appeal as its own.

Heroes and Freaks of Everyday Life: Morning News as Entertainment

Television has a number of different modes, different forms of presentation that work well on the medium: action, usually involving vehicles or gross body movements—fights, car crashes, and the like; collage—the rapidly succeeding images of the modern commercial being the classic example; irony—achieved through the juxtaposition of contrasting statements or images ("I don't know of anybody being oppressed," said an American businessman in Guatemala, interviewed by Ed Rabel for the CBS documentary *Central America in Revolt*. "I think this is just something that some reporters have thought up." Cut to visuals of Guatemala's shantytowns, and a murdered reformer); and finally, intimacy of a certain kind—intimacy carried on at just enough social distance that it is all right for a third person to listen in. This is the mode of morning news. Friendly and interesting people have conversations with other friendly and interesting people, and the viewer is invited to "join them." From time to time, other friendly people fill the viewer in on matters of public interest—weather, sports, and the news.

Good Morning America is produced by ABC's entertainment division; NBC's *Today* and the *CBS Morning News* are produced by the news divisions. But all three morning news shows are entertainment first and journalism second. In 1985, for example, during the May rating sweeps, Bryant Gumbel, Jane Pauley, and NBC's *Today* traveled around the country on an Amtrak train. It was no doubt a difficult and expensive technical feat. But it produced exceptionally good morning television. It meant, for one thing, that there would be plenty of little crises that would enhance the aura of informality so important to the intimacy of morning news. In Memphis, for instance, it rained intermittently, forcing Jane and Bryant to explain apologetically that the show might be a little chaotic—just as "real" hosts often have to do. Putting the show on the road also added a new twist to the symbolic participation of the audience. People could actually come down to the railroad stop to greet *Today* and be seen on the air; this they did, cheering and waving signs as fans do at a football game when the cameras point at them. The relation of television to its audience involves a kind of mutual flattery, which, as we shall see, is important on many levels.

Aside from the rain and the presence of the audience, though, the *Today* show was not particularly unusual during the Amtrak trip. From Memphis, one hour-long segment included the following stories: a feature on people who had lived on boats in the Mississippi; an interview with Tennessee Senators Albert Gore, Jr., and Sr.; a story on the tourist industry centered on Elvis Presley's birthplace; a story on Memphis race relations; and an appearance by singer Jerry Lee Lewis.

As entertainment, the morning news deals relatively little with the political conflicts which are the stock-in-trade of front pages and the evening news. Typically, unless some particularly dramatic political event is going on, each one-hour segment will contain one feature on a political topic. In this case, it was the race relations story (the story on the Albert Gores, father and son, was a human interest, not a political, story). The balance of the items will be "soft" feature stories of one sort or another. Even the "hard news" bulletins, which typically take up about ten minutes of each hour, focus fairly heavily on certain kinds of stories considered to be good material for entertainment television. During May and June of 1985, for example, the stories that received special emphasis on lead news segments of the morning news included the Frustaci septuplets (the lead story the day *Today* was in Memphis), the "Walker spy family," the trial of the socialite and accused wife murderer Claus von Bülow, a cyclone in Bangladesh, the introduction of the Reagan tax reform plan, and of course the TWA hijacking.

What is it that these stories have in common? Each is in some way about everyday life. The tax reform story belongs to a familiar special category. It is "news you can use," like the consumer and medical reporting that occupies a large niche on the local news. The morning news, like much other television coverage, emphasized not the tax plan's impact on economic growth or social equality or priorities, but "what it will mean to you."

The rest of the stories are about perversions, exaltations, interruptions, or crises of everyday life. The birth of seven children to one family is not an everyday event; if it were, it wouldn't have the fascination that makes it news. But it is a twist on something that is an everyday event. People can imagine what it is like for an ordinary person to go into the hospital and suddenly have seven sick babies, just as they can imagine what it must be like to be flying home on an airliner and suddenly be taken hostage. Most of these stories are positive. Most are about heroes of everyday life—people who, though they seem ordinary and easy to identify with, either deal gracefully with an extraordinary crisis or else rise above the usual boredom of life, like the people who lived on the Mississippi, or a man who appeared in the second hour of *Today* in Memphis, pursuing a dream of restoring the steam engine. In this category also is the celebrity, whose life, which we as "friends" are privileged to share, is like our own projected onto a higher plane.

The Walker and von Bülow families, on the other hand, are freaks of everyday life—a seemingly normal American family which begins to spy for the Soviets; a marriage gone awry like so many others, but a fabulous marriage gone fabulously and grotesquely awry. Many stories combine images of heroism with the fascination of the freak show. The story of the Frustaci septuplets combines the courage of the family, which occupies the foreground, with the freakishness of a multiple birth. Another of the great morning news stories of 1985 also falls into this category—the story of Cathleen Webb, who recanted the testimony that had put her former boyfriend, Gary Dotson, in prison for rape, both of them subsequently appearing together on all the morning shows. A particularly clear example appeared on the local news in New York in July 1985 when WABC ran a series on rare diseases. The emphasis was on how people coped with illnesses that made parts of life most of us take for granted extremely difficult; in this sense, those who appeared were clearly heroes. But at the same time, each of the two episodes I saw was about diseases that produced gross physical deformities, including the "elephant man" disease.

The morning news does do some political stories, and it is interesting to consider what happens when it brings political issues into the intimacy of its small circle of friends. At times, the result is much more substantial coverage than would normally be found on the evening news. In 1981, for example, when Ground Zero Week was organized to publicize the danger of nuclear war, arms control advocates were much happier with the coverage they got on the morning than the evening news. Why should this be? The morning news, for one thing, is much slower-paced than the evening news, which is so tightly edited today that it is extremely rare for anyone other than the correspondent to speak longer than ten or fifteen seconds. The average "sound bite" is about ten seconds, and this has important consequences for what can be said. One can express a stripped-down feeling or attitude in ten seconds, but it is rather difficult to make an argument. It is also very difficult to step outside of conventional modes of thought: to frame an issue in a way that is unfamiliar to the audience requires time for explanation. It might be added that the ten-second sound bite seems likely to promote a particularly passive relation of the audience to the news: it is necessarily prepackaged thought, "like a cartoon bubble," in the words of David Marash, a maverick local anchor with a reputation for bucking the powerful trend in recent years toward faster-paced evening news broadcasts. Compared with the evening news, the five minutes of unedited conversation permitted by the talk show format of the morning news seems virtually a luxurious opportunity to discuss issues in depth.

Because it is not primarily journalism, moreover, the morning news is not bound by a number of journalistic conventions that made it difficult for arms control advocates to put the nuclear issue on the national agenda in the 1980s. "Serious" journalism is primarily concerned with issues being debated in Washington. This is not to say that TV news at any level is concerned exclusively with the affairs of Washington officials. The concern of television with ordinary people and ordinary life spills over to the evening news as well. This is one of the things that is distinctive about American TV news compared with that of other countries. About a third of those who appear on American TV news are citizens without official position. In Italy, by contrast, virtually all are officials of government, political parties, or other organized groups. Still, the ordinary citizen is brought into the evening news primarily to react to certain official policies, or else to appear in human interest stories, which are included in the evening news to "lighten it up." Washington controls the agenda for political reporting, and it is relatively difficult for a movement pushing an issue not on that agenda—as arms control was not in 1981—to get itself taken seriously as "hard news."

For the morning news, on the other hand, Ground Zero's very lack of Washington roots made it excellent material. Few things are as deadly to the intimate format of morning news as interviews with the likes of Caspar Weinberger and George Shultz. This is not to say that no Washington officials appeared. The morning news enters a mixed mode when it deals with an issue like arms control, and many standard conventions of journalism apply. There would, for instance, be no question of discussing a defense issue without presenting the main lines of policy debate about it in Washington. The final day of Ground Zero Week, for instance, *CBS Morning News* set up a debate between Richard Perle, assistant secretary of defense, and Sidney Drell, a physicist supporting the freeze movement.

What made Ground Zero a good story, though, and paved the way for the concluding discussion of arms control policy, was the fact that it emerged from a grass roots movement concerned with an issue that anyone could relate to on some level. The people behind Ground Zero were precisely the sort who normally appear on the morning news: articulate and upscale—it was largely a movement of the professional middle class—yet also ordinary people for whom politics was only a sideline. In a way, such a story fit perfectly with the formula of crises and perversions of everyday life. People tend to think of nuclear war, after all, as something like a natural disaster, which is one of the major categories of human interest story—think of the way it was later presented in the ABC film *The Day After,* as an unexplained event that disrupted the lives of ordinary people. So along with the debate about policy, *CBS Morning News* also included a segment on "living with fear," which included interviews with high school students about how they felt growing up in a nuclear world, and with bomb shelter developers who described the features of underground living (balanced, it might be added, by a statement from a psychiatrist, another articulate nonofficial voice, who made the case that a nuclear war was not survivable).

"Serious" journalism tends to treat politics as a contest rather than a discussion of social values: it asks "Who is winning?," not "Who is right?" or "What should we do?" This is related to the principle of "objective reporting" (particularly important in election coverage). So when the evening news covered Ground Zero, it focused not on the argument the movement was making about nuclear war and nuclear policy, but on the question of whether the movement would be politically effective; CBS, for example, interviewed California pollster Mervin Field on that subject. On the morning news, on the other hand, in part simply because the antinuclear advocates were part of a live conversation, they had many opportunities to emphasize their own central issue, "the urgency, the determination," as Drell put it, "to get back to the negotiating table." An entertainment medium cannot pose as an authority the way an information medium can, but must enter into dialogue with the public, represented in the case of the morning news by the guests. So the morning news is in some ways more open than the evening news even in the coverage of politics.

But consider the following story from ABC's *Good Morning America*. On May 23, 1985, Joan Lunden interviewed Sylvester Stallone about *Rambo,* the "action-adventure" film in which Stallone plays a Vietnam veteran on a crusade to rescue Americans still held captive, naturally killing plenty of Vietnamese in the process. Here is part of the interview.

LUNDEN. And Sylvester Stallone is joining us from Los Angeles. Good morning. Gee, I love those simple drawing-room comedies. This thing is action-packed! How *hard* was it to make a movie like this?

STALLONE. This was probably the most difficult film. . . . Because of the heat, the inherent dangers of the stunts . . . and the terrain—people were always coming across tarantulas in the bushes, or coral snakes, or whatever.

LUNDEN. You go through, I know, a pretty rigorous training period before each film. But you went through the most grueling, rigorous training for this one. How long and what was it like?

STALLONE. I wanted him to look like the terrain, hard and cut up but very inflexible, almost like a piece of machinery.

LUNDEN. I think you succeeded on that one. [*Then speaking more quickly*] It's getting good reviews. Now the only thing is, is that the movie does maintain of course that the Vietnamese still have POWs, American POWs. And a few critics have said that that "exploits the emotions of relatives whose families are still listed as missing in action." What do you *say* to that criticism?

STALLONE. What we're trying to show is . . . they are there. From all the data that has been compiled from the people that have been working with the film, which is from very reliable sources, there are men there. So I think a dramatization to show this only helps put the spotlight on a very darkened area. . . .

LUNDEN. So it's more than an action-adventure film. It's a statement.

The conversation then put politics aside and moved on to a more typical celebrity interview "issue," the question of whether Stallone was "stuck in a rut" with the image of a "larger-than-life hero."

Rambo was among the most popular films of 1985. It was also a political phenomenon whose significance goes well beyond the dubious claim that the Vietnamese hold American prisoners. It belongs to a genre of Vietnam revenge stories which has long had powerful appeal to the *Soldier of Fortune* crowd, but which with *Rambo* broke into the mainstream of American popular culture. The response has been powerful—audiences often cheer with Rambo and chant "USA, USA." And the "stab in the back" mentality is chillingly similar to that of Germany in the early thirties, not only in its aggressive nationalism, but in the particular kind of vigilante spirit it portrays: in the end, Rambo turns his violence on the "wimp" civilian who betrayed him, while a chorus of faceless "little men" cheers, and the colonel, the one authority figure who has always respected Rambo, looks on understandingly. Rambo, moreover, is a strange kind of hero whose only mode of expression is violence. He is, as the colonel says, a killing "machine." Stallone has been described as the new John Wayne, but he is in fact a significant break from the John Wayne image: the machismo of John Wayne was always bounded by a sense of connection to a human culture—usually symbolized by the nuclear family Wayne could not be part of—and an idealized vision of political order. Rambo's violence is profoundly antisocial.

The United States is not so far gone that the implications of *Rambo* have escaped the notice of at least some critics. (*Variety*, reporting on gross returns at New York theaters one week, described *Rambo* as an "all-American on-screen war machine manipulating the masses for $450,000.") But to have raised this kind of issue on the morning news would have disrupted its friendly atmosphere. Stories on popular culture fall unequivocally in the entertainment mode of the morning news. In the celebrity interviews, the morning news avoids controversy in the same way, and for largely the same reasons, that casual acquaintances avoid it when they are trying to make conversation. As entertainment, television is a consensual medium. It focuses on what people are assumed to share. Even the reporting of Ground Zero was not really an exception. Nuclear war was good material for the morning news in part because it was at one level a consensual issue. Everyone is against nuclear war; Bill Kurtis was even able to get Richard Perle and Sidney Drell to agree on that. But Vietnam remains far too touchy an issue to bring into a story that is intended essentially as diversion from the cares of the world.

The Evening News: Journalism on an Entertainment Medium

The evening news as we know it today began in September 1963 when CBS and NBC expanded their news broadcasts from fifteen minutes to half an hour (ABC followed in 1967). The quiz show scandal of 1959 had tarnished the networks' public image, and an activist chairman of the FCC, Newton Minow, had called television a "vast wasteland," warning that the license renewal process would cease to be treated as a formality. In this atmosphere, the expanded evening news, along with a new commitment to live public affairs programming and documentaries, gave the networks a claim to be something more than a high-tech way of selling detergent. It made them a part of the fourth estate, or as modern journalism is sometimes called, the "fourth branch of government." It associated them with the prestige of the state; each of the new half-hour shows was inaugurated with an interview with President Kennedy. At the same time, reflecting the ambivalent political heritage of American journalism, it associated them with the tradition of the press as a defender of the public *against* the state—and hence an institution protected by the First Amendment against government interference.

The news was initially seen as a "loss leader" whose function was more to restore prestige than to make money. As a result, the news divisions were largely freed from the commercial considerations that dominate most television production, while television journalists came to enjoy a degree of professional autonomy not so different from that of their counterparts in the "prestige" press. A network news ethic developed of giving the public "what it needed" more than "what it wanted."

Despite its ambitions, however, television journalism was very primitive in the early 1960s. This was most evident in Washington reporting, which makes up the bulk of "hard news" coverage. As late as 1965, at least to judge from the little TV coverage which survives from that period, most television reports from Washington consisted of little more than unedited film of official speeches and press conferences, introduced by the anchor and followed by his commentary, which usually summarized and reiterated what officials had said in public. The major print media, by contrast, were much more active in the gathering and presentation of news: Washington coverage in the "prestige press" made use of a variety of sources (albeit still official), many of them unnamed, which the journalist would put together to reveal "the real story" which was presumed to lie behind the surface of official proceedings. This wasn't so much an adversarial stance; that would develop, to a limited extent, a few years later. It was simply the mode of operation of a form of journalism written for an audience that was assumed to follow politics fairly closely. By the mid-1970s, as Vietnam and then Watergate opened the gap between official statements and the "real story" wider and wider, television journalism began to catch up with the more active and sophisticated journalism of the "prestige press."

But if television reached journalistic puberty sometime around 1970, it also became more commercial. By the end of the sixties, the evening news shows were already making small profits, and in 1968, in an augury of dramatic developments to come, 60 *Minutes* arrived on the scene, and soon began to gather large audiences. 60 *Minutes* was television's original contribution to the increasingly active journalism of the era. It also rocketed to the top of the ratings charts by 1969, putting the entire CBS news division into the black for the first time. And then in the early 1970s, local television, for which news had become far and away the primary source of profits, entered an intense competition for ratings that would bring all the tools of commercial television, from graphics-generators to market research, into the news business.

All of this began to catch up with the network evening news in the mid-1970s. The most important event was ABC's 1977 appointment of Roone Arledge to head its news division. Switching from ABC Sports in defiance of a tradition of promoting news division heads from within the news division, Arledge turned ABC News from an also-ran into a serious ratings competitor of NBC and CBS. The news divisions entered a new period of intense competition, still in progress, during which the old barriers isolating news from commercial television have progressively weakened. A number of network producers, interviewed for this article, said they felt the pressure to keep an eye on the ratings had accelerated in recent years, citing as major landmarks in this shift the first appointment of Van Gordon Sauter as head of CBS News—Sauter has moved back and forth between the news and other divisions of CBS, making him, many journalists feel, a television person first and a news person second—and the turnover of anchors that finally ended with Dan Rather, Peter Jennings, and Tom Brokaw competing head-to-head.

It is nothing new for American news organizations to combine the functions of journalism—in the sense of providing information and commentary, primarily about political affairs—and entertainment. On the contrary, the American newspaper, which has been primarily a commerical enterprise since the 1830s, has a long history of doing exactly that. That television now shows this duality most sharply has to do with the structure of the television industry. In the newspaper business, the tension between entertainment and journalism was sharpest in the days depicted in *Citizen Kane* and *The Front Page,* when urban newspapers competed head-to-head for readership. Today, most papers have monopolies, or nearly so, in their primary markets; in other cases, New York for instance, where a number of papers compete in the same urban area, the market is stratified by class.

But in the television business, the three networks compete head-to-head for the same national market, and in each major urban area at least three television stations fight for the advertising dollars. Television's consumers, moreover, are volatile. They are like the newspaper reader of years ago, who bought the paper on the newsstand rather than by subscription, and might buy one paper today and another tomorrow depending on the headlines. The audience for an evening news show can fluctuate considerably from day to day. And though the news is not a major money-maker compared with prime time, the financial consequences of fluctuating ratings are considerable. In the early 1980s, when ABC News made its run at the other networks, a slide in ratings for the *CBS Evening News* from a 27 to 24 percent share of the audience cut the value of a thirty-second spot on the show by as much as $10,000. Add to this the fact that the evening news is an integral part of the "audience flow" that channels people into the network's prime-time programming, and it is clear that the networks have strong incentives to act aggressively to maximize the audience for the evening news. The result has been a significant convergence of news toward the conventions of television entertainment, with news broadcasts becoming faster-paced (one product of this period is the ten-second sound bite, compared with an average of over forty seconds in the 1960s and early 1970s), more visual, and with greater emphasis on the kinds of stories—usually, like morning news stories, those with a human interest angle—the audience is assumed to enjoy watching.

The Power of Television

The network's very success at creating a form of news that would have both the prestige of elite journalism and the mass appeal of television has produced new problems for them. In the early 1960s, they were criticized for their lack of concern with public issues. Today, they face the opposite criticism: television news is widely seen as a dangerously powerful political institution. In part, this is because of the size and national scope of television's audience. The networks introduced the first daily news coverage to reach a broad national audience (the *Wall Street Journal* and the *Christian Science Monitor* have long had national circulations, but their readerships are smaller and more specialized). Even with the advent of *USA Today* and the national edition of the *New York Times,* they have by far the largest daily exposures.

Television, moreover, presents the news differently than print media do, in ways that have led many to argue that it has greater impact on its audience than other kinds of news. Television, it is said, is personal: the news is brought to us not by anonymous writers but by individuals selected in no small part for a persona that combines authority with likability. It is well known that polls once showed Walter Cronkite to be the most "trusted" man in America. Television is also visual; people may feel they are "seeing it for themselves" on television. And television is more "interpretive" or "thematic": unlike most newspaper reports, television stories tend to be tightly organized around a particular "story line" or interpretation.

Many of the claims made today about the power of television are so sweeping (the cover of Barbara Matusow's book *The Evening Stars,* for instance, says of the anchors, "They influence our opinions more than any politician—and can do so with the mere flicker of an eyebrow") that it is worth introducing a note of caution. The main evidence for television's preeminent power over public opinion is a set of polls conducted by the Roper Organization which showed, as of 1984, that 64 percent of the public said they get most of their news from television, while only 40 percent named newspapers, and many fewer radio or magazines (people could name more than one medium). According to the same polls, most people say they find TV more believable. But this, as Lawrence Lichty has pointed out, simply shows that most people *think* they get most of their news from TV. Whether they really do is another matter; on any given day, only half as many people—about a third of the population—watch any TV news, national or local, as read a newspaper. A similar percentage of the public, about a third, reads *Time, Newsweek,* or *U.S. News & World Report.* A quarter read *Readers' Digest.* It is one of the ironies of the CBS-Westmoreland libel case that more people read *TV Guide*'s attack on *The Uncounted Enemy: A Vietnam Deception* than saw the documentary itself. The circulation of *TV Guide* is 17 million; the audience for the controversial documentary was about 8 million.

As for the impact of TV on those who do watch it, it is clear that it can be substantial. It was once the standard view of academic media researchers that the mass media did not have much impact on people's opinions. But this view has been discredited in recent years as researchers have become more sophisticated about *how* the media might influence public opinion. The researchers of the 1950s

were interested primarily in propaganda; that is, direct efforts to
change people's political opinions. Modern media research is concerned with more indirect forms of influence. A recent experimental
study, for example, found that altering television broadcasts to
emphasize or deemphasize particular issues affected not only people's assessments of the importance of the issues (the "agenda-
setting effect") but their evaluation of presidential performance as
well. At the same time, though, there is no real confirming evidence
that television indeed affects people's opinions more than print. And
it clearly often happens that people reject what they hear and see on
the news. At the Democratic Convention in 1968, Walter Cronkite
not only flickered his eyebrow but called the Chicago police
"thugs." Surveys, nonetheless, showed that the public sided with
the police.

Nobody can say for sure how powerful television actually is, but
television does present the news in a way that may make it particularly important as a carrier of ideology and social values. The crucial
thing here is the unified, thematic nature of television presentation.
A newspaper story, particularly a "hard news" story about a political
event, is traditionally organized in the form of an "inverted pyramid." The "who, what, when, where" is given in the lead para-
graph, and the article then moves on to fill in details, reactions, and
pieces of background, theoretically moving from the most to the
least important facts, on the assumption that most readers will not
get to the end of the story. A certain "angle" or point of view will
of course guide the sifting of "important" from "unimportant"
facts, and this will usually be expressed at least implicitly in the
lead paragraphs. After that, though, a story will often strike out in
a number of different directions; the theme of the lead paragraphs
need not carry through the entire piece.

Television has a very different relation to its audience. A newspaper reader can browse at will from story to story; television must
"carry the audience along" from the beginning of each story to the
end and on to the next. So a television story is often more like a
circle than a pyramid. It introduces its central theme at the beginning, develops it throughout the story, though perhaps with twists
and turns dictated by problems of balance or ideological tensions
the journalist may consciously or unconsciously be trying to resolve,

and returns to it in a closing line that "wraps the story up." This is often true not only of the individual story but of "segments"— groups of stories placed together between two commercials—and even of the news broadcast as a whole. This of course was the case with the *CBS Evening News* on the day of the hostage press conference and the guerrilla attack in El Salvador. In the newspapers, the stories from Lebanon and El Salvador shared the front page, but were reported with little reference to one another, except in quotations from administration officials, who sought to connect them. On television they were treated as part of the same story (with the result that the El Salvador story, which a year or so earlier might have been framed as "deepening American involvement in El Salvador's guerrilla war," became instead "America held hostage"). And the newspaper had nothing like the refrain that again and again hammered home the theme of the CBS broadcast: "For President Reagan and all Americans, one more tough situation . . . one of the most turbulent weeks for our country . . . volume of terrorist violence against the United States . . . American servicemen going peacefully about their peaceful rounds and being murdered for it."

Television and Political Authority

Television is no mere headline service. It plays a special role in assigning ideological meaning to political events. But what kind of ideology does it promote? Television's ideology, to summarize very roughly, descends from the liberalism of the Progressive era. It is reformist, and stands ready to expose violations of ideals of fair play, equal opportunity, and prosperity. It is also populist in the sense that it is suspicious of power and those who seek it, and will often praise the wisdom of the "common man" against the cynicism of the "politician." But reformism and populism coexist with a strong belief in order, consensus, moderation, leadership, and the basic soundness of American institutions and benevolence of American world leadership. I shall focus here on one facet of this "reformist conservatism" of American TV—its ambivalent attitude toward political authority.

Since the late 1960s, conservatives have been crusading against the "liberal media." The charges against the media are many, but central among them, particularly for the more moderate academic conservatives, has been the argument that the media serve to undermine political authority. Reflecting on the rise of television for a 1975 Trilateral Commission report on the "governability of democracy," Samuel Huntington wrote, "the themes which are stressed [in TV news], particularly the focus on controversy and violence, and, conceivably, the values and outlook of the journalists, tended to arouse unfavorable attitudes toward established institutions and to promote a decline of confidence in government." And in 1983, in a book sponsored by the American Enterprise Institute, Austin Ranney argued, as have many others: "Television newspeople have an anti-establishment bias; that is, they view with special suspicion whatever political leaders and organizations seem most powerful at the moment . . . Television's constant denigration of politicians' motives, words and deeds does more than merely confirm politicians' already-established poor reputation; it also lowers public confidence in government itself."

This isn't altogether wrong. Since the mid-1960s, influenced by Vietnam and Watergate, American journalism has become more "adversarial"—more inclined to question political authority. The change has been particularly dramatic in the case of television, though this is in part because television news started out with a much more deferential attitude toward government officials than comparable national media. One of the most dramatic changes in the structure of television reporting, for example, has to do with the way statements by the president and other top administration officials are handled. As late as the first Nixon administration, it was common for the White House correspondent simply to introduce a presidential statement with a brief summary and then to show the president's remarks unedited, often for two minutes or more.

A similar practice continues in such countries as France and Italy today. But in the United States now, as a consequence both of the increased pace of the newscast and the post-Watergate attitude that the journalist cannot be a mere conduit for official views, TV reporters routinely cut an official's remarks into ten- or fifteen-second sound bites, then weave these into their own narration. It is the journalist, not the official, who speaks to the news audience. And there is no doubt that journalists are much bolder than they used to be about putting those remarks in a context which may not be one the official would have preferred. Often this entails pointing out the political motivations of a statement or a "photo opportunity." "President Reagan's visit to the German military cemetery in Bitburg now is called by many the greatest blunder of his administration," reported Dan Rather in 1985. "Before leaving West Germany today, Mr. Reagan tried to deflect some of the criticism leveled at him by criticizing the Soviets." (Rather missed the deeper significance of Reagan's remarks, which was that throughout his V-E Day trip, he had tried, to the extent that it was politically possible, to focus attention on the cold war instead of World War II.) A year and a half earlier, in November 1983, NBC's Chris Wallace, summing up a report on a Reagan trip to South Korea, said, "Any trip a president makes is political, and officials traveling with Mr. Reagan were clearly delighted with pictures of him on the front lines. At one point, an aide motioned to the president to move more into the sunlight."

But this is only half the story. Chris Wallace, for instance, continued his remarks on Reagan's Korea trip this way: "Still, it was clear that Mr. Reagan was genuinely moved by what he saw here today—the choir of orphans, young American soldiers ready to fight far from home. It's safe to assume Mr. Reagan will be speaking and thinking of this place for a long time." The president is the prime character in television's personalized presentation of politics, and even setting aside the fear of crossing a popular president that journalists share with members of Congress and other political figures, TV has the same interest in presenting him sympathetically as in presenting Sylvester Stallone that way. What Wallace does here is to separate "Reagan the person" from "Reagan the politician," and protect the former from the negative image of the political role. This, of course, is precisely what politicians have tried to do since Vietnam, Watergate, and the rest deflated the more patriarchal image of authority that prevailed in the 1950s and 1960s: to project an image of personal sincerity and effectiveness while being a "regular guy" in contrast to a "Washington politician." Jimmy Carter tried to do this and failed; Reagan succeeded. It is an image that

works well on television for someone who can play the part, the
more so as TV news drifts toward a more entertainment-style format.

Does this mean, then, that television recognizes only celebrity,
rather than authority in the traditional sense? Not really. Television's cynicism about politicians—it is really not television's exclusively, but part of American culture—coexists with a strong belief
in leadership and the importance of public support for it. A good
illustration of this can be found in an ABC "Status Report" on the
May 1985 bombing by a police helicopter that burned to the ground
a city block in Philadelphia. Here are excerpts from that story,
reported by Richard Threlkeld:

THRELKELD. For the cradle of independence, William Penn's City
    of Brotherly Love, this seemed terribly out of place. Combat on
    the streets. A police helicopter drops a bomb—*a bomb*—on a
    house full of men, women, and children. . . . There was outrage
    here.
ANGRY CITIZEN. How do you justify a bombing in public? Is this
    a war zone or is this Beirut? What's up, man?
THRELKELD. And a lot of Tuesday and Wednesday morning quar-
    terbacking from outsiders who saw these pictures. [New York
    mayor Koch appears, here in the role of politician rather than
    leader.]
        In some other cities we can think of, perhaps including Mayor
    Koch's New York, that awful sequence of events might have
    started a riot. . . .
        That didn't happen here in Philadelphia. Quite the oppo-
    site. . . .
        Yesterday, the city's black clergy prayed for the mayor. The
    polls indicate most Philadelphians actually endorse what he did,
    although not the tragic, unintended result.
        Half the explanation lies in the people the police were trying
    to evict . . . members of MOVE, a tiny, bizarre cult whose
    members wear Rastafarian hairdos and have all changed their
    name to "Africa." . . . Police moved in after days of negotiation
    failed and people in the house started shooting. . . .
        Despite what happened and all the unanswered questions,

people have been uncommonly forgiving of Wilson Goode, the mayor. . . .

The mayor has promised that all the homeless will have brand-new homes by Christmas. And in the meantime, the whole city, black and white, has pitched in to help. . . . America's fifth-largest city is suddenly behaving with all the good-neighborliness of a little town. . . .

An event like the Philadelphia bombing, as Threlkeld conveys in setting the scene, is potentially damaging to the society's self-image (for the cradle of independence . . . a *bomb* . . . What's up, man?). What television tends to do in a case like this, far from focusing on "controversy and violence," is to emphasize unity and the restoration of normality, and reassure the viewers that nothing is fundamentally wrong. American culture being strongly populist, the restoration of normality is attributed in part to community self-help. But we are reassured as well that government institutions are responding to the crisis; Peter Jennings introduced the story by reporting that officials from various agencies were touring the area and had promised aid. The mayor appears not as a politician but as a symbol of the unity of the community. (Goode's blackness, of course, makes him a particularly important symbol in a crisis that raises the specter of a renewal of black-white conflict.) The causes of the conflict, meanwhile, Threlkeld pushes outside the mainstream of society, onto the "tiny bizarre cult." Threlkeld calls MOVE "half the explanation." But whatever the other half is—a sense of hopelessness in parts of the black community, the machismo of American culture that leads to escalation once confrontation begins, failure of city officials to deal with the crisis sooner or to think out the consequences of their tactics—Threlkeld says nothing about it.

Those who believe a show business medium inevitably tends to emphasize conflict rather than harmony should think about what television entertainment is actually like. There is conflict, of course; drama can't exist without conflict. But the portrayal of conflict by no means always casts established institutions or authorities in a bad light. A great deal of television's conflict is good-against-evil conflict, evil being located outside the mainstream of society—in "faceless enemies" and "bizarre cults." Here the message is often precisely the necessity of order and authority. When conflicts take place within the community of major characters—the community we are expected to identify with—it is normally resolved in the course of an episode or two, proving the strength of that community and the legitimacy of the familylike relations within it, including authority relations.

A television drama is like certain dreams: it enacts a fear and provides an idealized resolution of it. TV news often has this character as well. It is more in its journalistic than its show business mode that television focuses on controversy. A paper like the *New York Times* or the *Washington Post,* dealing with an event like the Philadelphia bombing, tends to focus on issues, that is, things that people disagree about. This is true not because they are "antiestablishment," but because their kind of journalism is oriented toward policymakers or people who follow politics closely. But as a medium oriented largely toward a huge and politically inactive mass public, television tends to be consensual.

A Populist Medium in the Age of Reagan

Television's populism hasn't always helped Ronald Reagan. In the depths of the recession of 1982, for example, the news was full of little vignettes about the unemployed and the despair of "rust-belt" America; this was television's effort to humanize economic news. Still, in the end, to the extent that Reagan's worldview has shaped the tone of TV news, it has done so in large part because of television's deep fear of offending the mass public.

Reagan is often seen as having nearly unlimited power to manipulate the media, but this has never been accurate. Television is not going to call Reagan a liar or a militarist or a right-wing ideologue. It isn't going to call his policy in Central America imperialistic, or his domestic policy systematically class-biased. It isn't even likely —with the exception of an occasional appearance on *Nightline*—to throw in such a view for the sake of "balance." The rules of "objectivity" require the television journalist, like any American journalist, to stick to narrower issues which do not bring the legitimacy of the state into question. Do the budget numbers add up? Can the

Salvadoran government beat the guerrillas? Will Congress buy the proposal? By historical standards, though, coverage of Reagan has not been particularly softer than coverage of any post-Watergate president; indeed, one often has the impression that journalists are at pains to demonstrate that the "Great Communicator" does not have them in his pocket. Rather's and Stahl's comments on the aftermath of Bitburg were certainly as barbed as anything Jimmy Carter suffered from the media, and they are not really exceptional.

Television has not been particularly deferential to Reagan or his specific policies. But *Reaganism* is another matter. It is not only television, of course, that has been affected by the Reagan era. Reagan's success and the disarray of the Democratic party have, in effect, shifted the center of gravity in American politics to the right. Since "balance" requires that the journalist straddle this center of gravity, the news has also shifted to the right. Nobody in the mainstream of American politics is about to deliver a ringing endorsement of the public sector in the current climate, so aside from an occasional piece on the op-ed page, no such view is going to get into the news. And the impact could be long-lasting: there appears to be a trend at a number of news organizations, including the *New York Times*, toward hiring and promoting more conservatives; the *Times* meanwhile canceled the column of one of its best-known liberal writers, Sydney Schanberg, who subsequently resigned.

The element of Reaganism that has most dramatically affected television, though, is not ideological conservatism, but the "America Is Back," "We're Number One" nationalism that has exhibited such deep appeal for the mass public. Television itself did a good deal to lay the groundwork for this political current, above all through its daily coverage of the Iran hostage crisis ("America Held Hostage, Day 276") and its presentation of that event as a national humiliation. The reaction came most strongly in another great media event, the invasion of Grenada. During the first day or two, television treated Grenada as it would treat a tax plan or budget proposal, with a neutral tone and a modest amount of skepticism of the administration's rationale. But as the positive public reaction mounted, television's emphasis quickly shifted away from political issues to the patriotic celebration—medical students kissing the ground, soldiers coming home to a heroes' welcome, and the like.

The public, moreover, not only cheered for the invasion of Grenada, but, according to a number of polls, endorsed Reagan's decision to keep the press from covering it. A year later, after a campaign that stressed the restoration of national pride, the "Great Communicator" was overwhelmingly reelected. Since that time, television has been scrambling to get on the right side of the "new patriotism."

One consequence has been an increasing stridency in coverage of consensus enemies—terrorists and the more traditional cold war enemies. The same day Rather and Stahl said Reagan was attacking the Soviet Union to deflect criticism from himself, for instance, CBS also had a story on the memory of World War II in the Soviet Union. The story itself was ideologically ambiguous, representing the Soviet mood as paranoiac, but at the same time treating with some respect the psychological impact of twenty million deaths. But Rather's introduction was as heavy-handed as anything his counterparts in the Soviet Union dish up: "The militaristic and totalitarian Communist party that rules modern Russia constantly emphasizes its version of the war as a lesson for its people and a lesson for others." (What it was about the Soviet "version" of World War II he considered false, Rather did not say.) The rules of "objectivity" have never applied to "militaristic Communists" any more than to "faceless enemies" or "bizarre cults"; but this kind of colorful prose had for the most part faded out in the mid-sixties. Its function here seems to have been to balance the liberal skepticism of the Bitburg story with a bow to the spirit of the new cold war. And this was just the beginning: as 1985 progressed and the Reagan-Gorbachev summit approached, the news, like every other part of television, was increasingly filled with cold war rhetoric and imagery.

The most important way television has "balanced" its liberal image, though, has been to adopt the imagery of Reagan's principal campaign theme: "America Is Back." One particularly interesting example occurred on CBS the day after the broadcast discussed at the beginning of this essay. Most of the news that day, of course, was about the Beirut hostage crisis. Near the end of the broadcast was a rather nervous piece of self-analysis, a story by Bob Simon recalling the press conference the day before—at which the hostages and the Amal militia had lectured journalists to behave in a civilized manner—and detailing various criticisms of the role of the media in the hostage crisis. Then came a "tease bumper" (one of the new techniques the networks have used to liven up the evening news) announcing the closing story. The tease showed the TWA plane on the ground in Beirut, and in an inset—cowboys on the range; the title was "Song of America." The story that followed bore remarkable resemblance to the Reagan film at the Republican convention that CBS and ABC had declined to televise the previous summer: it began with a soft-focus shot of a crew rowing down a river at sunrise, and then moved on to the Statue of Liberty surrounded by scaffolding and a series of shots of Americans going happily about their everyday life, concluding with a cowboy who reflects, "There's a lot to be said for the freedom that's involved in this lifestyle, and realizing that there's people like [the hostages] that don't have that opportunity, it stays on your mind." The theme was that America was strong despite the hostage crisis—morally strong, that is, in the sense of the City on a Hill, not strong in the sense that its immense political and economic power was unchallenged, an emphasis which would have given the story a very different slant. "There is a lot of concern in the country this week," Bruce Morton concluded. "But there is strength and order too."

Earlier the same month, on June 3, 1985, NBC reported on the aftermath of a tornado that hit Newton Falls, Ohio. The story focused on the way the community pulled together to help those in need; and in this respect it was a very standard story. There is nothing new or unusual about upbeat news on television, though it may be particularly common in periods when television has been under political attack. ("Happy news" began appearing on the local news not long after Vice President Spiro Agnew's 1969 assault on the media.) The story of how neighbors pull together at a time of crisis is one of the most common genres of good news. But in this case, there was a twist: Community Spirit became transformed into Nationalism. The last line of the story was supplied by a resident who said, "Everybody's interested in helping. And I say that's what makes America great. There's no country in the world like the United States." Then a shot of an American flag standing amid the rubble.

The response people in television generally give when asked

about the impact of Reagan is familiar. "Reagan has brightened the national mood; I don't think there's any question about that," said Bruce Morton. "And I think that clearly is reflected in the news coverage. As it should be: we're supposed to be kind of a mirror of what's going on." But the notion of "mirroring" hardly does justice to stories like Morton's or the NBC story from Newton Falls, which was reported by Jack Reynolds. Mirrors do not start out in soft focus. Television has not only mirrored but *identified itself* with this element of the popular mood. Morton's story, as its title indicates, was a song, a paean, not a mere report. So was Reynolds', closing not with a correspondent's wrap-up but with the views of the patriotic resident, reinforced with a symbolic visual. In each of these stories, television was in a sense doing what the morning news does in a less political way, with its folksy celebration of everyday life, and what Ronald Reagan has done with such powerful political effect: flattering the public.

To say that television responds to or even flatters the public mood is not necessarily to say that it gives a *voice* to the ordinary American. The hostage crisis is a good example. The hostages and their families were clearly the stars of television's drama. Their lives became immensely important. They were elevated to heroic proportions. But their role on television was primarily symbolic, and to the extent that they began to become participants in political discussion, rather than symbols of American courage, this made television people quite nervous; even as the hostages were being lauded as heroes, quite a bit of commentary was devoted to explaining them away ("the Stockholm syndrome") and counteracting some comments that were proving politically uncomfortable.

The American public mood, like any "public mood," is complex. Why does television choose to "mirror" the spirit of "We're Number One"? Surely there are a number of reasons, not least of which is that television people, like other Americans, sincerely believe in the image of America Reagan has invoked. But this kind of reporting is also very useful for television. In a way, Dan Rather is as much a politician as Ronald Reagan, not personally, but on behalf of his news organization. He goes before the public every day to appeal for "votes." And just as politicians have often found that it is more effective to wrap oneself in the flag and praise the wisdom of the People than to get involved in controversial political issues, so in recent years has television.

And what's wrong with "feeling good?" The danger is easy to see if we keep in mind the fact that the emphasis on the moral strength of America has been combined both with escalating rhetoric against consensus enemies and with an image of America as a nation under siege. In this context, the celebration of the new American "optimism" (it could, of course, be called "complacency" or "chauvinism" just as easily) has produced a strong trend toward a more black-and-white view of the world, partly reversing a shift toward more nuanced reporting that resulted from the movements and crises of the sixties.

This can be seen in the reporting of the Beirut hostage crisis, which is worth one last look. Despite all the furor about television becoming a hostage and an instrument of the terrorists, the most powerful theme in television coverage was the simple contrast between evil terrorists and good Americans going about their apolitical lives. This theme dominated coverage in the early days of the crisis, faded a little as reporters focused on the negotiations with Amal and the conditions of the hostages, and then returned with a vengeance—in part, no doubt, as a response to criticism of the networks for their slippage from the earlier theme—at the end of the crisis. The night the hostages were released, Dan Rather closed the live CBS special with his own summation of the event, which contrasted "profiles in cowardice" (the terrorists) and "profiles in courage" (the Americans). Conservatives lamented television's focus on the hostages, arguing in effect that it made it more difficult for the administration to treat them as expendable. And so it did. But personalizing the hostage crisis in the way television did also fed conservative rhetoric about the singular evil of terrorism.

There was, of course, evil here. The Americans were indeed innocent victims of political violence; and it is one of the strengths of television that it can convey a powerful sense of the human costs of terrorism, as it can the costs of war or recession or of apartheid in South Africa. But in two important ways, television's populist portrayal of the meaning of terrorism in Beirut, as in a number of other incidents, has been highly distorted. It is, in the first place, highly selective. There are, after all, tens of thousands of innocent victims of political violence in the world in any given year, only a tiny proportion of them American—and only a tiny proportion of them mentioned at all on television. Even the seven Salvadorans killed along with the six Americans in the attack that coincided with the TWA hijacking were hardly mentioned.

What sends television into a mode of high human concern and moral indignation—and here we come to the second way television's portrayal of terrorism is distorted—is not political violence against innocent human beings, not even necessarily violence against Americans (a number have died in political violence in Central America without this sort of attention), but the fact that this particular violence was seen as directed against *America* itself. As with Iran, the story in Beirut was not "people held hostage," not even "Americans held hostage," but (as ABC titled its half-hour nightly special on the Iran hostage crisis, which eventually became *Nightline*) "America held hostage." This is not to say that there is anything insincere about television's concern with the hostages and their families; what does happen, however, is that human concern is adapted to the service of political symbolism. The hostages were symbolic of America. The hostages were innocent victims of political violence. So it appears, in television's personalized portrayal of terrorism, that America is an innocent victim of political violence.

But at the political level, it is not clear that the language of innocent victims, of uncomplicated good and unadulterated evil, of courage and cowardice, is appropriate. Directly and indirectly, American policy has taken its share of innocent victims in the Middle East, as it has in Central America and many other places. The terrorists hardly have a monopoly on the killing of innocents. Terrorism, moreover, does not come out of nowhere—nor is it a result simply of the fanaticism or "cowardice" of certain individuals. It has political roots; and, again, American policymakers certainly bear some share of the responsibility. (Never in the course of the Beirut hostage crisis did I hear a television journalist mention the decision of the Reagan administration to use U.S. forces in Lebanon, initially brought in as peacekeepers, to intervene against Shiite forces in Lebanon's civil war.) But all of this complexity is pushed into the background once the story has been defined in terms of violence against the symbolic American everyman; to mention it comes to seem morally insensitive and unpatriotic.

In 1985, CBS was promoting its news broadcast with the slogan "We Keep America on Top of the World." Perhaps the double entendre was sheer coincidence; perhaps it was intended to capitalize on the "new patriotism." But it expresses a disturbing truth about television news in the age of Reagan: the news has in important ways shifted back toward the days when journalism was the strident ideological arm of cold war foreign policy, presenting the world as a great and simple battleground between good and evil, with America as the unique embodiment of good. One would think the nation would have learned over the course of forty years of cold war the dangers of this kind of perspective, which include not only the risk of war, both "limited" and cataclysmic, but also damage to democracy and complacency about festering problems within the United States. In the age of Reagan, however, television shows strong signs of repressing this history.

There are, fortunately, some countertendencies to Reaganism and the recent shift toward a more black-and-white view of the world. The post-Watergate ethic of independence and depth in news reporting, for one thing, is deeply entrenched and not likely to disappear altogether, at least without a drastic escalation of world tensions. There is also an element in the public mood now that has connections with Reaganism, in that it is related to the desire to have the old, idealistic America back, but which also runs deeply counter to the individualism, privatism, and bravado that have characterized the 1980s so far. This is the idealism that has manifested itself in the public reaction to South Africa and the famine in Ethiopia. These are of course distant and ideologically easy causes (particularly since Ethiopia has a Marxist enemy to denounce). But it is probably a good guess that some of this sentiment will begin spilling into more controversial areas. Already the print media show signs of rediscovering poverty in America. Television, contrary to the mythology about its immense power, rarely takes the lead in anything; rather, as a shift occurs, television follows cautiously behind. For now, however, television is being swept along, and helping to sweep the country along, on a dangerous journey into an idealized past.

Search for Yesterday

RUTH ROSEN

In 1942, a jury sentenced to death Toni
Jo Henry, a twenty-six-year-old woman convicted of murder. During her final days, the *New York Post* asked about her last thoughts. "I'm worried about *Abie's Irish Rose,*" she explained. "Every day I used to listen to it. But they discontinued the serial until September and I won't be here in September." Shortly thereafter, the producers of the soap opera *Abie's Irish Rose* sent the condemned woman a synopsis of the story covering installments from September through the following June.

Although extreme, Toni Jo Henry's immersion in the fictive world of soap opera was not—and is not—unusual. Ever since soap operas began as fifteen-minute radio serials in the 1930s, they have been astonishingly successful at converting normal, unsuspecting Americans into loyal addicts. When soaps shifted from radio to television in the fifties, their audiences remained loyal. In the eighties, the soaps expanded to one-hour dramas and captured a far more diverse following. Like Toni Jo Henry, many of these viewers willingly suspend their disbelief in an imaginary world and find, much to their surprise, that they care at least as much about soap characters as about people they know.

For some viewers, the world of the soap and their own daily lives begin to blur. Early in my research, I encountered one such fan. At a local supermarket, I picked up *Soap Opera Digest,* a magazine that offers weekly synopses of soap plots and articles about the stars. The cashier, in her late teens, quickly spotted the magazine I had hidden between the detergent and the broccoli. Its cover featured a famous couple from ABC's popular soap, *General Hospital.* As she rang up the items, the cashier commented, "I think Grant and Celia will work it out, don't you?" Stunned, I nodded. She bagged my groceries and continued her monologue on Grant and Celia's marital problems, offering suggestions and advice. Imperceptibly, I had slipped into the curious world of the soap opera. The cashier simply assumed that I too was a "resident" of *General Hospital*'s fictional Port Charles.

She was not entirely wrong. Fifteen years ago, confined to a hospital bed for nearly a month, I found solace and stimulation in the daily crises of Port Charles' residents. I began to care about the characters, to wonder about their fates. Their problems seemed infinitely more interesting and, yes, comforting, than the real medical world that surrounded me. Since then, I have kept contact. You could say I am an occasional abuser, not a confirmed addict.

That experience helps me understand the intensity of viewers' feelings about *their* soaps. An actor on *All My Children* says that "viewers feel they know more about you. . . . They feel they have some kind of ownership of you." A fan of the same program threatens: "I'll stop watching the show if May [a character] is killed off!" The long-postponed marriage of Luke and Laura on *General Hospital* produces mounds of letters from frustrated viewers.

Viewers frequently confuse the character with the actor. An actress who played the wicked Lisa on *As the World Turns* for sixteen years is punched by an irate viewer in front of Manhattan's Lord & Taylor department store. CBS finds that viewers send carefully wrapped "Care" packages to actors who play impoverished characters. An actress on *All My Children* reports that fans begin their letters by addressing *her* and then imperceptibly slip into accusatory condemnations of her character's actions. When Julie, in *Days of Our Lives,* wonders whether to have an abortion, actress Susan Hayes receives pictures of fetuses in the mail.

Every week, an invisible nation of more than fifty million Americans watches soap operas. Eighty percent are women. Although soap producers, as well as advertisers, mainly seek a female audience between eighteen and forty-nine years of age, daytime drama has broadened its appeal during the last decade. Stereotypical viewers of the past—the housewife, the infirm, the retired—have now been joined by teenagers, professionals, and college students, both female and male.

Soap operas have even attained a chic status among celebrities, who increasingly own up to what was once a secret passion. Supreme Court Justice Thurgood Marshall, for example, is reported to find time to watch *Days of Our Lives*. Sammy Davis, Jr., became so entranced with *Love of Life* and *General Hospital* that he agreed to make several guest appearances. Elizabeth Taylor, also a fan of *General Hospital,* spiced up daytime drama by making several well-publicized cameo appearances. Former Texas Governor John Connally and avant-garde artist Andy Warhol are two of the ten million fans who follow *As the World Turns.*

Many people, however, embarrassed about their addiction, still take considerable efforts to hide their secret. As I pass the word around that I am investigating the world of the soap opera, closet addicts, assuming my tolerance, confess their passion. A well-known writer admits that she routinely schedules early lunches to avoid missing *One Life to Live.* One of my male colleagues sheepishly reveals that he heads home in the middle of the day to catch his two favorite soaps. A female executive shyly discloses that she keeps a tiny portable TV in her office so she can catch *All My Children* while lunching in private. A distinguished editor who became addicted to a soap expresses great relief when the program is canceled: "I've never dared look seriously at another for fear that my life might slowly trickle away. . . ."

But the furtive maneuvers of such closet viewers are gradually becoming unnecessary. Many viewers already tape their favorite soap or soaps on videocassette recorders. Daytime soaps consistently join such prime-time favorites as *Dynasty* and *Dallas* among the ten most commonly taped television programs. Some viewers even convert the "screenings" into social events. A well-known daytime actress tells me that soaps are very popular among the Malibu set. One actress, unable to watch *General Hospital* during the week, tapes the programs and offers an all-day screening for her friends on Saturday, complete with hors d'oeuvres and champagne. But VCRs are no longer the monopoly of the upscale. I walk into a dark recreational hall where university students watch television on a giant screen. It is the middle of the afternoon. There, sprawled amid their books, coats, and day packs, are several hundred devotees watching *General Hospital* in complete silence. On some college campuses, the daily happenings of *All My Children* are reported in the campus newspaper. In many cities, synopses of all the daytime soaps also appear in the daily paper.

There is no doubt that soap operas have moved closer to the center of American popular culture. The source of their popularity, however, has puzzled researchers ever since the days of radio. Herta Herzog, an early investigator of radio soap culture, concluded during World War II that soaps give viewers emotional release, vicarious wish fulfillment, and advice about how to conduct their lives. Others have pointed to the soaps' suspense; one becomes addicted to the characters' unfolding fate. As in life, one never knows how it will all turn out. Still others have suggested simplistically that soaps help viewers overcome loneliness and escape the predictability of daily routine. Some argue that viewers enjoy identifying with the characters' successes or, alternatively, with their suffering.

Undoubtedly, each of these notions does explain part of the soaps' mass appeal. Soaps can ease the loneliness and boredom of life. They do offer advice, sometimes implicitly, often explicitly, on what to wear, how to conduct love affairs, how to save a marriage, how to handle one's children, how to cope with heartache, how to enjoy the intrigue of romance. But soaps do more: they provide a surrogate family and social life, a stable network of friends and neighbors. Soaps offer continuity. People don't just watch soap operas; they live with them. Day after day, "as the world turns," soap characters bare their struggles without making any real-life demands upon the viewer. With almost no effort at all, the viewer can participate vicariously in love affairs, friendships, and intrigue that seem intimate but are safely remote. Soaps, for example, create an illusion of

male-female intimacy that many women seek from baffled and re-
luctant husbands. The interior world of soap characters is often more
accessible—and less risky—than the feelings of one's actual friends
or family.

Viewers frequently "see" soap characters more often than they
visit their friends or relatives. Agnes Nixon, who created *All My
Children,* now a campus favorite, asked students at Duke University
why they watched the soaps. One young man replied, "It's the only
constant in our lives." The writer Renata Adler, who became addicted to *Another World* during a prolonged illness, says, "I saw the
characters in the soaps more often than my friends. It had a continuity stronger even than the news." A Princeton University historian who started watching *All My Children* while teaching a new
course on American popular culture now admits, "I feel like it must
be an illness with me. I've got to have my fix every day."

It should not be surprising that all sorts of Americans—not only
the bed- and house-ridden—find solace in the mythically stable
communities of soap operas. Some soap communities, after all, have
lasted over thirty years. All potential viewers are members of a
society that has been in constant transformation through geographic
mobility and the loss of extended families. Loneliness, we are repeatedly told, has become pandemic in America, and the longing
for community is a palpable need. Whether through religion, clubs,
associations, or support groups—or through daily immersion in a
favorite soap—many Americans search for some kind of communal
life to counter varying degrees of social isolation and alienation.

Nor is this quest new. There is no golden past in America,
despite the continuous effort to look back to one. To be an American
has meant uprooting oneself from the old country, then struggling
to adjust again to new settings, new cultural trends, new jobs, and
new technologies. And, for the most part, Americans do it rather
well. "Newness" long ago acquired a sacred place in the national
iconography, as did "opportunity." But individual success, when it
came, was often at the expense of the continuity of family and
community. The tension between the American commitment to
individualism and the perennial search for a communal and collective life is at the heart of American social and cultural identity: it
has sparked reform movements and instigated cyclical periods of

national anxiety and introspection. It has also given us apparently contradictory myths: the ascent of Horatio Alger, and the small American town that no one ever wants to leave.

How did men ever move up and out? One way of resolving the conflict between individualism and communal life was to assign one sex to govern public life and the other, the private sphere. In the middle of the nineteenth century, as home and work gradually became separated, Americans increasingly identified women with the emotional values and needs of family and community life. In the national mythology the home became a refuge. At the hearth one could find the noncommercial, Christian values of a preindustrial, precapitalist society. There the individual could count on the nurturance and caretaking missing in the cruel utilitarian world of commerce. There family and community took precedence over private calculation, the home becoming the repository of all that was no longer valued in public life.

As men's work increasingly drew them away from family life, they gradually became identified with the commercial values, the dangers, and the competition of the market economy. But the public sphere was strewn with risks as well as opportunities: a man could strike it rich or lose his job. Whatever the result, Americans increasingly held a man responsible for the consequences of his own actions. In the secularized world of the nineteenth century, Americans seldom took Providence for granted. God's will had become man's, to do with as best he could.

In this sexually bifurcated world, men were obligated to seek an individual destiny that often conflicted with the female world of home and community. The national mythology required that a man move on, restlessly pursuing financial success at every chance. But the price of such relentless ambition was the disruption of family and community life. Americans, however, were resourceful. As early as 1835, de Tocqueville noted that Americans were busy creating a vast network of associations that would provide a surrogate communal life. Still, as the cities expanded, Americans mourned the passing of the small towns they had left behind. The more they were forced to confront the anonymity of urban life, the more they mythologized the stability, face-to-face recognition, shared values, and moral accountability of the village. By the early decades of the twentieth century, this myth had grown to such proportions that it inspired Progressive reformers to attempt to make over the American city into a small town. In their struggle to end gambling, eliminate liquor, and abolish prostitution, reformers held up a communal past in which men and women, as well as different classes, knew exactly where they belonged—and stayed there. Ironically, all this was attempted as the suffrage movement was nearing success, labor was challenging the hegemony of business, and the poor began dressing according to fashion rather than class position.

Throughout the twentieth century, the ideal of the American town has grown stronger, even as such actual communities have dried up. In the end, Americans sanctified the memory of the village as a stand-in for the moral community. In times of poverty, Americans kept alive the hope that family and community would sustain the individual. Radio soaps, as cultural historian Warren Susman has noted, "played a role in reinforcing fundamental values . . . they provided a sense of continuity, assuring the triumph of generally shared values and beliefs, no matter what 'reality' in the form of social and economic conditions might suggest." In times of relative plenty, moralists insisted that traditional values should and could constrain lust and greed. As contemporary life became more atomistic and less communal, more private and less public, the myth of the community survived and prospered.

Amid rapid social and cultural change, many Americans have suffered from a kind of social vertigo. It is a perennial theme in sociology that, as Lyn Lofland puts it, "the transformation from the world of personally known others to the world of strangers has been and continues to be an emotionally painful one." Warren Susman has observed that the main drama of twentieth-century America is the supplanting of the Puritan-republican, producer-capitalist culture by the leisure-centered culture of consumer society. The consumer culture, predicated on abundance, emphasizes pleasure over work; it defines pleasure, moreover, as a matter of individual consumption. Despite a public ideology of "togetherness," people sort out their identities less through relations, more through purchases and the fugitive identifications of popular culture.

Here lies the extraordinary appeal and irony of the daytime soap opera; it is circulated by the very commercial culture which has engendered the need for it in the first place. As the stable small town fades, the soap opera keeps alive its idealized replica, the image of a community in which everyone knows or is related to everyone else, where continuity counts more than transience, where right and wrong are unambiguous, where good triumphs over evil. It is a world dominated by the domestic values of the family. Loyalty to family and community ultimately matter more than the individual's quest for success. Not that personal passion and ambition are missing. On the contrary, most of the drama turns on situations in which individual greed or lust conflicts with a family's best interests. While the monogamous heterosexual family is idealized, for example, love and passion, daily soap subjects, take place largely outside it. Moral failure is tolerated, but never condoned. As long as sinners bow to the community's idea of itself, they can belong and be redeemed. At the end of each strand of plot, all conflict is resolved so that the traditional values of the community and family are reaffirmed.

If this sounds like a good old-fashioned morality play, it is. But unlike the morality play, it has no beginning and no end. Soaps are like the serialized morality novels of the eighteenth and nineteenth centuries which also exaggerated the ordinary, examined every problem from everyone's point of view, and extended plots for months, even years. The most immediate roots of the contemporary soap opera, however, are the radio soaps of the late twenties and thirties. Irna Phillips, who is credited with creating the conventions of the American radio soap opera, explained her philosophy shortly before her death: "The essence of the drama is still conflict, of course—conflict within each person, conflict between two people . . . I'm trying to get back to the fundamentals; for example, the way in which a death in the family, or serious illness, brings members of the family closer together, gives them a real sense of how much they're dependent on each other." Her successor, Agnes Nixon, who continued the nearly matrilineal hold on American soap opera creation, agrees about the importance of family and communal life. When she came up with the basic story line—"bible"—for *All My Children,* Nixon decided that "the community of Pine Valley is almost as important in our story as are the characters themselves."

On daytime soaps, characters value old-fashioned "honesty," "fidelity," "loyalty," and indeed "character," at least in principle. In return for good behavior, they expect membership in a community that will always forgive, always come to the rescue. They need never suffer alone. As in the Bible, they live in a world saturated with ultimate meaning. Even the small, daily problems of the individual become the concerns of the community. Perhaps this is what is most conspicuous about the soaps. Nowhere else in American popular culture do people spend as much time discussing and analyzing the personal problems of other people. This is, in short, a female world, one in which women's culture, with its traditional emphasis on interpersonal relations, takes precedence over business and public life.

In her research on human development, cognitive psychologist Carol Gilligan found an essential difference between the sexes: while men tended to make judgments according to abstract moral principles, women were much more likely to decide on the basis of how their actions would affect other people. On daytime soaps, the split dissolves: both men and women are judged by the values of the women's world. Men discuss romance, family, and personal problems with the same intensity as women. Only on soaps do men value the verbal intimacy that Lillian Rubin, in *Intimate Strangers*, found lacking in most traditional marriages. In the soap's world, everyone is preoccupied with personal life, and the community is the family writ large. It is a community no one is supposed to leave. Many covet wealth, but happiness is defined by the bonds that bind.

The uniqueness of this domestic rule becomes clearer when we compare daytime soaps with their prime-time counterparts. On *Dynasty* or *Dallas*, family loyalty is encouraged, but easy wealth and sex are often pursued at the expense of loyalty to community. The dazzling Sunbelt cities of prime-time soaps are also a long way, economically and spiritually, from the mythical northeastern towns of daytime soaps. True, the melodramatic evening and daytime soaps have in some ways begun to converge. Adventure stories, fancier production values, and more on-location scenes have come to daytime. Rich family dynasties—whose wealth is mysteriously based in the Sunbelt—increasingly take up residence in northeastern soap communities. The evening soaps, for their part, have drawn on typical soap opera cliff-hangers to sustain audience anticipation from week to week. Even so, daytime and evening soaps remain a world apart. Evening soaps are about the pursuit of power more than happiness. With only one hour a week and a much larger male audience, they rely far more on glamour and fast-paced action than on the endless analysis of personal conflicts. The extreme wealth and cutthroat ambition so lovingly—if at times ambiguously—portrayed at night contrasts sharply with the humdrum domesticity of the daytime soaps. Most important, the difference between daytime and evening soaps has to do, as Agnes Nixon put it, with the "suffering of consequences." On evening soaps, there is no time to experience the consequences of stupid or sinful behavior; during the day there is time for little else.

Enter, then, the peculiar world of the daytime soap opera. *General Hospital* makes a good case study: it has lasted more than twenty years on television, and since the late seventies has been one of the most popular of the approximately fifteen daytime soaps. As a trendy soap, moreover, *General Hospital* seems to be about lust and greed, while it in fact reaffirms traditional loyalties.

General Hospital made its television debut in 1963. After twenty-six weeks, its poor ratings caused ABC to consider cancellation. The network relented, however. (Unlike prime-time programs, which can be yanked in a few weeks, soaps are given two or three years in which to attract a loyal following.) Like most soaps of the fifties and early sixties, *General Hospital* was deeply melancholy, somber, and moralistic. The production was bare bones; in simple kitchen and hospital settings, sipping endless cups of coffee, people mulled over each other's problems and beat their breasts. Actress Emily McLaughlin, who has played nurse Jessie Brewer for over two decades, remembers that "we never smiled or very seldom, organ music was playing almost all the time, and no good person drove a sports car. There was an idea among all soap producers or the networks that the audience was totally women and the women got their frustrations out by crying along with us." Plots reflected the Manichaean mood of the cold war era: people were either saints or villains. The regenerate were redeemed by vaguely religious values.

Then, in the late sixties and early seventies, a few soaps began to reflect the massive social changes that were sweeping the country. Agnes Nixon, in particular, transformed the look of daytime soap opera with two new ABC creations: *One Life to Live* and *All My Children*. She brightened the sets, introduced faster-paced dialogue, injected controversial and racy subjects into the story line and, as a result, not surprisingly earned the network top ratings.

By contrast, *General Hospital*'s ratings were faltering. Rather than cancel the program, in 1977 ABC assigned Gloria Monty, a talented former theater and soap director, to revamp the show. Lavish sets and fashionable costumes brightened the program's formerly bleak look. The writings became snappier; rapid repartee and streaks of humor enlivened and modernized the characters. Rock music, the electronic synthesizer, even orchestration replaced the previously ubiquitous Hammond organ. The sexual revolution arrived in Port Charles; *General Hospital* earned a new reputation as the sexiest daytime soap on television. To the staple of romance—adultery, love triangles, and unrequited love—Monty added fantastic adventure and mystery stories that heightened the suspense and successfully appealed to a growing male audience. On-location filming—even in foreign countries and on exotic islands—added glamour to the usual interior sets. Most important, Monty appealed to young people by introducing in the late seventies two of television's hottest young daytime stars, Luke Spencer and Laura Webber.

Things develop slowly on the soaps. Luke and Laura took a few years to surmount the many obstacles that blocked their romance. By the early eighties, their lurid and frustrated liaison (which began with his raping her) became a national sensation. In September 1981, the star-crossed lovers appeared on the cover of *Newsweek;* that November, fourteen million people, a full 43 percent of the television-viewing audience, made daytime rating history as they witnessed the couple's long-awaited wedding, adorned with a guest appearance by Elizabeth Taylor.

With such publicity, a daytime soap for the first time fully entered the mainstream of American popular culture. *Southwest General,* the soap featured in the film *Tootsie,* was, to the cognoscenti, a transparent parody of *General Hospital.* (Dustin Hoffman even spent time on the *General Hospital* set preparing for his role.) Students at Harvard University invited Monty and several actors to discuss the program at a public forum. (The auditorium was jammed.) A series of soft-rock stars—including Rick Springfield and Jack Wagner—made soap opera debuts on *General Hospital*. Theme songs used to identify certain characters and romances on the show became popular hits. During Luke's ill-fated romance with Holly, an unknown melody entitled "Baby, Come to Me" accompanied their every encounter. Within months, the song zoomed to the top of the hit list and went "gold," selling over half a million records. In 1984, Jack Wagner, in his role as Frisco Jones, Port Charles' local rock star, created another musical hit when he sang a sweetish ballad, "All I Need."

Monty's efforts have netted handsome profits for ABC. Soaps are among the networks' most profitable enterprises. The soaps are relatively inexpensive to produce: five days of *General Hospital* can be produced for the cost of a single episode of *The A-Team*. Daytime soaps also bring in huge advertising revenues: the networks allot twice as much commercial time to daytime drama as to prime time. At its peak in 1981–82, for example, *General Hospital* grossed more than $253 million in advertising revenues and commanded $60,000 per minute of commercial time. In 1983, ABC reportedly cleared $1 million a week from *General Hospital*'s $2.7 million in annual advertising revenues. In 1984, the three networks together reaped over $1 billion in annual advertising revenues from the soaps.

Many soaps, like *General Hospital,* are owned directly by producers, not leased from independent production companies like primetime shows. Procter & Gamble, once the major producer of soaps—hence their name—now creates only a handful which are, by current standards, old-fashioned and targeted at an older audience. When soap companies produced their own programs, they dictated much of the content and even integrated their products into the story line. In contrast, no brand names appear on today's soaps. Nor do soap products dominate the commercials. But the commercials do extend the tenor of the soaps. Like the serials themselves, these commercials are upbeat, didactic tales which advise women how to glamorize themselves and deodorize their homes. Fake nails and creams promising eternal youth teach women how to emulate the soap stars and hang on to their men; spotted glassware warns of the calamities that endanger the perfect dinner party. Even men do some housework now; the dreary housewife of the old-fashioned soaps has been expelled from the commercials as from the program itself.

Although ABC's soaps are commonly viewed as the most daring and trendy on television, they still observe the conventions of day-time serial drama. For one thing, with the exception of a few new daytime serials—*Capitol, Santa Barbara,* and *Ryan's Hope*—most soaps are still set in small northeastern towns like Port Charles, where the four seasons and traditional holidays are observed and a respectable distance separates the community from the evils of the Big City.

No longer a town, Port Charles has gradually expanded into a small city that somehow retains the values and intimacy of a sheltered community. Where is Port Charles? From the dialogue, we imagine that it is conveniently close to, but safely distant from, the political corruptions of Albany and the cultural seductions of New York City. Producer Monty says it is "somewhere on the Great Lakes." The viewer never sees Port Charles, however. The opening shot is of the large, sprawling hospital. Although some soaps (*One Life to Live,* for example) now open with a panoramic view of the town, most leave the soap community entirely to the viewer's imagination. And why not? The community, after all, is more an idea than a physical place. It is known largely through the inner lives of its inhabitants and the physical interiors of its hospitals, offices, restaurants, and the comfortable rooms of its middle-class homes. The community consists of interlocking networks—thirty or forty people, most of whom know or are related to each other.

To the novice viewer, their complicated relations are at first incomprehensible. This community has a history; its present refers to its past and its past is filled with revelations, intrigues, and love affairs that resonate through every conversation. The uninitiated viewer must also disentangle a web of six or more interrelated stories, some just beginning, others approaching their dramatic climax. How is one to make sense of a dramatic form that has no beginning, no middle, no end, and no protagonist?

The inexperienced viewer is "positioned," in a sense, like a new-comer to a community. When one moves into a new town, it takes time to ferret out relations and events that older residents might prefer to forget. Fortunately, the structure and conventions of the soap opera make it relatively easy to pick up in the eternal middle. In the past, a narrator explained at the beginning of each program what had just happened. Today, soap operas seduce the viewer with a few short scenes introducing some of the day's stories. After a few commercials, a sequence of scenes begins. In each scene, the characters recite news of recent events and tell how they feel about them, as in the hackneyed maid scene that established the plot line of the standard drawing-room comedy. Four or five minutes later, a new scene begins. Different characters react to another problem. To maintain social cohesion, the soap community makes sure that all the members keep up with all the problems. Day after day, Port Charles' residents spread the word. As each person learns, with the aid of overheard conversations and flashbacks, so the viewer learns. Gradually, the viewer is drawn into the circle of insiders.

Often the viewer sees from a position of privilege, discovering a character's secrets and deceptions months before the rest of the community. The delayed denouement of each subplot allows the viewer to speculate on the outcome of individual behavior, to imagine hypothetical solutions, to form judgments. In this way, the viewer gains an intimate knowledge of the community. In this way, the viewer gets addicted.

The surface realism of the soap opera conjures up an illusion of "liveness." The domestic settings and easygoing rhythms encourage the viewer to believe that the drama, however ridiculous, is simply an extension of daily life. The conversation is so slow that some have called it "radio with pictures." (Advertisers have always assumed that busy housewives would listen, rather than watch.) Conversation is casual and colloquial, as though one were eavesdropping on neighbors. There is plenty of time to "read" the character's face; close-ups establish intimacy. The sets are comfortably familiar; well-lit interiors of living rooms, restaurants, offices, and hospitals. Daytime soaps have little of the glamour of their prime-time relations. The viewer easily imagines that the conversation is taking place in real time.

But, of course, this "liveness" is a contrivance. Soaps give us not a mirror reflection of reality, but a bent and stylized dailiness filtered through hundreds of peculiar conventions. To name a few: Soap characters rarely eat meals; they nibble snacks and sip coffee.

When they do eat, it is usually in restaurants. Motherhood is glorified, but women are rarely seen caring for children. Children are often raved about, but seldom put in an appearance. Child care is invisible and seemingly not problematic. Family life is extolled, but divorce occurs twice as often as in actual American society. There are more doctors than patients in the hospital. Professional people mainly discuss their personal problems, not their work. No one ever swears; no one ever goes to the bathroom; nothing is out of place unless a burglary has taken place. Illicit sexual relations often result in pregnancy, usually followed by a convenient miscarriage. People rarely die of familiar or lingering diseases (which would frighten viewers), but succumb to "mountain fever" or sudden car accidents. Men are particularly plagued by paralysis of the legs. Plots are byzantine and bizarre: blackmail and amnesia happen commonly; once-lost-now-found relatives show up frequently; a woman who has a hysterectomy becomes a mother; a woman spends seventeen days in a revolving door having flashbacks; an astounding number of people develop split personalities; cliff-hangers always occur on Fridays.

And so it goes. The soap opera is in fact a highly idiosyncratic version of reality. The lurid aspects are those most easily parodied by unfamiliar voyeurs. But what is more peculiar, in some ways, is the nature of the community itself. Most of Port Charles' residents are white Anglo-Saxon professionals who live middle- to upper-class lives. As in many other soap operas, the audience is privileged to know the power elite of Port Charles: the mayor, the police commissioner, the hospital chief of staff, the chief cardiologist. Each of these men is married, each lives in a bright, well-decorated, and tidy home.

Sandwiching this middle-class community are a few of the very rich and the poor. The rich are often too stuffy; the poor, too gauche. Nevertheless, both rich and poor share problems plaguing the middle class. The Quartermaine family, the wealthiest family in town, is not exempt from suffering. Like everyone else, its members have skeletons in their closets; they endure blackmail and the consequences of their own greed. Their lives, moreover, can be tedious. Monica Quartermaine, a heart surgeon who has married into the family, expresses the subtext for much of soap drama when she confesses her disappointment with her superficial life: "I don't think happiness lasts very long."

If the rich are not made happy by their wealth, the poor are sometimes made strong by their lack of it. In Port Charles, the poor, mostly white, eke out their living in a depressed and seamy area called "the waterfront." When the working class is not being used for comic relief—such as suggesting idiotic solutions to problems—they are there to demonstrate what true community is really like. Kelly's Diner, run by the indomitable Ruby Spencer, is a waterfront joint where the working class gathers and the middle class seeks solace. A former madam, Ruby is a straightforward working-class woman who dispenses, along with her excellent cooking, wisdom about what really matters: honesty, integrity, and loyalty to family and community. Her niece and nephew, Bobbie and Luke Spencer, grew up on the street and fell into criminal activity, but ended up winning the respect of the community by becoming hardworking and devoted citizens. Unlike the rich or most of the middle class, these people have guts and conviction. The poor, alas, also have their skeletons and heartaches. Because of their poverty, they are especially vulnerable to greed. Their distrust of respectable society, moreover, makes them an ornery group to help, as the rich discover when they seek to establish a waterfront clinic.

Class conflict, however, is minimal in Port Charles. Since nearly everyone knows or is related to everyone else, relations among the privileged and the waterfront folk are characterized more by irritation than by any hint of class hatred. Marriage between classes, and the camaraderie of hospital work, also make for social cohesion. This is a community held together by the deep belief that there is a shared solidarity beneath all petty squabbles and past wrongs. Rich and poor may not celebrate holidays in the same way or in the same place, but all feel they belong to the same community.

Until recently, few even token ethnics or racial minorities lived in Port Charles. When asked why, producer Gloria Monty resorts to truism: "We can't do everything." The explanation, however, is far more complex. Soap communities have to be believable; it is simply not credible that a community filled with mainstream Anglos as well as ethnic and racial minorities could live together in intimate harmony in present-day America. Nor does interracial or even interfaith romance seem to "work" on daytime drama. Romance, we must remember, is a key element of the soap world. Elusive and dangerous, it can enter people's lives at any moment. To cross the boundaries of color or religion, even vicariously, is apparently unacceptable to the soap audience—or so traditional TV wisdom has it—and therefore to network executives. For a while, for example, *General Hospital* featured a hot love affair between a sensitive Jewish attorney and a charming Irish Catholic woman. Although the soap community generally accepted them, the woman faced serious ostracism from close friends and relatives who remained largely offscreen. According to one actress, ABC faced similar offscreen problems—from irate viewers. In the end, the love affair was cut short and the actress left the show.

As a result of the civil rights movement of the sixties, most soaps now include one or two black couples in an otherwise all-white community. They are usually middle-class professionals, indistinguishable from their white counterparts—except for color—and fairly well integrated into the white community. Their romantic involvements are limited by the scarcity of other black people.

On rare occasions, though, soaps do deal with issues that actually reflect on the pain of the black experience. On *One Life to Live,* a young light-skinned black woman, Carla Gray, "passed" as white until she fell in love with a black man and had to confront her racial heritage. *General Hospital* has explored the issue of different class backgrounds among blacks. Claudia, raised in a wealthy family, has little patience with her husband, Brian, who comes from a less affluent background and remains preoccupied with the problems of the poor. Despite a few such imaginative efforts, ethnic and racial minorities are marginal characters hovering at the periphery of the community. Audience response, moreover, inhibits further racial integration of the soaps. In the seventies, *Search for Tomorrow* introduced a story line about a black youth center. Negative audience response, however, resulted in the story being dropped.

In a rare departure from its presentation of its usual homogeneous community, *General Hospital* in 1985 suddenly introduced an Asian quarter in Port Charles. With the exception of two token characters who are integrated into the hospital crowd, the Asian quarter mainly reinforces hackneyed stereotypes of competing gangs and a mysterious Asian Godfather figure who, as a clear villain, extorts the shopkeepers of the quarter and threatens the law and order of Port Charles. Predictably, the story line plays upon contemporary fears of immigration even as it espouses equal opportunity for all. Good will triumph over evil when the mysterious Mr. Woo is eliminated; then, each member of the quarter "will have the choice to become rich or poor."

Ethnics were not always such marginal characters on the soaps. Those who remember radio soaps will wonder what happened to *The Rise of the Goldbergs, Abie's Irish Rose,* and other ethnic serials. *Ryan's Hope,* an exception, continues the tradition of setting a soap in an urban ethnic enclave and exploring the heartaches of a subculture that is marginal to the dominant society. Radio soaps aimed at specifically rural or ethnic audiences. Today, soap producers rightly or wrongly think they have to avoid ethnic characters in order to reach their maximum audience in the South and Midwest. "We want to appeal to everyone," says Monty emphatically.

Monty is not alone in seeking the broadest possible audience by limiting controversial subjects or objectionable characters. All soap producers are extremely responsive to their audience. In addition to ratings, networks use viewers' letters to measure the popularity of particular characters or stories. An absence of letters condemns an actor to unemployment, a story line to the dustheap. Many viewers, moreover, *want* comfort, not controversy. One Pittsburgh viewer explained in a letter to a soap producer:

> You may not think so, but most of us like the more down-to-earth story and characters than all too many added "way-out" concepts. We all need to feel and know that there is still normal, average day-to-day living out there . . . what is badly needed today is a comfortable feeling. There are already enough sadistic novels, television plays, news, and "what have you" to make you want to run and hide.

In addition to offering harmony and homogeneity, the community also delivers considerable stability. Despite constant divorce and remarriage, the community, we are assured, goes on forever.

Strangers come and go, but Port Charles' core of families continues. In fact, the stranger serves an important function by reinforcing and reaffirming the values of the community. Through the eyes of the stranger, the viewer is able to behold the full-blown virtue of Port Charles. Usually a stranger is introduced as a relative of a Port Charles resident. Often he or she arrives as a villain intending to exploit or otherwise threaten the community. If the character is not to be written out of the story line, a conversion must eventually take place. After causing much trouble, the villain must recognize the superior virtue of the community and decide to win the respect of his or her neighbors.

The story of *General Hospital*'s Grant Andrews is a particularly good example of such character transformation. When first introduced, Andrews is a foreign agent sent by the "motherland" to spy on the United States. (This cold war spy story began, not surprisingly, in the Reagan era.) He impersonates a former Port Charles resident who lies helpless in a hospital suffering from—what else? —amnesia. The impostor marries, assumes a respectable position as an orthopedic surgeon, begins to appreciate the values of the community and country, and ultimately defects. When the real Grant Andrews recovers from his amnesia and returns to Port Charles, he turns out to be a deranged and murderous lunatic. The impostor villain, after paying dearly for his deception, earns the community's forgiveness and becomes a respected member of Port Charles.

Such conversions are extremely common. Some of the most central characters in Port Charles initially arrived with sinister intentions. Chris Robinson, an actor who plays the highly respected Rick Webber on *General Hospital,* notes that on soaps, "murderers, whores, prostitutes can become heroines. I believe that can happen in real life. I think the percentages are 1 in 1000. On *General Hospital,* it's 10 out of 12." At the same time, respectable people may suddenly be seized by lust or greed that flips their lives around. At one point, the virtuous Rick Webber jeopardizes his family and career by having a passionate love affair with the beautiful and seductive Monica Quartermaine. In the end, they return to their proper spouses (a common but by no means predictable resolution). As in life, people change and the reasons are not always clear. On soaps, however, people change with greater frequency; to sustain dramatic tension, individuals are daily threatened by temptation.

In the world of the soaps, life is not easy. Despite efforts to make daytime drama more upbeat, there is still much suffering. Problems, after all, are what the soaps are about. And there are many: bigamy, adultery, betrayal, illegitimacy, love triangles, deception, and sexual rivalry, to name but a few. Within the last decade, the soaps have also started to explore such topical issues as drug addiction, obesity, incest, mastectomy, child abuse, wife beating, career versus family, plastic surgery, and rape. Fear of hinting at a large, grim, public reality excludes such issues as infant mortality, plant closings, unemployment, homelessness, and war.

Whatever the problem, it is always treated as personal rather than social or political in its origins: people bring on their own pain by succumbing to temptations that they know are in conflict with the best interests of family and community. To preserve her hard-won respectability, Ginny Blake hides her sordid past from her new husband. The past, however, always catches up on the soaps; so she is blackmailed, and her lie nearly wrecks her marriage. In the end, she realizes that a lie—however well meant—is wrong.

The emphasis on personal problems, of course, obscures the social and political culture in which Americans actually live. In the soap world, the victim is always blamed. Dealing with social or political problems, Gloria Monty insists, "is not our job." In Port Charles there is no institutionalized racism or sexism; the struggle over the Equal Rights Amendment never happened and one never knows if the United States happens to be at war. This mythic community, turned in on itself, is obsessed solely with its private agonies, drawing unity only from its individual pains.

The exclusive emphasis on personal problems is not inherent in the genre of soap drama; rather, it is an accurate reflection of the peculiarly apolitical culture of the United States. In Brazil, for example, where evening soap operas are a national obsession shared by gatherings of friends and families, current political and social debates are commonly woven into the story lines. Brazilian soaps are not about mythic communities that endure forever. They are dramas situated in modern cities, exploring contemporary social

problems, lasting six to ten months, then replaced by completely
new plots and characters. As evening fare, they are produced by
some of the best talent in Brazilian television, and appeal to a more
diverse audience.

Along with the sexual revolution, the therapeutic culture has also
arrived in most American daytime soap communities. Problems are
not only personal; they also are interpreted—and cured—through
psychological insight. Therapeutic redemption has replaced religious salvation. Evil is no longer unexplained; it is understood
through an excess of psychobabble. Characters continually ask each
other how they "feel" about everything. Couples are encouraged to
"communicate"—not because honesty is the best policy, but because marriage will falter without "open discussion." Soap characters insist that good sex makes a good marriage; if the marriage
sours, one of the partners must be hiding something. The danger of
psychological repression is ubiquitous. When rock singer Frisco
Jones finds he cannot make a serious commitment to Felicia, she
begs him to reveal what he has repressed. After considerable pressure, he pours out his sordid memories and is cured. The past, in
other words, creates emotional constipation; psychological revelation is the purgative that frees characters to go on with their lives.

Many of the evil deeds committed by soap characters are also
placed in psychoanalytic perspective. Most soap communities have
a resident psychiatrist or therapist who, along with other characters,
uses the authority of therapeutic language to explain the sources of
peoples' fatal flaws. Monica Quartermaine's relentless pursuit of love
and wealth is understood as a result of her childhood traumas as an
orphan. Ginny Blake's ruthless ambition originates from her youthful poverty on the wrong side of town. D. L. Brock beats his wife
because of problems he has failed to resolve in his past. Evil, while
still unpredictable, is no longer inexplicable. But the past only
explains, never excuses, individual behavior. Luke Spencer, for example, once a partner in organized crime, starts out as a menace to
the community. Later, when he undergoes the obligatory conversion
and saves the city from a bizarre scheme to destroy it by freezing it,
he becomes a hero and is elected mayor. His sister Bobbi, once a
conniving prostitute, becomes a respectable and ambitious nurse.
Their pasts are explained as a result of early years spent as streetwise

orphans on the wrong side of the tracks. Although their sins are forgiven, their flaws are remembered, not explained away by childhood poverty. The underlying flaws serve to remind others of the consequences of wrongdoing, indeed to shore up the community's virtue as a ministry of forgiveness.

Such individualism also frames the way soaps depict feminism. Along with the sexual revolution and the therapeutic culture, feminism—or at least the white, middle-class, professional version of it—has also arrived in Port Charles. No longer do female characters sit at home discussing their problems over the kitchen table. Now most women characters work as lawyers, surgeons, and journalists, and discuss their problems over business lunches or hurried snacks in the hospital cafeteria.

They are not the power elite of the community, but through their friendships with each other these successful women keep the social tapestry of the community intact. In this and other ways, they don't threaten audience preconceptions. Each of these career women either has or craves a husband and children. Too much attention to career is soon punished—by a wandering husband or errant child—until the woman refocuses her concern onto her family. Most important, these professional women are rarely shown doing their work. What concerns them most are the problems of their family and friends and their own romantic and sexual adventures.

Despite their high status, well-paying careers, and liberated sexual behavior, then, these are tradition-minded women who take their families and community seriously. If they threaten housewives in the audience, it is not because they work outside the home, but rather because they play the role of superwoman with such appalling ease: they are competent and successful in their careers; their dress and coiffures are impeccable; their children, whom we rarely see, do not normally disturb their routines; they are able to prepare magnificent dinners and elegant community celebrations at the drop of a hat. This is the media's version of feminism: women can have, and do, it all—without help from men.

Problems women encounter with men, at work or at home, are explained like all others in individual terms. Derek, a television producer, constantly makes sexual advances toward his employee

Ginny, but this is acceptable because they were lovers twenty years ago. When Ginny gets promoted, her husband Rick is concerned that *she* won't be able to handle it all. She then knocks herself out becoming a perfect journalist, loving mother, and sexy wife. On the other side of town, Bobbi, whose violent husband has just died, is alternately admired and ridiculed when she demands independence from men.

Stories on *General Hospital,* however, are generally sympathetic to women, even though conversations ridicule any direct references to feminism. Grant Andrews loses his beloved Celia when he refuses to take her new career seriously. Ginny wins Rick's respect through her superb journalistic reporting. Holly Scorpio, one of the female characters who does not work outside the home, forces her husband, the police commissioner, to let her help him on cases. Behind the scenes, she proves that her "female intuition" is often more effective than his systematic investigations. Frustrated by her merely vicarious involvement in working life, Holly secretly takes on the police-women's fight for equal pay. Against her husband's wishes and behind his back, she helps organize a strike that results in equality for women in the police force. At a testimonial dinner for him, she is honored by the Women in Blue for being "her own woman." This is Holly's compensation; she has been a dutiful wife and successful sleuth; at the same time, she has struck a blow for women's equality.

Men are not the enemy on soaps, but their bravado and machismo are often subjected to ridicule. On one occasion, two *General Hospital* husbands befriend one another at a bar to lament the neglect they suffer at the hands of their successful and beautiful wives. Their drunken complaints are undercut, however, by the viewers' knowledge that the real problem is their sexual insecurity. The men appear ridiculous when they make their drunken accusations, while their wives appear soberly rational and justifiably irritated.

Feminist issues are generally used for comic relief in the battle of the sexes: a male character makes a nasty comment about all women; a woman verbally protests with a laugh; the man, also laughing, apologizes. Just as race or class cannot come between members of the community, so sexual conflict is strictly personal, to be understood and resolved with good humor and goodwill.

Problems must also be resolved in a manner that affirms the values of the family and the community. This is where the strong emphasis on individual problems fuses with the community's interest. Soaps thrive on the anticipation and frustrated desires of the audience. For months, the choreography of a soap plot keeps starcrossed lovers apart; obscures the truth from a deceived lover; tangles the conflicting desires of a love triangle; contrives to punish an innocent person who has been cleverly framed. At every turn, the social cohesion of the soap community is endangered by a flood of individual moral failings. But at brief intervals, subplots come to an end with a temporary resolution to the conflict: a husband returns to his wife; an adulteress realizes her mistake; a too ambitious man recognizes that family and community are more important than riches; a liar realizes that deception has only worsened her problem; a couple find brief happiness before another obstacle emerges; an illegitimate child is finally acknowledged by a parent who preferred to bury the past.

From the chaos of personal failure and confusion comes moral consensus. Honesty, fidelity, and loyalty are reaffirmed. The community's very capacity to overcome these troubles certifies it as the true repository of decency. The lucky audience gets to have it both ways. For months, or even years, they have been entertained and titillated by the lustful, greedy quest for self-fulfillment. Then, for a brief moment, the audience is comforted, perhaps absolved, by the temporary affirmation of marital love, united families, and community solidarity. No matter that the fabric will soon unravel again. Love has won out; good has triumphed over evil. The good exists to be tested, after all, Everything is, for the moment, as it should be.

Or is it? Despite the occasional affirmation of a particular moral order, the more persistent lesson is that life is mostly *not* as it should be. In other words, the dramatic tension of soaps thrives as much on moral ambiguity as on moral consensus. Viewers have ample opportunity to identify with both—or many—sides of a problem. Nor is this accidental. When Agnes Nixon decided to deal with the controversial issue of peace activism, she purposely designed the story line so that viewers with opposing beliefs would think that *their* values were being affirmed by the plot. A female character who is torn by obligations to career and family can successfully appeal to both feminists and antifeminists. Even if a particular moral order must be affirmed in the end, there is, until the denouement, plenty of opportunity to walk both sides of the street.

Life hurts on the soaps, but there is always the possibility of improvement. Despite hard knocks, everyone gets a second chance. That is the essence of soap entertaining for Gloria Monty: "I think we have a certain moral duty at times, but one of the things I do believe in so much is to give an optimistic viewpoint to life and philosophically to bring hope into people's existence and, if anything, to educate people to look at the positive side rather than the negative side of living."

Ronald Reagan could not have said it better. Nothing is more American than optimism accompanied by a pervasive sense of dread. The belief in a second chance is a cornerstone of the American dream. It also makes for addictive entertainment. "This at bottom," says Agnes Nixon, "is the ingredient responsible for the audiences being hooked, for their tuning in to the next episode. The serial form imitates life in that, for its characters, the curtain rises with birth and does not ring down until death. . . . There is always tomorrow."

Hope, finally, is what the soap opera is all about; the usually illusory hope that maybe, just perhaps, tomorrow will deal a new hand, that circumstances will change, that life will be easier; that romance will triumph over loneliness, that communal needs will rise above individual desire. But if, as the soaps teach, life is hard and filled with personal suffering, then there is one final consolation: that the community will ease the burden of the individual, that the time-honored solidarity of the past will strengthen the individual to face the pain that the future, alas, will all too predictably bring.

Day after day, the soaps encourage viewers to escape their own lives, to ignore the actual problems in their own community and nation, and to yearn for perfect love in a mythic community. In contrast to epidemic loneliness, soaps offer vicarious participation in an illusory world where family and community still count, where a moral and social order provide stability. Even if the rules are broken daily, the soap world affirms values that are in reality trampled by a consumerist, businesslike society. Long before Reagan rose to power manipulating such values and myths, Americans clung to the memory of a world in which people knew where they belonged. To those like Reagan who would, if they could, turn the clock back to the turn of the century, the soaps offer comfort. To those who enjoy the self-indulgent atomism of modern life, the soaps provide a respite, the comforting illusion that they are not alone. In a sense, the popularity of soaps testifies to a subterranean despair which paradoxically finds hope in a past that cannot be resurrected.

The Shortcake Strategy

TOM ENGELHARDT

I

Imagine a teddy bear. Not just some old, fuzzy, nondescript brown bear, but a modern creature provided with his or her own special "tummy symbol" and "tushy tag," and carefully named for a single "heartwarming" emotional state or act. The particular one in question is called Secret Bear and he has many Care Bear brothers and sisters, all of whom live in a rainbow-filled cloudland called Care-A-Lot. Last year, just down a rainbow river, the Care Bears discovered "a very special place called the Forest of Feelings, a beautiful world of pastel-cloud trees and colorful rainbow pools," inhabited by a previously unheard-of set of relations called the Care Bear Cousins. But let's stay with Secret Bear for a moment. ("Do you have a secret? You can tell me anything. You're my secret friend.") He stands thirteen inches tall. He's mostly light orange and very soft. On his white belly is a beautiful, red, heart-shaped lock graphic with a keyhole just for *you* to unlock. He is a cub sired by the American Greetings Corporation by way of Kenner Products, itself owned by General Mills, and he's waiting to appear, as have many of his brothers and sisters, in a highly successful TV special, or like his cousins in a smash animated movie. He's part of a very recent, highly successful, extremely emotional, distinctly upwardly mobile family. If you pull the little string that dangles from his plush back, you will hear six randomly recorded messages that talk about sharing secrets or being part of the Care Bear Family.

Children's television is filled with hundreds of similar creatures: furry bears and fruit-scented little girls, robots and Smurfs, musclebound blond princes and antiterrorist teams, talking unicorns and shrill chipmunks elbowing each other off the screen every half hour or so to demonstrate their unique buyability while mouthing extracts from a random loop of recorded messages: be polite, be happy, be sure to hug, be a good student, consult with others, respect your elders, cheating doesn't pay, watch out for too friendly strangers, don't fight, follow the rules. On and on.

Few adults, of course, look at children's television carefully. Early weekday mornings, after-school hours, and Saturday until 1 P.M. are basically times to park the kids. For any adult who looked, however, it would be hard to avoid the impression that these animated shows are strangely like Secret Bear. Plots repeat each other from one show to another, no matter who produces them. Whether aimed at little girls and syrupy sweet, or at little boys and filled with "action" sequences in which the forces of Good triumph, however provisionally, over the forces of Evil, they involve an obsession with theft, capture, and kidnapping (emphasis on the "kid"), with escape, chase, and recapture, with deception and mechanical transformation from one shape or state of being to another—all strung together to make each show a series of predictable permutations. Lame homilies (what the industry calls "prosocial messages") are then tagged on and the shows are set in partial motion with crude animation techniques.

Our mythocultural past is ransacked to concoct a tiny, preset group of images (rainbows for happiness, red hearts for warmth, unicorns for magical regeneration, blondness to indicate superiority). A few worn-out characters and stories from a Disney childhood are thrown in. The Classic Comics version of the *Iliad* is recalled by a constant reuse of the Trojan Horse as a plot device. Some frog princes, witches, and demons are introduced. Hollywood-medieval costuming is added (jerkins, crusaders' crosses, and leisure boots as well as Nordic helmets from *Conan the Barbarian*). *Star Wars* is stripped down for everything from Darth Vader–like voices to Death Stars and space-battle special effects. And that's kids' TV: a simple set of almost interchangeable parts, authorless in any normal sense, even peopleless—living adults and children having been banished to PBS, cable programming, and an occasional network special.

One would pardon visiting aliens from the planets Eternia (*He-Man*), Arcadia (*Voltron*), or Thundera (*Thundercats*) if they mistook such crude, repetitious, and heavy-handed fare for badly done propaganda put together by some unseen (and certainly uninspired) hand. But our aliens might then wonder, as critics of kids' TV sometimes do: If this is propaganda, what is it for? If it's meant to convince, why are the shows so lacking in conviction that even their most violent sequences are without resonance or emotional consequence? And, finally, if these shows are so bad, why (as the industry constantly reminds us) do earthling young choose to watch them in such extraordinary numbers?

2

The fact is, there has probably never been a more creative moment in children's TV than the present one; more creative, that is, as long as what appears on the screen is seen as a listless by-product of an extraordinary explosion of entrepreneurial life force taking place elsewhere—in the business of creating and marketing toys. In fact, to answer any of our aliens' questions, we must first grasp that burgeoning business world behind the screen, whose story has all the elements critics claim are missing from children's TV. It is original, daring, and educational, filled with action as well as breathtaking experimentation. It's the story of how "authorship" as a business concept shifted from television studios to the toy industry as well as to greeting card companies, advertising agencies, cereal makers, and home video distributors; and how, in only a few years, a relatively small-scale business of licensing popular kids' characters to appear on products has been transformed into a multibillion-dollar industry. This neat trick has been accomplished by unleashing the corporately minted "licensed character" and with it, for television, the program-length commercial.

But to begin this real-life story correctly: Once upon a time, in a land called America in the long-gone year of 1904, the Brown Shoe Company purchased the rights to use the name of Buster Brown, a popular comic strip character, to promote its children's shoes at the St. Louis World's Fair, and so the idea of "character licensing" was born. The selling of a popular name and image into potentially infinite repetition on other buyable products was not long in coming into its own. Charlie Chaplin, perhaps the most popular "character" of the silent film era, franchised himself out as dolls, toys, books, and even a not terribly successful comic strip by Elzie Segar, later the creator of "Popeye." Walt Disney took up the idea almost as soon as, in 1928, he set Mickey Mouse sailing in *Steamboat Willie.* Initially, licensers commonly thought it a good deal simply to get the free advertising value of having their "image" on a product—no payment required. But by the 1930s, with crazes like Shirley Temple dolls, all that had already changed totally.

Character licensing was, however, made for children's television and sprang practically full-grown from some of its earliest programming. For those who nostalgically remember the 1950s as a golden age of kids' TV, it's easy to forget the crude huckstering of those early years; the announcers like Buffalo Bob of *Howdy Doody* who did the ads themselves, pressuring enraptured viewers to "have your Mom or Daddy take you to the store where you get Poll Parrot shoes, and ask for *your* Howdy Doody cutout!" So it's hardly surprising that popular children's TV characters quickly spawned enormous lines of products to which their images were affixed. Among the most successful of these licensing ventures was the marketing of Hopalong Cassidy, whose face stared out from pajamas, wallpaper, candy bars, watches, toothpaste tubes, and cowboy paraphernalia produced by over one hundred companies to the tune of $70 million annually. This was a trend that only gained momentum in the following decades. Take that cartoon favorite Scooby-Doo, the Great Dane detective, who, in the 1970s, was turned into hundreds of licensees worldwide producing literally thousands of products making millions of dollars annually; or even Jim Henson's *Sesame*

Street (not to speak of its commercial spinoffs, *The Muppets* and *Jim Henson's Muppet Babies*), whose fourteen years of royalties from licensed products (including Sesame Street theme parks) provided, by 1983, more than half the cost of producing the show.

That was the height of old-time TV merchandising. The process started with a successful show; a toy company then came along and paid for the right to make a doll of its main character; a clothes company came along and paid to make pajamas featuring the character; and so on. These toys and other products might or might not, in turn, be advertised on TV. The coordination was minimal, the sums of money involved relatively modest. As Joseph Barbera, co-founder of the Hanna-Barbera cartoon studios, Saturday morning TV's largest producer of animated programs, put it in the late 1970s when his characters appeared on more than forty-five hundred different products: "When a program is on the air for more than one year, we stand the chance of selling merchandise. If it doesn't stay on the air, and the networks don't renew it, then merchandisers just aren't interested."

Then came the first of several breakthroughs that changed the face of children's television and the nature of child consumerism. A young director named George Lucas formed Lucasfilm, a company part of whose purpose was to license his own creations, the characters which were about to appear in a film called *Star Wars*. In 1977, as the movie blasted off into the war-film void of post-Vietnam America, the small, plastic figurines of Luke Skywalker, Han Solo, Princess Leia, Obi-Wan Kenobe, Darth Vader, and their various minions, licensed out to and created by Kenner Products, took the toy world by storm, becoming the most coveted and most often acquired boys' toys of that time.

Not long after, two employees of the American Greetings Corporation, art director Tom Wilson and vice president Jack Chojnacki, came up with a new concept. They would set up under American Greetings' aegis a separate licensing branch called Those Characters From Cleveland whose task would be to create new characters imbued with instant, strong public identification possibilities. These characters would then be put on American's greeting cards as well as licensed out to various manufacturers. Basing their first attempt on a specially commissioned survey of all the qualities young girls supposedly found most appealing, they created a pink-ishly garbed little girl with an oversized head who lived with her other "berry nice friends" in a place called Strawberryland, and they christened her Strawberry Shortcake. Developed jointly with M.A.D., the Marketing and Design Division of the Toy Group at General Mills, she was introduced to the 1980 American International Toy Fair in New York by General Mills' own Kenner toys and soon after given her own animated TV special, also produced by Kenner (and rejected in those innocent days by the networks who correctly saw the show for the ad it was).

But Ms. Shortcake needed no network to make her way in the world. She quickly became America's number-one baby doll, star-ring in special after special on over a hundred independent stations around the country and appearing on hundreds of products selling an astronomical aggregate of more than $1 billion worth of herself before, as one of her ads put it, "other four year olds learn to count." In short, two corporate dads had summarily turned an industry upside down, while reversing the time-honored order of character licensing. They had shown that a salable image could be created out of relatively thin air and that the product could precede the show. Even more important, they had created a whole new strategic frame-work for marketing not simply a toy, but (like Ronald Reagan himself) an image. In this strategy, your corporate research com-pleted and your ersatz character in existence, every licensed or pro-duced element from doll to lunchbox to mall appearance to TV show will reinforce the others, creating for that tiny being a sense of ubiquitous stardom and desirability. The advertising and pro-motion budgets of all the producers add up to an advertising and promotion campaign of unheard-of size and coordination in the world of child consumerism. The result: a child surrounded by an advertising image reflecting off every object that catches the eye.

Naturally, it quickly dawned on the toy industry, card compa-nies, cereal companies, and others that if they too were to create their own characters, each with his or her own "backstory" (or elaborated fantasy), they could make all the licensing money previ-ously taken in by the TV companies who created the shows. Where the first corporate explorers ventured at their peril, others soon rushed to their profit. Among the earliest entrants in the licensed-character sweepstakes, the Smurfs and Pac-Man confirmed and extended the Shortcake strategy. Seven-plus cutely named dwarves without Snow White, the Smurfs are little blue creatures who live in mushroom-shaped cottages, eat smurfberries, and avoid an ineffectually evil wizard named Gargamel. Although they were spun from the imagination of a Belgian cartoonist named Peyo, their blandly sweet adventures might easily pass for a purely corporate creation. Adopted by the American licensing firm Wallace Berrie, they were in any case quickly treated that way. A host of smurfable products and a 1981 debut on NBC's Saturday morning cartoon lineup quickly garnered more than $1 billion in sales and turned *The Smurfs* into America's most-watched children's TV program.

Meanwhile, an insatiable little yellow mouth by the name of Pac-Man had gobbled his way out of the video arcades and onto Saturday morning TV as well as into spaghetti cans, vitamin bottles, and bubble gum packs. Pac-Man's rise indicated that in the emerging new video technologies might lie ingenious marketing possibilities, and proved as well that a licensable character might become a marketing and TV success even if it initially lacked a "backstory." (Who has time for a story when a bleeping energy pellet may do you in at any second?) Of course, corporate imitators were soon at work: Donkey Kong, Jr., Pitfall, Q*bert, Dragon's Lair, and other games quickly followed Pac-Man's route from video screen to TV screen.

Despite such individual programming successes, the dominance of the program-length commercial still seemed by no means assured. By 1982, only two and a half hours a week of them had made it onto the screen, concentrated in the Saturday morning kids' ghetto (plus a few odd specials in other time slots). It took the strongest man in the universe, an action figure named He-Man, to make the final breakthrough. To understand his impact, we must first explore the ways this wave of nascent entrepreneurial strategizing, fueled by Reagan-inspired deregulation, blasted the program-length commercial into orbit.

3

The program-length commercial has a prehistory, though like that of the rest of TV, it is infinitely forgettable. In 1969, ABC aired a cartoon called *Hot Wheels*—also the name of a line of toy cars produced by toy-industry giant Mattel. Topper, one of Mattel's competitors, filed a complaint with the Federal Communications Commission (FCC) claiming that the ABC show was, in effect, a thirty-minute commercial. Congress has given the FCC the task of licensing the airwaves in the "public interest, convenience, and necessity," and the ability to enforce the "public interest" by actually taking away a station's license to broadcast. Although this ultimate sanction has been invoked only a couple of times, the FCC's various recommendations, policy statements, guidelines, and rulings do nonetheless often carry the weight of law—and are certainly carefully noted—in the world of TV broadcasting. In the case of *Hot Wheels,* the FCC issued a ruling stating that "there can be no doubt that in this program, Mattell receives commercial promotion for its product beyond the time [allowed] for commercial advertising. . . . We find this pattern disturbing . . . for [it] subordinates programming in the interest of the public to programming in the interest of salability." *Hot Wheels* was subsequently taken off the air.

In the 1970s, prodded by Action for Children's Television (ACT) and other activist groups, the FCC took a significantly more interventionist stance on children's issues. Adopting a policy statement in 1974 emphasizing that "broadcasters have a special obligation to serve children," it began a process of pressuring the industry to adopt codes regulating some of the worst excesses of children's advertising, to tone down the "violence" of the cartoons, and to introduce throughout the week a greater variety of educational and informational programs directed at specific age groups rather than vague masses of children two to eleven years old.

But in 1981, newly elected President Ronald Reagan appointed as head of the FCC Mark Fowler, "a journeyman communications attorney . . . with few credentials beyond his association with the Reagan campaign team," and the whole thrust of the agency reversed itself. Under the banner of deregulation, Fowler announced that "it was time to move away from thinking about broadcasters as trustees. It was time to treat them the way almost everyone else in society does—that is, as businesses." For, as he said on a different occasion, "television is just another appliance. It's a toaster with pictures." At Christmastime 1983, the FCC finally lifted its children's policy guidelines from 1974, and followed up in 1984 by allowing TV stations to air as many commercial minutes in a given time period as they choose to, a ruling which, in effect, sanctioned the program-length commercial. It was hardly surprising, then, that in 1985 the FCC rejected an ACT complaint about program-length commercials based on the FCC's own 1969 *Hot Wheels* ruling.

The networks did not, however, wait for these FCC decisions to act. As soon as the direction of Fowler's FCC became clear, they began to unload children's programs. In 1982, CBS fired twenty people doing alternative programming for children, dropped the children's news show 30 *Minutes,* and began phasing out the low-rated *Captain Kangaroo.* The other networks heaved a collective sigh of relief and followed suit, ABC cutting *Animals, Animals, Animals* and *Kids Are People Too,* its low-rated Emmy-award-winning weekend shows, while NBC pulled the plug on *Project Peacock,* its prime-time children's specials. In fact, an FCC study showed that from 1979 to 1983 the average time commercial stations allotted to children's programming dropped from 11.3 to 4.4 hours a week, and the after-school time slot was left without a single regularly scheduled network children's series.

As the networks pulled out, Prince Adam, a.k.a. He-Man, moved in. A plastic figurine developed in 1981 by Mattel, a company that has about a 14 percent share of the U.S. toy market, it had a fantasy scripted around it by Filmation Associates, a TV production company previously best known as the producers of Bill Cosby's *Fat Albert and the Cosby Kids*—with Mattel retaining licensing rights to the characters while Filmation controlled what they did on the screen. The action figurines and the TV show *He-Man and the Masters of the Universe* were both based on Mattel research which indicated that "boys from three to seven spend a fourth of their time fantasizing about good versus evil."

Turned down by ABC, Mattel and the Westinghouse-owned Filmation took a novel approach to distributing the show. They syndicated their first sixty-five half-hour daily shows to independent stations around the country for their after-school time slots. Syndication is a deal in which, in return for a ready-made show, local stations pay out cash plus a set number of minutes of advertising time which the show's producers can then sell to advertisers. (Many of the wave of cartoons which followed *He-Man* into the afternoon hours took a similar route called "barter-syndication" in which stations are offered a "free" show in return for salable advertising time.) He-Man made his debut in September 1983 at the very moment when late afternoon commercial TV was denuded of network kids' programs and filled with reruns of defunct adult shows. And so was born the first daily cartoon tailor-made for afternoon syndication in which every object you see on screen can promptly be bought in a nearby store.

"I never knew it was possible," said Lou Scheimer, president of Filmation. "I didn't know there was enough money out there. No one knew there was enough money out there." There was. As Prince Adam, blond hunk from the planet Eternia, fought off the evil Skeletor, defended Castle Grayskull, and preserved the secrets of the universe, daily uttering "I have the power!"—the words that turned him into the golden hulk of He-Man—the show set instant ratings records. Within a year, it was being shown on 120 stations covering 82 percent of the nation, and in 32 other countries as well. Since 1984 these figures have risen, while Mattel has managed to license out He-Man to innumerable licensees, who now produce everything from lunch boxes to Halloween costumes. Mattel sold 35 million of the action figures alone in 1984: 95,628 a day; 66.4 each minute. "If you lined up the 70 million 5½-inch Master of the Universe figures sold since the toy was introduced in 1981," claimed Richard Weiner of Richard Weiner, Inc., which promotes the toy, "they would extend from New York City to Los Angeles and back again." No wonder that in their sales pitch to retailers, Mattel's brag is "*We* have the power!"

Certainly, it was fitting in the Age of Reagan that the strongest character in the universe—not some plush baby doll or namby-pamby low-rated educational show—should conquer new territory for the new marketing strategy first pioneered by American Greetings. He-Man had, in short, smashed into the soft underbelly of television, where ad rates for adult shows sink to near insignificance, and he took it the way Reagan took Grenada. In his wake, a whole industry locked into place.

The simple increase in program-length commercials gives some sense of the success of this process. On Saturday morning, they jumped from two and a half hours in 1981–82 to six and a half hours in 1984–85; and in the 1985–86 season the Disney organization has weighed in for the first time with two shows—for CBS a coventure with Hasbro toys called *Wuzzles* ("the most wonderful license that ever Wuz"); and for NBC, *The Gummi Bears* based on a popular candy. At the same time, Lucasfilm, of *Star Wars* fame, has brought to ABC *Droids: The Adventures of R2-D2 and C3PO* and *Ewoks* ("one full hour weekly of network television support for the strongest, most proven film-licensed characters in the marketplace"); while the after-school slots or independent stations are filled to the brim with new action-adventure animated serials.

From fourteen shows two years ago, licensed-character cartoons jumped to forty or more in 1985, with scores still under development. In fact, with almost all the afternoon time slots already committed through the 1986–87 season, action-adventure producers are scrambling for new media strategies like releasing directly to the home video market and skipping TV broadcast altogether. Such programming is also creeping into what may be one of the few remaining available time slots—the otherwise somnolent Sunday morning period normally turned over to religious programming and lame reruns. Hanna-Barbera Productions, which with Ruby-Spears Enterprises (both owned by Taft Entertainment) has until recently produced almost three quarters of all Saturday morning kids' shows, is for the first time ever producing new animation "specifically designed for Sunday morning viewing"—a single ninety-minute bloc called *The Funtastic World of Hanna-Barbera* that includes *Galtar,* a "mythological action/adventure series starring a young, blond-haired hero who battles villains in an imaginary land," and *The Paw Paws,* the animated adventures of a tribe of tiny bears "whose purpose in life is to protect newborn forest creatures from danger and to teach survival to all animal life." Taft ads say that with Wallace Berrie (of Smurf licensing fame) as "the property's anchor licensee," the Paw Paws are expected "to 'bear' rich profits."

Such profits are evident in the toy industry itself, where retail sales jumped from $10.4 billion in 1983 to $12.8 billion in 1984, before leveling off in 1985. $8.5 billion of the 1985 sales were "character products," a jump of almost $1 billion over 1984, and well "more than the retail sales for the entire, multi-faceted licensing business as recently as 1978."

If you take single lines of toys backed by TV programs, enormous advertising budgets, and a universe of product tie-ins, the results are similarly impressive. For instance, robot toys, brought over from Japan only two years ago, and backed by reedited, rewritten, product-specific Japanese space-robot cartoons, became the fastest-growing toy category of 1984–85. Boosted by *The Transformers* TV series, Hasbro's Transformers toy line alone—the robots turn into vehicles and back again—made more than $100 million in its first year, which some consider the most successful toy launch ever.

In such a world, Mattel, Hasbro, and Coleco, the toy company giants with the most resources, are obviously at an enormous advantage. (It has been estimated that the three accounted for a whopping 36 percent of wholesale toy shipments in 1985, up from 13 percent five years earlier.) An industry ad for Rainbow Brite, a character created by the Hallmark Card Company, gives some sense of the magnitude of the financial and other resources now mustered behind a successful licensing line. "Find gold at the end of this rainbow all through 1985," the ad begins. ". . . With over $35 million worth of support, Rainbow Brite will be one of the most visible characters your customers will see all year. For beginners, there's a more than $10-million Mattel Toy Co. advertising campaign about to break in print—and on television. Then, look for Rainbow Brite to star in her own five-part mini-series on national TV. She'll tour extensively and appear on exciting new products. She'll even debut on the package of a new Ralston-Purina breakfast cereal named just for her!"

The linking of such giant toy companies into TV production companies into advertising companies, now often overseeing the actual production of TV series for their toy company clients, tied into distribution companies (some owned by the above) linked either to a nation-embracing set of independent television stations or directly to the networks, linked to a series of product licensees (sometimes up to one hundred or more per successful character)—this whole chain has had the effect not just of creating a few simple, recognizable images, attachable to almost any object in a child's world, but also of vastly upping the ante for successfully launching new toy lines, which now need an estimated $20 million to $30 million in start-up backing. In the process, many smaller toy companies have been pushed, or will soon be pushed, out of the business altogether. (Sales of "no name" dolls, for instance, fell by something like 50 percent in 1985.)

With so much at stake, corporate managers have hedged their bets by attempting to discover beforehand what children will like in toys, in TV shows, in characters, in fantasies. But this "research" itself seems to be little more than a closed loop proving that variations on what already works will work—until eventually they no longer work. If, for instance, you ask little girls what they think fairies are, as Tonka Toys' researchers did in preparing for Star Fairies, their new entry in the "minidoll segment of the $1 billion doll market," and discover that fairies are "beautiful, magical creatures who live in the sky and ride unicorns," what have you found out? Perhaps no more than that most little girls, already assiduous buyers of similar lines of dolls and watchers of similar TV shows put on by similar toy companies, have noted that the magical little girl characters tend to live in magical cloud-cuckoo lands and tend to ride magical horses or unicorns. In other words, such research by companies already in the business of prefabricating children's culture may not so much be uncovering archetypes of desire as creating them.

In the hands of present-day corporate toy managers, however, such research does help direct companies into increasingly frenzied cycles of recombinant planning as bizarre in their own ways as the wildest attempts at genetic recombination could be in the world of biology. Corporate research, for example, showed that although Mattel's He-Man was aimed at boys aged four to eight, about 30 percent of those watching the TV show were girls. What to conclude from that? Well, why not mix a bit of Wonder Woman with a sizable dollop of He-Man, add lots of Barbie, and lo! you have He-Man's sister Adora, alias She-Ra, Princess of Power, from Mattel, or Golden Girl from Galoob—two "fashion-action" figurines for girls. And what do both of these warrior women ride? Why, horses that turn into unicorns with "groomable manes."

There is, however, another type of recombinant planning and experimentation to be found in the toy business—not in corporate research departments but in the actual creation of a vast web of supporting product, advertising, and promotional tie-ins, a TV show being simply the premiere. They include:

Traditional Product Licensing. Here the licensed image is slapped onto buyable, everyday objects. A typical partial list of such licensed products from M.A.S.K. (Mobile Armored Strike Kommand), a new action-toy set and daily TV cartoon from Kenner Products and the General Mills Toy Group, includes pajamas, blanket sleepers, robes, hosiery, totes, backpacks, soft-sided luggage, belts, hats, wallets, underwear, sheets, slumber bags, bath sheets, play tents, blankets, wall coverings, plastic dinnerware, clocks, watches, audio equipment, school supplies, greeting cards, party goods, gift-wrapping paper, and lunch boxes with hidden compartments meant to play on the M.A.S.K. logo, "Illusion is the ultimate weapon!"

Cereals and Cereal Makers. Cereal makers have been one of the few major advertisers on children's TV since its earliest days. Recently, as their TV advertising budgets have soared—cereal giant General Mills' rose 470 percent in the last decade, a lot of it targeted for Saturday morning—they have become more and more closely tied in to all aspects of the licensed-character market, including joint ventures in the creation of the characters themselves. They have also put licensed characters on cereal boxes and backed them with massive advertising budgets. Examples are General Mills' Strawberry Shortcake, Pac-Man, and Hugga Bunch cereals; Ralston Purina's Rainbow Brite, Cabbage Patch Kids, and G.I. Joe; Kellogg's C3PO's. These have captured 5 to 10 percent of the $4-billion cereal business, though their staying power is in question. Quaker Oats' Mr. T cereal has, for instance, already fallen by the wayside despite a $10-million ad budget. If licensed-character cereals ultimately sog out, "one major side effect of the upheaval," *Advertising Age* suggests, "could be marketeers' return to the drawing board to create their own characters," as Kellogg's did with Tony the Tiger years ago, but this time with TV shows, toys, and who knows what else in mind.

Character Appearances. There is nothing new about character appearances, but they too have turned into a significantly bigger business, a particularly effective means of promoting properties. No one who has ever taken an awestruck, slightly shy child to meet a "live" character, whether at Disneyland or at a local mall, could deny the evident, tangible power of that living, moving, breathing, three-dimensional image. As a result, licensed characters now travel the country's malls, ride in parades, visit toy and department stores, stop at the White House, and generally sweep across the land all year long. For instance, Mattel's Rainbow Brite fifteen-minute traveling musical show appears in six hundred in-store events a year.

Movie Appearances. Movies are in, a newly discovered stop along the increasingly complex route of appearances made by licensed characters. Whether introducing a new set of toys/products and a new TV series *(She-Ra, Princess of Power),* introducing an upcoming TV/product season (He-Man's *The Secret of the Sword* or *GoBots: Battle of the Rock Lords),* or playing off already seen TV specials *(The Care Bears Movie, Care Bears Movie II: A New Generation,* and *Rainbow Brite and the Star Stealer),* movies are opening up new vistas in the world of licensed-character marketing.

For example, *The Care Bears Movie,* a $4-million coproduction of American Greetings, General Mills, Kenner Products, LBS Communications, and Nelvana Ltd., was initially released to one thousand theaters by The Samuel Goldwyn Company in March 1985. Meant mainly to introduce American Greetings' new line of Care Bear Cousins, it had an advertising budget of $4 million while, as *Variety* put it, "the beneficiaries of [the film's] merchandising tie-ins have earmarked a claimed $20,000,000 to promo Care Bear products in step with the film's release."

With $20 million in proceeds in the till within a few months of its opening, the film was considered a kiddie success. Home video distribution rights were promptly sold to Vestron Video for $1.5 million; within the year, the film would also be released to one of the pay cable channels, following which it might go either onto network TV or into barter-syndication to independent stations, each money-making appearance another ad for the whole line of Care Bear products. Not surprisingly, a variety of animated films linked to various toy lines are now in preparation, all guaranteed an endless life on a variety of screens.

New Technology. Arcade video games, story tapes, and home computer software all take the licensed-character explosion beyond the TV channel, but none more powerfully than the videocassette recorder, which by the end of 1985 was installed in 30 percent of American homes. Because children love to see popular shows many times over, home video, a market that didn't exist just a few years ago, now seems likely to quickly pass cable as the next major outlet for first-run, licensed-character animated series. Already, of the top six bestselling children's cassettes listed by *Video Insider* on August 30, 1985, five (*The Care Bears Movie,* two *Transformers* shows, and one each for Rainbow Brite and Strawberry Shortcake) are program-length commercials. "Our 'Masters of the Universe,' a television show that can be recorded off the air free, has incredibly sold over 300,000 video cassettes," said Lou Scheimer, president of Filmation. At an average of $19.95 to $39.95 per cassette—although prices as high as $59.95 are not uncommon—this is a financial bonanza. Certainly, it's unprecedented in advertising history to be able to sell an ad directly into the home and get people to play it again and again.

As a result, what *Variety* calls "kidvid deals" are now an everyday part of the start-up life of the licensed character, and even more innovative deals are on the way. For example, LBS Communications, considered the leading barter-syndicator in TV, was reported to be exploring with the Coca-Cola Company kiddie video programs which would be sold directly at supermarkets, and with Kenner products "the distribution of advertiser-supported VCR cartoons via toy retail chains"—both ways to circumvent not just the TV screen, but the corner video rental store as well.

All this only begins to touch on the endless array of tie-ins that barrage the child consumer: there are comic books, sometimes sold in stores, sometimes simply given away in toy packets; there are books, often connected to tapes, sometimes licensed out to a large publisher like Random House, sometimes produced directly by a toy company; there are board games; there are daily comic strips; there are magazines like *G.I. Joe, He-Man and the Masters of the Universe, She-Ra, Princess of Power,* and *Muppet,* which are themselves little more than "magazine-length ads"; premium tie-ins where the kids find stickers of their favorite characters in cereal boxes or licensed character meals at their favorite fast food restaurants; slides, decals, sweepstakes, and countless other tricks, scams, and spin-offs, each adding its bit to an overall strategy of marketing blitz.

Apologists for the new order of children's things will no doubt liken it to the traditional order of myth and fairy tale (or at least to the traditional world of children's cartoons and their subsequent licensing histories). And it is true, possibly because human beings are so naturally vulnerable, and small children more vulnerable than the rest of us, that we seem always to have needed to imagine a mythical world of both large protectors and greater-than-life-size threatening figures. Traditional fairy tales and even classic children's literature certainly have had their share of interventional "super-heroes" and dastardly, magic-wielding villains—from helpful giants and fairy godmothers to witches and demons. They have also had their share of early technowizardry—capes that guarantee invisibility, seven-league boots, pumpkin coaches, and magic spells. Nonetheless, today's children's TV fare only superficially represents or even draws on this tradition, because at the heart of the fairy tale and of children's literature in general is a human journey or struggle involving the exhibition of human courage, cleverness, slyness, trickery, or even betrayal. It is the human, often the human child, who makes the trip, who in some sense confronts, evades, or possibly solves the problem; it is the human, often a child, not the superhero or a magical instrument, who is transformed in the end. And if a lesson is drawn from all this, often in rather unsocial terms by our contemporary standards, it does emerge in some fashion from the crosscurrents of the human tale itself.

None of this holds on kidvid. For the first time on such a massive scale, a "character" has been born free of its specific structure in a myth, fairy tale, story, or even cartoon, and instead embedded from the beginning in a consortium of busy manufacturers whose goals are purely and simply to profit by multiplying the image itself in any way that conceivably will make money. Not everything tried so far works, and perhaps someday the whole structure will collapse from overlicensing; but right now, no idea is too wild to pursue.

Do you expect to have problems getting your new action-adventure series on the air? Then do what Telepictures did for *Thundercats* (half-human, half-animal action figures with glowing eyes and a $15-million TV production budget): offer independent TV stations willing to make a long-term commitment not just the show itself, but a share in the profits from the sale of Thundercats' licensed products. And if Sunday morning fills up and no obvious time slots are left, well, what about prime time? Kids already spend a significant portion of their twenty-seven hours a week in front of the set watching prime-time shows anyway. And haven't the critics always said that most of prime time is kids' TV? And who says adults wouldn't watch cartoons that sell them something other than toys, cereals, and candy?

Haven't the critics been charging for years that children's TV is a hideously syrupy medium mainly aimed at advertising sugar products to kids? Well, then, why shouldn't Walt Disney and Hasbro go all the way and simply market the Gummi Bears candy as a Saturday morning character? And why couldn't some forward-looking aerospace corporation like Lockheed polish up its image and make itself a little money besides by creating its own talking-plane action-figure with TV show and licensees? And if research shows that there's an opening in the minidoll segment of the doll market for a warrior woman who turns into a pink robotic vehicle, then how about it? Or a show in which the Smurfs and Strawberry Shortcake join licenses to battle Marvel's evil Darkseid to everyone's profit? Maybe licensed-character videos with prosocial messages could even be sold directly through pediatrician's offices. Who knows?

Of course, the ceiling on the licensed-character market may already have been reached, or perhaps it will be reached in 1986–87 when all the imitations of the copycat shows of the present moment saturate the airwaves, when overlicensing sates children and disgusts their parents, and sets are flicked to PBS or cable's Nickelodeon, or off altogether; but don't bet on it. And in the meantime, the card companies have hit pay dirt; the giant toy companies are selling their dolls by the millions; the advertising agencies, as in radio of the thirties and forties and adult TV of the fifties, are once again deeply, lucratively involved in overseeing the production of TV shows for their clients; the film production companies that used to make thirteen animated episodes of a kids' show each season to be played over and over again are now doing a booming business year-round producing sixty-five to ninety episodes of all the action-adventure daily shows; second-level independent stations have gotten a giant afternoon boost from essentially free daily shows with a built-in, instant-recognition audience of children; due to recent FCC decisions, even the networks may soon be able to pressure for a cut of the licensed-product profits; and other businesses beyond enumeration are profiting from the situation. In fact, everybody's profiting—except perhaps the kids watching the TV screens where a stream of licensed characters flicker by in programs so flaccid it's hard to believe they bear any relationship to the juiced-up world that generates them.

Yet for an adult viewer, their very lack of inspiration, their authorless, randomly repetitive, interchangeable quality gives them a strange sort of fascination. Just as the industry has been deregulated economically, so in some sense what appears on screen has been deregulated emotionally to produce a sort of crude twilight zone of present-day American consciousness.

Several vivid urges and anxieties leap from the screen of the supershow to which children's commercial TV adds up: an explosive release of aggression as superheroes and robotic saviors solve all human problems while playing with fantasy versions of the Reagan military budget; unfettered acquisitionism as advertisers pull out all the stops to induce kids to really *want*; and managed emotion in which tiny humanoid beings intervene to correct our inability to feel, love, hug, and care—that is, our assumed state of emotional deprivation. Along with these go a pervasive sense of nuclear anxiety, an uneasiness with science and technology bordering on paranoia, and a stance of passivity (perhaps mirroring the child's act of watching TV) in which humans are shown to be totally resourceless and must rely on nonhuman creatures to help, nurture, and defend them. In sum, it leaves us with a TV-generated vision of Americans as a nation of overarmed, trigger-happy, grasping, anxious, and love-starved people who feel deeply sorry for themselves and beleaguered in the world—something, that is, of a self-portrait of the Reagan era.

4

Kids' TV can be divided into four zones, each of which fills in parts of that self-portrait: action-figure superheroes syndicated in afternoon time slots (with some carryover to Saturday and Sunday mornings); specials aimed at little girls; the network Saturday morning schedule; and, finally, the ads.

The Universe of the Action-Figure Superhero. Once upon a time, there were a series of soldier figures made by Hasbro and sold to little boys under the name of G.I. Joe. Then came the post–Vietnam War period, not a propitious selling atmosphere for a "real American hero," whereupon in 1978 Joe and his ilk were quietly retired. Now G.I. Joe is back, this time with his own daily afternoon show. He is a bit smaller—perhaps due, as Peggy Charren of ACT says, to inflation—but he comes equipped with a sort of animated A-Team pitted against a group of international terrorists (acronym: COBRA), that great Reagan-era bogeyman, and armed to the teeth. As the *Wall Street Journal* describes it, Joe's arsenal includes "a 7½-foot G.I. Joe aircraft carrier—a toy behemoth, Pentagon-priced at about $100. The toy can carry up to 100 Joes, at $3 each, and several Skystriker jets at $19 apiece. A fleet of 100,000 aircraft carriers is planned."

In fact, the fall 1986 toy-and-TV season is highlighting terrorism, with Rambo and his Force of Freedom bursting onto the afternoon screen locked in daily combat with General Terror and his S.A.V.A.G.E. terrorist group. Coleco Industries, creator of the Rambo action-figure line, even beat Reagan to the conceptual punch with a character named "Mad Dog," conceived and designed well before the raid on Libya. *Advertising Age* reports that this year more than $40 million may be spent on ads supporting terrorism-related toy lines, "more than President Reagan wanted to send to Nicaraguan rebels for weapons."

Most action-adventure shows, however, have snubbed this somewhat more conventional sector of the defense budget, preferring the world of Star Wars first envisioned as a fantasy by George Lucas and only later promoted by Reagan's High Frontiersmen. Reagan himself clearly feels safest in space, and the producers of these shows still tend to agree that outer space, high tech, and faraway enemies in a distant future are a safer, tidier, less complicated way to turn after-school TV into a war zone.

A composite show would look something like this:

On the idyllic planet of Eternia *(He-Man)*, Arcadia *(Voltron)*, or even Earth *(M.A.S.K.)* . . .

Lives an intrepid blond prince named Adam *(He-Man)*, a blond hulk of a freelance scientist *(M.A.S.K.)*, a blond warrior-prince named Dargon *(Sectaurs)*, a blond princess *(She-Ra)*, "a real American hero" *(G.I. Joe)*, a superforce of space explorers representing a galaxy alliance *(Voltron)*, an intrepid group of space explorers representing the United Planets *(Mighty Orbots)*, a "true hero of pure heart and purpose" named Jayce representing the Lightning League *(Jayce and the Wheeled Warriors)*, a group of friends able to transform themselves from inane teenagers . . .

Into power superheroes *(Superfriends)*, into the strongest man in the universe *(He-Man)*, into a "heroic team of armed machines" *(M.A.S.K.)*, into "a mighty robot loved by good, feared by evil" *(Voltron)*, into a mighty robot that "protects the world from the shadow of evil" *(Mighty Orbots)*, into mighty armed warriors, the Autobots *(Transformers)*. . . .

Locked in mortal combat with them are the evil, black-eyed Skeletor *(He-Man)*, the evil, yellow-eyed Lotar and his evil, blue-faced father from Planet Doom *(Voltron)*, General Spidrax, lord of evil, master of the Dark Domain's mighty armies *(Sectaurs)*, the evil, red-eyed Darkseid of the Planet Apokolips *(Superfriends)*, the treacherous Miles Mayhem, head of V.E.N.O.M.—the Vicious Evil Network of Mayhem—from the Contraworld *(M.A.S.K.)*, the evil Monster Minds *(Jayce)*, the evil Decepticons *(Transformers)*, the evil, many-eyed Umbra and his Shadow Star *(Mighty Orbots)*. . . .

In this struggle between Good and Evil, light and darkness, blondness versus purpleness (or sickly yellowness), blue-eyedness versus glowing red-, purple-, or yellow-eyedness, what is at stake is nothing less than "the secrets of the universe" *(He-Man)*, "the universe" *(Voltron)*, "the destruction of the universe" *(Jayce)*, "the ultimate battle for survival" *(Sectaurs)*, "the fate of the entire world" *(Robotech)*, "the ultimate doom" *(Transformers)*. . . .

The actual episodes revolve around a series of evil plans to loose havoc on innocent planets (metal-eating bugs, froglike "Robeasts," and so on), or to trap the hero and deny him his transforming powers, or to stop the mighty robots from being assembled, or to kidnap a friend of the superheroes, or to steal something so powerful, dangerous, radioactive, death-dealing that it will destroy the earth/planet/galaxy/universe or alternately turn it into a world of slaves/zombies at the service of the Evil Force. . . .

All of which results in a series of chases and battles with techno-wonder weapons—space stations, laser beams, harnessed black holes, assorted yet-to-be-invented and never-to-be-invented megaweapons—and a final withdrawal by the forces of evil, muttering curses and threatening to return, followed by a prosocial message, often not obviously related to the show, or perhaps a "safety tip" by the show's hero.

Such a summary only begins to touch on the similarities among these shows. To the extent that they are driven at all, the forces driving them are three—the introduction of new characters with their accompanying weapons, castles, and other accoutrements; the necessity for "teamwork"; and the displaying of the show's techno-weaponry through special effects. Each is a larger imperative linking the show into the energy field of licensed-character marketing.

The need to introduce new characters is cyclic and seasonal, the problem arising not from the shows' plots at all, but from the voracious selling needs of the licensed character and perhaps from the intense consumption patterns of our society as well. Competing for shelf space against a flood of new characters arriving each season, an ongoing line must respond by featuring new sets of characters while at the same time providing new megaweaponry and other paraphernalia for established characters. For *He-Man* last season, this meant finding a place for Hordak and his Evil Horde as well as weapons/vehicles with names like "Land Shark" and the "Bashasaurus." Making room for new characters forces the show's writers to offer a certain minimal level of drama at the beginning of each new season, similar to the tension generated in a soap opera when an actor leaves and a new character must be inserted and given a sudden pedigree.

Teamwork, the second plot element in this world, is equally connected to toy selling. Rugged individualism is as little a part of kid's TV as it is of the rest of TV's fictions, or indeed of the corporatized adult society of the Reagan era beyond the tube. After all, no one wants to sell one action figure. The whole point is to get the child to buy whole teams of good guys and teams of bad guys (color-, price-, and weapon-coordinated to the ads that follow on other shows). No longer the masked man and his lone sidekick, but the M.A.S.K. team and its V.E.N.O.M. opposites. So the program writers must find not so much plots as strings of team-action sequences.

It is in these sequences with their explosively animated displays of technoweaponry that kids' TV comes alive, however momentarily. Approximately twice per show, for instance, the blond leader of the Voltron force issues some version of this order to the other four space explorers (including one blond princess), each already seated in his or her own powerful robot lion: "Ready to form Voltron! Activate interlocks! Dynotherms connected! Infracells up! Megathrusters are at go!"

The others respond, "Let's go, Voltron!" and the screen bursts into a riot of violent colors to a rock beat, flashes of lightning, odd camera angles, vivid cuts, and suddenly, to a cry of "Form blazing sword!" there emerges from the five lions a single awesome robot being with a glinting double-pronged phallic object of monstrous proportions that cuts through the enemy in a blinding, screen-filling flash of white-yellow light which can be nothing but an atomic explosion.

The similar robotic figure on Saturday morning's *Mighty Orbots* is often formed no less than four times a show, with battle effects to follow. The M.A.S.K. team dons its elaborate mask-weapons, each with special powers, in a sound-and-light ceremony which takes up more time than anything but the programmed fights to come. Prince Adam is encircled in vivid, dancing, lightning flashes as he pulls his sword and shouts out in a deep, echoing, computer-enhanced voice, "By the power of Grayskull . . . I have the power!"

and transforms into He-Man; ditto Bruce Banner into the Incredible Hulk, the teenager Brett into Turbo Teen; and so on. One could say that the "plots" are no more than excuses to trigger these transformations and show the characters strutting their buyable wares.

So much effort is expended on the thrill of the transformation and the *Star Wars*–imitation special effects, and so little animation effort is put into the rest of the show, that the effect is strange. In a given set of frames, only a few things may move: legs churning in a chase, or eyes rolling in a speech. For much of any show, the various badly animated, stiffly drawn beings, especially the humans, tend to lurch about with choppy, robotic motions. This robotic effect is emphasized by awkward dialogue and monotonal voice-overs. At the same time, the robots, weaponry, and vehicles involved in the special-effects sequences gain an almost human fluidity.

In fact, in every way—vitality, size, power, ability, intelligence—humans cede center stage to their technology, or its slightly more human superhero relatives, who use superscience and unheard of weaponry to solve all human problems. Lacking a giant robot, an advanced fighting missile-armed truck or a magical Rubik's cube, humans are invariably helpless and deeply passive in the face of crisis. Passivity is not a happy state, however, and underneath the miraculous curative interventions of good technology lies a half-hidden world of fear, suspicion, and anxiety about a science which dwarfs humanity; a world in which you can never trust what you see because it may instantly metamorphose into something else; a world in which genetic experiments gone awry create frightening mutants and a scientist's well-meant formula in the wrong hands turns a house pet into a slavering wild beast; a world alive with a pseudoscientific language as ominous in what it promises as it is perverse in its absurd inaccuracies. ("That was incredible, Firestorm, your holographic image of a black hole did the trick!")

"My car skidded into a government laboratory, where a top secret experiment was underway. I swerved into the path of Dr. Chase's Molecular Transfer Ray, causing me and my car to become one . . ." begins the voice-over for *Turbo Teen* as you see car and boy meld together, hands transforming into wheels, smile into a grill, like a Michelin tire ad or Renault car commercial gone bonkers.

(See Todd Gitlin's article in this volume.) Meanwhile, in an episode of *The Incredible Hulk,* "brilliant" scientist Bruce Banner, alias the Hulk himself, a sort of unjolly green giant, "prepares to test his amazing Transmat, a superpowerful beam that can transfer anything that lives from one place to another. . . ." "Doc? Are you sure this Transmat is safe?" "It worked on the guinea pigs," Banner answers all too ominously, for instantly the experiment goes wrong. "The powerful beam has triggered the gamma rays within his body that change Bruce Banner into"—and the voice-over pauses dramatically as we see the experiment wreak its havoc—"the Incredible Hulk!"

Such unease about the role of science and technology in our world is everywhere evident on children's TV. A once-dreamed-of, machine-produced life of leisure has somehow transformed itself into a perilous vision of imminent disaster. TV science, in its hydra-headed technological form, has completely taken over our on-screen lives—and the unspoken message is that it may turn on us at any second. The ultimate form of this scientific betrayal is, of course, nuclear cataclysm, perhaps particularly ascendent on kids' TV right now (as in video games) because of the increased fears of nuclear war the Reagan presidency brought with it. Such fears permeate action-adventure shows the way they once did the grade-B mutant-bug films of the 1950s: the daily use of nuclear threats as plot elements (stolen plutonium, radioactive death-rocks, radioactive sun creatures); the superweapon destruction of whole planets by the forces of evil (a direct theft from *Star Wars*); scenes like one in *Dungeons and Dragons* in which the good teenagers are saved from a harpylike evil spirit by a blinding explosion which leaves them "safe" in a desert landscape; the upping of the stakes in all these shows to the Fate of the Universe; constant, vague references to an ultimate battle for survival or an ultimate destruction, past or future. ("But then, technological experiments went wildly out of control, the Ancients' paradise began to collapse and a Great Cataclysm began.") Indeed, the whiz-bang technoexplosions which dot these action-adventure cartoons, while often not explicitly nuclear, are clearly routinized dress rehearsals for the ultimate Big Bang. Such nuclear devastation is so overused, so banal, that it is as taken for granted in these shows as the existence of the magical box itself. Presumably simple creations of "the Ancients," they both precede history.

Nuclear menace has, in short, become a fixture of kids' television life—yet it has scarcely been remarked upon either by the producers of the shows or, more interestingly, by the critics. On the face of it, this omission is curious, given academic, critical, parental, even official alarm about "violence" on television. Millions of dollars have been spent on social-scientific studies that demonstrate the seemingly obvious: there is some correlation (often contradictory from study to study) between viewing TV violence and aggressive behavior in children. However carefully tabulated and studied such TV acts of violence may be, the category of "violence" itself is almost meaningless, covering as it does anything from the total destruction of a planet to Miss Piggy hitting Gonzo with a pillow. Such "violence" floats in an abstract space conveniently uncoupled from the real world. The category, by omitting distinctions, leaves no opening to explore, for instance, the obvious parallels between the Reagan-era military budget and the increase in violent acts and baroque weaponry in these shows; or to compare this sort of TV violence with violence elsewhere in media history—in silent film comedies, to take an example, where it was certainly just as prevalent though of a far more subversive nature, or in the violent world of the comic strip from the moment Krazy Kat first picked up a brick (to say nothing of a previous generation's experiences at shooting galleries and in penny arcades). The scholarly literature is not interested in the links between violence and authority, violence and power, violence and the Good on kids' TV. Perhaps most important, no one mentions that this on-screen "violence" is of a strangely ritualistic and utterly unconvincing nature. Nor does anyone seem to wonder whether such convictionless mayhem induces in children an indifference to suffering in the real world, some strange form of visual pleasure or some utterly unexpected set of reactions. "Violence" is simply a catch-all category that allows moral crusaders to vent their displeasure without either analyzing what's really going on in front of our kids' eyes or discussing why and how it gets there.

In fact, the only place where violence on kids' TV doesn't seem utterly antiseptic is in the ads for the action-figure toys on which the shows are based. Only there do we sense real aggression, some actual human venom at work. A few years ago, these commercials were little films about kids playing with their toys. Now they are tiny ritual outdoor battles among three or four usually white, mostly blond boys (never a girl) in vaguely suburban settings. Each holds a Transformer or a GoBot or a He-Man figure on a "stage" of uneven rocks. Grimacing and growling, the boys insult each others' figures, exchange oaths and curses ("Next bash is on you, boneface!") while parading their toys, often to the crushing drumbeat of Japanese-style background chants for the product. Only here, in the ads, can you actually *feel* the urge to smash, insult, destroy—all connected to the urge to rush out and buy.

How children sort these shows out, and what their impact might be, can be little more than speculation. How the industry reacts to the periodic studies of "violence" that lead to outraged articles in the media and then cries for reform in Congress, is clearer. Under fire, the producers begin to tag "prosocial messages" onto their shows. Typically, *M.A.S.K.* has its safety tips (moreover, it's the first first-run cartoon series to be closed-captioned for the hearing impaired), while *He-Man* has its final homilies urging respect, politeness, or some similar value. These messages and tips are so dissociated from what's of interest about the shows (special effects, robots, toys to buy) that they can clearly only have been designed as ammunition for future congressional hearings on the responsibilities of broadcasters.

Their minimal links to the shows are living proof, however, that the attack on "violence" misses the point. Were someone to come up with another formula guaranteed to attract boys two to eleven to licensed-character products, the mesh of toy companies, card companies, advertising agencies, and film production companies that make TV's violent shows would abandon them in a minute—and what would be the result? We already know part of the answer: Rainbow Brite, Strawberry Shortcake, the Care Bears, and all their "nonviolent" ilk, the sort of shows so sickly sweet, so poorly made, and so obviously false that a viewing adult almost yearns for the Incredible Hulk or Skeletor or the Monster Minds to land in their midst and tear the place to bits.

Managed Emotion. As superweapon-wielding specialists in aggression dominate center stage in boys' TV, so a group of bossy, demanding, doll-like creatures dominate the relentlessly "happy" realm of girls'

TV. These psychotherapists of children's TV (and their accompanying voice-overs) are intent on teaching such evidently unknown skills as "the magic of hugging," or "caring," or "getting through the tough times in life." Without the special effects of the action-adventure shows to light up the screen several times each half hour, what's left are shows so ritualized, so perfunctory that they hardly seem to happen at all. A review of five of these shows found them remarkably alike. Each involved "very innocent, sweet, high-voiced creatures that lived in a pleasant, happy land. They were threatened by bad people (giants, things from dark swamps, or creatures without good feelings). In each story, one member of the happy land was captured by a bad guy and the rest of the do-gooders got up enough courage to rescue their friend."

Of course, these shows are still driven by two of the imperatives of boys' TV: the introduction of new characters (like the Care Bear Cousins); and the need for teamwork, which in these shows shades over into the more emotion-laden areas of togetherness, cooperation, and sharing. (In fact, one of the worst emotion-crimes you can commit in any of these happy lands is to be alone.) Thus, these shows are intimately linked to the seasonal launching and selling of new lines of dolls and other licensed products—not singly, but in bonded groups: ten or more Care Bears; scads of My Little Ponies; eight Hugga Bunch plush dolls with their own baby Hugglets in their arms, each carefully linked to a single valued emotional state or trait that the producers declare to be somehow lacking in the world of kids.

Such shows have one advantage over their action-adventure cousins. The gaping holes of inaction in them allow producers to do what critics have demanded and parents have asked for: throw out the "violence" (even the bad guys tend to be dopey rather than truly evil or frightening), and put in some *real* values in the form of prosocial messages. Of course, the traditional fairy tale sometimes culminated in a moral, though not necessarily a simple or "prosocial" one by present-day standards. Today, however, the TV-imposed superego speaks from on high. A painfully thin story is simply interspersed with a series of embarrassingly direct demands or even orders about how you should act, feel, and be. Take cooperation, for instance. Everyone realizes that kids should cooperate, while any fool (and TV producers are no fools) with child development experts and extensive research departments to call on knows that if your show advocates cooperation you can't easily be faulted. And if it so happens that you'd prefer to sell groups of little bears/puppies/fairies/ponies, then how useful to have wholly admirable reasons for suggesting that a parent plunk down a couple of hundred dollars. What better than urging kids to get into sharing and togetherness and cooperation by buying whole integrated, cooperative, loving sets of huggable, snugglable, nurturing dolls? ("Ten Care Bears are better than one," as one Care Bear special put it.)

In this oh-so-prosocial world, procreation is perpetual, no matter how many competing toy companies are involved, as Strawberry Shortcake and her friends begat Rainbow Brite and her friends begat My Little Pony begat the Hugga Bunch; while the Care Bears begat whole populations of little bearlike creatures, and the adoptable Cabbage Patch Kids begat adoptable Pound Puppies; and some forward-looking soul has even crossed a dollop of robot, two dollops of Care Bears, and a little drop of E.T. to sire Robotman from Robotland, "a magical place in another dimension as far away as the stars, but near as last night's sweet dreams. . . . His mission . . . to create an environment of happiness, while serving his new family and friends."

To take one show in more detail, the Charmkins are tiny buyable charms who live in Charmkinland, a world where the "skies are sunny all day," where rainbows are omnipresent and the landscape glows (or day-glos). The Charmkins, all flowers grown from the corporate soil of Hasbro, include Brown-eyed Susan (the leader); a little boy named Willie Winkie; a baby in a pink hat, pink shoes, and a white dress named Tulip; and Ladyslipper, a dainty, unbelievably high-voiced little ballerina with silver white hair topped by a crown of pink flowers, a pink tutu, and pink slippers. They naturally have supercute pets—a shaggy dog, a parrot, and a cat—and they are never alone. Across the river from Charmkinland live the Weeds, in Thistledown, a dark, gloomy, murky swamp. Dragonweed is their king, and they're all envious oafs with buckteeth who throw mud at one another and wear medieval rags. In this particular special, they capture Ladyslipper because Dragonweed wants her to "dance" for him. The Charmkins then venture into the swamp and, after a minimal adventure or two, free her. Meanwhile, various songs are sung, each with its own message. For instance, Brown-eyed Susan sings to Dragonweed: "Thistledown could be sunny too, if you'd let it. . . . You can find a rainbow anywhere. The world is rife with color when sunlight is in your heart." So get to it, kids! Throw out that gloom. Feel that bright, sunny joy inside. *Now.*

The ads on these shows are of a piece with the shows themselves, but livelier, better produced, more vivid. During this special, for instance, there were two ads for My Little Pony products ("I *love* to comb their curly hair . . ."), one introducing "new unicorn ponies" and the other, "rainbow ponies." Undoubtedly, they will be specials in their own right one of these days. You could, in addition, see an ad for *The Care Bears Movie*: "You can share our adventure as we journey to a strange land to meet new friends, the Care Bear cousins. . . . There's courage and caring as we set out to show that caring can save the world."

In the past few years, an endless stream of these happy little beings with their magical unicorns in their syrupy cloud-cuckoo lands have paraded across the screen demanding that they be snug-gled, cuddled, nuzzled, hugged, loved, and adored, generally entic-ing children to lay bare their emotions so that they can be examined and made healthy. As Al Kahn of Coleco (the maker of Cabbage Patch dolls) puts it: "All the psychologists are saying it's much better for children to get their emotions on the table. What these toys do is enable them to fantasize, to bring their emotions out in a very meaningful way. . . . Coleco has always been successful in selling emotions."

Emotions on kids' TV have largely been relegated to specials, miniseries, and ads. What love, caring, and other feelings do not yet have is their own syndicated show, perhaps because, to the writers and producers of kids' TV, love and the rest seem like scarcer, more difficult, less dramatic commodities to deal with than action and aggression. Nobody has yet come up with sixty-five half-hour episodes about a love creature who wields the weapons of caring and huggability to set the world aright. This can undoubt-edly be taken as symptomatic of the existence of a darker underside to the brittle world of happy licensed girls' characters. Promotional materials for these dolls and shows make this clear enough. For instance, Kenner, in a Hugga Bunch film promotion encouraging "the magic of hugging," also reminds us that "in the beginning there was love . . . but then something happened. . . . We grew up . . . lost touch with each other." Kenner wants to remind us that "you're not alone," that "hugs can bring us together."

One implication of all these shows surely is that you are alone, that you've got emotional problems you probably can't express, that you're not as happy, as loving, as caring as you certainly could be, that at the very least there's room for improvement; that, in short, we've all got at least one foot in that dismal swamp world with those dopey bad guys, and we could do a lot better, *if* we got some help. But it's going to cost. About twenty bucks a doll. And one doll won't do. Not by a long shot, not unless you're a one-emotion girl. Of course, when you think about it from a parent's point of view, it's still a lot cheaper than eighty dollars a session for a live therapist, and if it works, well . . .

The need to sell numerous little beings adds a special, unintended twist to the darker, more antisocial messages which underlie even the most relentlessly positive of these shows. If we all have trouble with caring or hugging, if intervention is called for, and if you also have to sell lots of licensed characters, then you have to present the managing (or healing) process as a highly complicated one that needs lots of cooperation by lots of highly specialized dolls, so specialized that instead of being complex individual personalities, they are no more than carefully labeled fragments of a personality: Tenderheart Bear, Share Bear, Cheer Bear, Grumpy Bear (who "understands those occasional tough times in life"). Together they must engage in a series of specialized interventions as complex as those of any real-life medical unit. If, in addition, you have to add new characters each year, then you must somehow create even more personality fragments, more acts of emotional well-being it is incumbent upon us to summon up. (And what happens next year, when the Care Bear Cousins get Second Cousins, and the Cabbage Patch Preemies get Fetuses, and the Hugga Bunch and their Hugglets spawn Squeezelets and Kisslets?) All this personality fragmentation reflects, in odd ways, familiar if less than pleasant feelings most people live with to one degree or another in our society: anxiety, helplessness, emotional flatness, a desperate need for self-improvement sustained by a lack of self-respect. Yet this is not simply us mirrored on the screen, but a particular version of us tailored to sell goods to kids. In such a TV world, the girls' shows amount to training in becoming passive creatures awaiting the ministrations of our dolls.

Saturday Morning. Saturday morning is the networks' ghetto for kids; and even if viewership is falling year by year (just as on adult TV), huge hunks of advertising money still flow in as the kids in their millions hunker down to watch their favorite cartoons.

In the last couple of years, the sacred precinct of Saturday morning has been overrun by licensed characters. Still, hidden away in its crevices, sometimes updated in incongruous ways, one can find traces of kids' TV history, even of that rarest of all elements, living human beings. For the relatively small audience of children watching between 7 and 8 A.M., there are still one or two programs with people: *Kidsworld* (CBS), *Vegetable Soup* and *The Kidalittles* (NBC). These, like the public service ads that surround them, are certainly the most integrated shows on children's TV, blacks and Hispanics naturally tending to cluster in those hours that make no difference to advertisers. In addition, during part of the period I was watching, CBS' *The Richard Pryor Show* (always well integrated) proved quite an enjoyable mix of real child actors, Pryor himself in a series of amusing bit parts, and puppets; its focus was on real-life problems, including watching too much TV. (It was, however, gone by the fall of 1985.) It was even possible to catch a glimpse of Bob Keeshan, formerly Captain Kangaroo, in his blue blazer, introducing *CBS Storybreak*'s cartoons adapted from books.

Then, too, one can still find a few old cartoon favorites like Bugs Bunny and the Road Runner cavorting on screen, and dolled-up versions of the oldest of our interventional superheroes like Superman and Wonder Woman, as well as their post-1960s superneurotic superhero friends, not to speak of the eternal Scooby-Doo (whose show is retitled every couple of seasons), the Pink Panther (and sons), and Alvin and the Chipmunks, still singing away in their shrill little voices. To describe the various Saturday morning shows in any detail, however, would be foolish, not just because of their repetitious nature, but because the season-to-season turnover is massive even by adult TV standards. Like licensed-character cereals, licensed-character shows (*The Smurfs* excepted) seem to fade in popularity relatively quickly.

Generally speaking, Saturday morning shows are more diffusely targeted than the boys' afternoon shows or the girls' specials, their goal being to pull in for their advertisers audiences of both sexes ranging from ages two to eleven (and possibly beyond, since some teenagers do watch). As a result, these shows try to offer a little of everything to everybody in the simplest, easiest, and usually cheapest ways possible. Any show may mix fake science with rainbows, or nuclear anxiety with unicorns. For instance, in CBS' computo-mystical *Dungeons and Dragons,* based on a popular game of strategy, a group of teenagers taking an amusement park ride break into a labyrinthine world of video arcade obstacles in which Norse helmets and A-bomb explosions mix with vampiric bad guys, Yoda-like gnomes, and cute little unicorns. NBC's *Kidd Video,* on the other hand, mixes a little MTVish music video by a teen band with animated action-adventures on the "Flip Side," lots of prosocial messages, magical fairies, your basic set of rainbows versus swamps, and so on.

With rare exceptions, production values are dreary at best. One or two shows like *Kidd Video* take a tentative stab at slightly out of the ordinary animation; *Jim Henson's Muppet Babies* (CBS) looks, in this barren landscape, like a work of near genius because it mixes striking juxtapositions (a cartoon door opens onto an old-movie *Tyrannosaurus rex*), odd angles (adults are seen as looming feet and ankles), crazy plot twists (the babies replay, with some humor, old movie and TV scenes), and messages that don't simply bash you over the head. But far more typical are the churning feet of characters chasing each other with stiffly immobile upper bodies, or the mouths that move in conversation while everything else stays still.

The best way to grasp Saturday morning TV, though, is to try to look at it as most children do. While a child may have a favorite show, the cry in the home is most likely to be, "Can I watch TV?"; and the result, the tuning in to a bloc of TV time, sometimes from mid-one-show to mid-another. So instead of looking at specific shows, let's follow a bloc of Saturday morning plots and prosocial messages (followed in the next section by a morning's flow of ads).

Take ABC on the morning of June 1, 1985, starting with *Super-friends, the Legendary Superpowers Show,* at 8 A.M. Its first half hour features a transformation device the villain Lex Luthor uses to escape jail by turning himself into Lois Lane. He then joins forces with some nuclear sun creatures who threaten to make Superman into a weakling and the earth into a flaming inferno. Half hour two involves an attempt by the Darth Vader—like Darkseid (even the name is borrowed from *Star Wars*) to steal the Superfriends' magic powers and invade the earth. At nine, in *The Mighty Orbots,* the evil Umbra attempts to take control of an earthlike planet with his "Shadow Star" (*Star Wars'* "Death Star") through a Trojan-horse plot to deactivate its defenses. Only the Mighty Orbot, a giant robot, stands in his way, if it can get itself put together! At nine-thirty, *Turbo Teen,* a red-sports-car/boy meld is once again chased by Dark Rider, a purple jeep driven by a Darth Vader—voiced bad guy. (It must be said that the sight of a cartoon boy in blue pajamas, chained to a wall, turning into a car is not to be missed.) At ten, *Rubik the Amazing Cube* and his three child friends are chased by robbers and their vicious dogs until Rubik transforms the robbers into cats whom the dogs chase in their turn. At ten-thirty, in the *Scooby-Doo Mysteries* and at eleven in *The Scarey Scooby Funnies,* the Great Dane detective is chased by a thirty-foot monster mouse (a genetic misexperiment), a prehistoric man, and a Chinese fire-breathing dragon. At eleven-thirty, *The Littles,* mouselike creatures who live in our walls but are never quite seen by us, try to save a little human girl whose mother is taking too many drugs. By mistake, Dinky Little ingests one of her pills and goes on an LSD trip-chase through a pie factory, while Lucy Little gets trapped in a pill bottle. And so it goes, Saturday after Saturday.

The sheer quantity of "prosociality" on these shows is awesome. Take NBC's morning lineup on April 20, 1985. At seven-thirty, in *The Kidalittles,* you are urged endlessly to be a positive thinker. At eight-thirty, *Pink Panther and Sons* recommends good treatment for old people. In *The Smurfs'* one-and-one-half-hour triple-header, the authoritarian though kindly Papa Smurf insists on all sorts of lessons: "Fun or no fun . . . there is no excuse for kicking. Kicking hurts and that's not smurfy. . . ." He cautions us not to break rules, reminds us that "if at first you don't succeed, smurf, smurf again, and again, and again." He tells us that we "must face [our] fears"; that, in dealing with a "Trojan Smurf" sent by the bad wizard Gargamel, teamwork is more important than individual glory, and so it goes right into ten-thirty's *Alvin and the Chipmunks,* where we are warned of the perils of boasting (though it seems to work for Alvin). Then on to *Kidd Video,* where Kidd, the lead singer of a teen band, befriends Cienega, a particularly ugly swamp monster, to make the very popular TV point that it's what's inside that counts. Many chases later, Cienega cries, her tears suddenly transforming her into a blond princess in a tutulike dress (Lucky Kidd!). In this new form, she bangs home the show's message: "Even though I was ugly, you cared for me. . . . The spell was broken because your caring was so strong." In case anyone misses the point, a band member who derided Kidd earlier for his kindness adds, "I guess we paid more attention to how you looked than to what you were doing." "And," another adds, "to what you were inside." The same theme is turned on its head moments later by *Mr. T* (eleven-thirty), as he frames his cartoon about kidnapping, chase, capture, escape, and recapture with a live warning that kids should always beware of whether there's a child-molesting monster inside a kind-looking stranger: "If a stranger stops you or calls you over to his car for something, take two steps backward and be ready to run. If a stranger offers you a toy, some candy, or a puppy, take off. . . . Take it from me, Mr. T."

Also scattered through these hours are a series of brief NBC-produced spots called *One to Grow On.* In each of these, an NBC-associated actor like Mr. T or Richard Moll, the dumb guard in *Night Court,* delivers a homily with a brief adlike film clip showing a couple of kids acting it out. (Some of these, in effect, are ads for shows kids are likely to watch.) On this particular morning, two involved stealing (first, don't do it; second, if you accuse someone else of doing it and you're wrong, "a little 'I'm sorry' goes a long way . . ."); one involved fighting ("Fighting's a loser's game because nobody really wins"); and the last advised kids "Take it one step at a time" . . . nothing comes easy."

Who knows what, if anything, kids make of this barrage of inane messages, platitudes, and high-flown sentiments, particularly from shows that are obsessed with theft, live off fighting, and feature superheroes for whom everything comes easy? Certainly, the contradiction between the message and the massage is as bizarre as it is unchanging. Still, it seems mild when compared with the ads.

The Ads. It's no news that ads are the life force of children's television. Only in them does the energy of the business itself break onto the screen in carefully constructed playlets, imaginative musical riffs, clever bits of animation with stunning production values, and fancy camera work. Perhaps the greatest compliment to their mesmerizing power was the decision of the creators of America's premier educational program for kids—*Sesame Street*—to base their program on the ad form, with the highly acclaimed but mixed results achieved to this day. (Lots of glitz and fun, but also an assumption that nothing can stay on the screen for more than a minute or two, that kids' attention spans just won't take it.)

Of course, the variety of kid-oriented products that can support the price of an ad on television is extremely limited. A thirty-second spot on Saturday morning in the autumn costs an average of $40,000; the same thirty seconds on the ever popular *Smurfs,* $60,000. Cereals (mainly presweetened), toys, and candy are the dominant advertisers, followed in fast-sinking order by other food products (cakes, cookies, and the like), chewing gum, carbonated drinks, fast food, toothpaste, and the odd sneaker or piece of clothing. This pretty much boils down to sugar and brand name toys, which can't help but make its own contribution to the repetitious nature of much of children's TV. (According to the Television Bureau of Advertising, $122 million were spent on TV advertising of toys and games alone from January to September 1984, up almost $40 million from the same period in 1983.) With show production costs relatively low—no human actors left to pay residuals to, very partial animation farmed out to cut-rate shops in Asia, the contractual right to repeat shows many times over—and ad rates above what the networks could get for adult programming at these hours, kids' TV is still considered profitable for the networks. Advertising money, however, is increasingly being siphoned off Saturday morning into the nonnetwork afternoon hours, and there have been rumors that one of the networks may actually pull out of Saturday morning children's programming altogether.

Studies have shown that really young children cannot distinguish between ads and shows. By the time they reach seven or eight years old, however, they not only distinguish, but often discount the ads, even watching them less carefully than the shows themselves. This is undoubtedly one reason why so much energy is expended to fill the ads with a throbbing life force. Such studies may be reassuring —don't worry, those 350,000 ads a typical child watches before high-school graduation don't really fool the kids—but they are also somewhat beside the point for two reasons. First, with the coming of the program-length commercial, the barriers between ad and show have been so broken down that often little more than a formal distinction remains; and second, even if kids can be shown to discount the more obviously false claims and messages of individual ads, what they actually see is ads en masse, a flood of ads which have their own larger messages to offer, their own story to tell about what is desired and not, valued and not, important and not in our society. Ads en bloc are, in fact, a heightened, crystallized, if unnoted, vision of just what the rest of children's TV is really selling.

Consider the flow of Saturday morning advertising, in which a particular tension exists between regular commercial advertising and public service ads, among which must be included network-created spots scattered throughout the morning hours to promote various good values and causes and to prove to kidvid critics, Congress, and the FCC that network hearts are in the right place. The public service ads cluster, for economically obvious reasons, in the unpalatable, low-viewer, early morning hours, slowly mixing with, and then being elbowed aside by, the paid ads as soon as larger masses of kiddie viewers come on board. So any Saturday, any network channel will begin with ads calling on viewers to eat well and build strong teeth, drink milk, "give a hoot, don't pollute," cook your own food "to build your body and build your health," eat snacks that are good for you, license your dog, help fight cancer, make sure teenagers don't drink and drive, use seat belts, prevent child abuse, and reject cigarettes or drugs because they are vicious destroyers.

Here, then, is a vision of life which involves these elements: problems (drugs, drunkenness, disease, accidental death, abuse, pollution); the dangers of the city; nonwhiteness, for problems and a dangerous urban landscape somehow go with blacks, Hispanics, and other minorities; drabness, partially because the world of old schools and tenements where these problems take place is dark and drab, partially because with rare exceptions the money to go into such spots is limited and the production values weak; and finally, in a more positive vein, the need for good eating, nutrition, and sound health.

By nine o'clock, however, this vision has been displaced by a contrasting one. Drabness has become Day-Glo brightness; the gray, ominous city has been replaced by a green, suburban country-side (the very paragon of those idyllic planets of action-adventure shows and the innocent cloud worlds of girls' specials); brown and black skins have been whitened (with blacks pretty much left to *Fame*-like dance numbers in which kids rock through school corri-dors for Fruit Chews, Hershey's chocolate, and the like, or to ap-pearances as, say, the fourth child at the edge of an action-toy fight sequence); and dark hair has been transmuted into a blindingly unreal silvery blondness.

In a typical ad, one sees an all-white porch with white settee or swing, just a hint of lush greenery, a flood of the yellowest sunlight, and four girls (at least two of them awesomely blond) hugging little dolls; or perhaps a glistening kitchen with glistening white children eating their cereal while cartoon animals hop around the table; or an all-white bedroom with little light-brown- and blond-haired children dressed in pastels romping with their toys on the bed—a window behind them letting in the same golden sun with the same hint of greenery beyond.

The unspoken message is overpowering. You want to be here, in an idyllic, almost rural suburb; not *there* in the dark, frightening city. These are the winners. *Those* are the losers, or why wouldn't they be associated with the good shows? And, of course, as this dream of the good life sells products, so it sells itself, unnoticed, unmentioned, unconsidered.

Only one thin counterthread runs through these hours: the net-work spots which pop up for a few seconds every now and then, functioning as an extraordinary barometer of an industry's defen-siveness and bad conscience. It's as if these spots, often with live actors or at least sprightly animation, were designed to register a sort of collective (but not too powerful) guilt over the TV vision itself.

ABC, for instance, runs a set of spots which feature a cat named Cap'n O. J. Readmore whose purpose in animated life is to urge children to "watch the TV in your head: read a book"; and another called *Scooter Computer and Mr. Chips* meant to promote "computer literacy" while convincing kids that computers can't think and are just tools for us to use. Could any action-adventure devotee take this seriously? Or for that matter, the plethora of spots that emphasize eating right, eating a balanced meal, not eating too many sweets, or in the case of a *One to Grow On* spot on NBC, not eating too much of one thing? Here a child who is warned against it orders three sundaes anyway and feels ill afterward. By itself, sensible enough advice, but the hour or so of ads on either side of it feature: McDonald's "Hot Fries," Bubblicious gum, 3 Musketeers bars, Bubble Yum gum, the Flintstones' Cocoa Pebbles cereal, Yoo-Hoo soft drinks, Rainbow Brite cereal, Hershey chocolate milk, Fruit Chewy Newtons, Pac-Man Macaroni & Cheese Dinner, and Hostess cupcakes. A case could be made, under the circumstances, for the three sundaes.

In any case, amid the *Close Encounters of the Third Kind* bubble gum ads; the frogs, tigers, and toucans bouncing on cereal boxes; the flying, dancing, prancing integrated feet desperate for candy, Fruit Chews, and Fruit Rolls; the sprightly interviews with sprightly kids who recommend cupcakes; the Hot Stuff Barbie and Dreamtime Barbie and Peaches 'n' Cream Barbie ads ("We girls can do *anything,* right, Barbie?"); the competitive Olympic-athlete Golden Girl ads ("I'm going to be Golden Girl, and I'll have prettier clothes than anyone!"); not to speak of the Heart Family dolls ("True fun is being part of the family that's a heart") and "The Animal" trucks with claws ("The Animal, clawing its way to the top!")—amidst this profusion, one ad, in particular, seems to sum up the world of kids' advertising in the Age of Reagan. It's an ad that links Post cereals to the children's discount toy store chain Toys-R-Us (which tends to locate in the suburbs) in a contest for a "one-thousand-dollar all-you-can-haul shopping spree at Toys-R-Us." Lots of kids with shopping carts burst through a "billboard" of Post cereals into aisles of toys, grabbing handfuls, armfuls of dolls, games, computers. You then see them in silhouette pushing wagons, buggies, whatever, piled high, along a sort of golden brick road. A small girl, arms filled, is the last to disappear, dropping a single toy as she goes. The screen is momentarily blank, then the girl ducks back for the toy as a voice intones, and the screen imprints, "It's all you can haul."

All you can haul. Every last toy. The real imperative. An unfettered industry bursting at the seams passes this self-image along to its viewers. It's what advertising's all about, but more demandingly so. Buy. Buy now. Buy lots. Not one doll, but ten. Twenty. Fifty. They're yours. You not only deserve them, you need them to feel good.

It captures a mood one could easily imagine in pre-1929 America, a frantic release of energy you can actually feel coursing through the veins of the industry's trade publications, the real emotions the Care Bears have gotten out onto the table, the real secret of Secret Bear. All you can haul before the roof falls in, because no one knows when the shake-out may come in the toy/licensing/TV industry, when—if at all—the corner may be turned, when one object too many may be printed up with a licensed character's image, when one too many of the same show may crowd onto afternoon TV, when one too many strange crossover creature may be created, and the whole multibillion-dollar edifice may crumble. But, hey, let the future take care of itself!

In the meantime, the kids' consumer industry has ingeniously solved problems with which adult TV and its worried advertisers are still struggling. It has made use of the latest technology at least as inventively as its superheroes, while protecting itself in an extraordinarily clever way from the dangerous underside of the same technology: the "zapping" of ads and the loss of viewers to VCRs, home computers, home video games, and other onrushing techno-wonders. VCRs which have for the first time created the possibility of a viewer actually fast-forwarding through the ads, and hand-operated remote controls which give viewers a chance to mute the sound during ads without getting up, have advertisers worrying. Through its licensed characters, however, kids' TV has so intertwined the ads and the programs that to zap them and still watch

TV would be next to impossible. The ads, after all, are little programs with one's favorite characters and the programs are giant ads, so what should be turned off anyway?

It used to be said that although adult TV might have a show called *Hotel*, it could not have a show called *Marriott Inn*. But with an ABC made-for-TV movie called *Club Med*, with the coming of Dynasty and Coca-Cola clothing styles, with Rocky IV clothes, stationery, and video games, with audiences eating up *Rambo* (a movie as crude as any kiddie superhero show), with scads of products and labels being slipped into every show imaginable, it's too soon to say what adults will actually stand for on TV, or for that matter at the movies. Kids' TV may well be pointing the way toward new adult solutions to the zapping of ads.

Certainly, by pulling the (nonlicensed) "character" out of its traditional environment, the kids' consumer industry has done a miraculous job of responding to loss of network viewership, even as the number of actual kid-hours spent watching TV has risen in the last decade from twenty-three to twenty-seven per week (11 to 12 percent of it weekend mornings; a portion of the rest, of course, spent watching "adult" TV). In fact, if one were to include hours spent in front of VCRs watching licensed-character shows, or simply hours with licensed characters in other forms (whether in fantasy play with G.I. Joe action-figures, listening to Berenstain Bears tapes, reading Wuzzle books, cuddling a Rainbow Brite doll, or going to bed in He-Man pajamas), product "viewership" can only have risen dramatically in recent years. While TV has clearly remained a central prop in the kids' consumer world, that world has covered its bets by spreading elsewhere. Turn off the TV tomorrow, parents, do your damnedest, everything the critics want you to do, and your kids still can't avoid us, because the Image, our images, are everywhere, smashed into a million identical bits and scattered throughout the world your children inhabit—so says the industry. Parents who try to duck this attack simply by denying the TV set to their children have missed the point.

Nor are there sufficient alternatives, though FCC head Fowler thinks differently, arguing that children's programming on PBS and the growth of cable channels have made further guidelines of any sort beside the point. This is what ACT's Peggy Charren calls the

Reagan administration's Marie Antoinette attitude toward kids: "Let them eat cable." It is true, of course, that PBS and cable TV —the lands of exile into which humans have been banished from the cartoon universe of commercial TV—harbor some real variety as well as some age-specific programming. On cable's Nickelodeon children's channel, for instance, a child can spin from *Pinwheel*'s cartoons to the fifties-style science of *Mr. Wizard;* on PBS, from the ultraspeedy *Sesame Street* to *Mister Rogers' Neighborhood,* which exists in a relaxing, slow motion, time-warp universe. But PBS, only a single stop on the TV dial, can hardly be a total children's channel for the very simple reason that if a given hour is programmed for preschoolers, then school-age kids have nowhere to turn. And these are, in any case, not exactly the best of times for PBS. The Reagan administration's budget-cutting pressure, the difficulty of getting corporate underwriting for kids' programming, and the drying up of foundation subsidies as foundations pull back to deal with other desperate areas of Reagan-era fund shortages, have made it hard for PBS to hold the line on children's programming, much less to expand to fill the void left by the commercial channels. And though cable reaches almost half of American homes, Nickelodeon with its 24 million-plus households reaches nowhere near all of them, and the expensive, upscale, "wholesome" Disney pay channel far fewer yet. In addition, Nickelodeon is suffering from a commercialization which is bound to lead it in expectable directions—starting in January 1984, it began taking ads—and from viewers going directly to the VCR.

In any case, the fact is that as far as kids are concerned (*Sesame Street* and HBO's *Fraggle Rock* aside), commercial TV is pretty much where it's at. The kids like it, and this is what critics have trouble explaining away; for if kidvid is really a flat, repetitious, utterly predictable backwater of some other far more energetic world, why do kids incorporate it into their fantasy life and fantasy play, into their desires and dreams?

As a strange sort of collective afterthought of the computer age, filled with interchangeable plots grabbed randomly from the junk-heap of culture, kidvid may be as close to myth as we can get. Perhaps its robotic transformations are our bizarre *Metamorphoses,* and what's on the screen reflects us in a purer way than any other cultural form. This, then, would be the sense in which children's TV is propaganda—propaganda meant to sell our own lives to our children. It may, in the end, be our truest educational television—because, unlike TV's prosocial messages, it does teach our children what we most value.

This may be why, every few years, the media suddenly get in a frenzy about the effect of TV on kids. *Newsweek*, for instance, cries out in its headlines about the "shame of kidvid" with a fervor it would never apply to the "shame" of American film or the "shame" of American culture. It's not that the critics are wrong, it's just that the periodic frenzy is cyclic enough to be suspect. However kids are actually treated in America, ideally we want to think of them as belonging to another race of beings, rather like the little denizens of Strawberryland, innocents open to the best we can possibly teach. We want to see them as different, more sensitive, somehow more human than ourselves, and so children's TV offends in ways the usual critiques do not touch. It disturbs because we shudder to see our children attracted to balder versions of what we are attracted to. Perhaps many of us also want to see ourselves as more immune to consumer dreams and Reagan-age fantasies than we are, so that it's like meeting yourself naked on a busy street in some hideously embarrassing dream to see your child love He-Man or Rainbow Brite with a possessing passion, or hunker down to watch a morning of kidvid. But why, after all, should the kids who live in our houses *not* be attracted to what, in only slightly more sophisticated form, is meant to attract us all: dreams of buying glitzy toys (promising more than they can ever deliver) with which to play out our fantasies. Why should children in our world appreciate shows that do not sell them anything?

The Reagan era has let loose dreams, fears, anxieties—of aggression and destruction, emotional deprivation, unfettered acquisitionism—let them loose with a passion. And who would claim, based on the results of recent elections, that Reagan's dreams (and fears) have no takers? No one could be untouched by them, least of all our children. For better or worse, childhood is not an immune age of life. If we want a different set of images on the screen, we'll have to produce not just better plots, but a different production system with different goals in a different world.

The Look
of
the Sound

PAT AUFDERHEIDE

Music videos are more than a fad, or fodder for spare hours and dollars of young consumers. They are pioneers in video expression, and the results of their reshaping of the form extend far beyond the TV set.

Music videos have broken through TV's most hallowed boundaries. As commercials in themselves, they have erased the very distinction between the commercial and the program. As nonstop sequences of discontinuous episodes, they have erased the boundaries between programs.

Music videos have also set themselves free from the television set, inserting themselves into movie theaters, popping up in shopping malls and department store windows, becoming actors in both live performances and the club scene. As omnivorous as they are pervasive, they draw on and influence the traditional image-shaping fields of fashion and advertising. Even political campaigning is borrowing from these new bite-sized packagers of desire.

If it sounds as if music video has a life of its own, this is not accidental. One of music video's distinctive features as a social expression is its open-ended quality, aiming to engulf the viewer in its communication with itself, its fashioning of an alternative world where image is reality. Videos are perhaps the most accessible form of that larger tendency known as postmodern art. That aesthetic-in-formation, signaled variously in the work of such artists as Andy Warhol, Nam June Paik, Thomas Pynchon, Philip Glass, and Keith Haring, is marked by several distinctive features. Among them are the merging of commercial and artistic image production, and an abolition of traditional boundaries between an image and its real-life referent, between past and present, between character and performance, between mannered art and stylized life.

When art, even self-consciously lightweight commercial fare, crosses that last boundary, it forces consideration of its social implications. And music videos have triggered plenty of such speculation, especially so since its primary audience is the young. Literary critic Fredric Jameson has suggested that the emerging postmodern aesthetic evokes an intense euphoria, a kind of "high," one that partakes in an experience rather than responding to an artist's statement. It is a provocative, and troubling, observation applied to music videos as they infiltrate the various domains of consumer culture, both on screens and on streets. A euphoric reaction is different in quality from the kinds of energizing, critical response once called up by rock music, hailed by Greil Marcus as triggering the critical capacity of negation, "the act that would make it self-evident to everyone that the world is not as it seems," and enthusiasts of rock culture wonder if music video heralds a new, more passive era for the young. Critic Marsha Kinder, for instance, finds the dreamy structure of videos a disturbing model for viewers who are stuck in real time. Not all agree; critic Margaret Morse suggests that the populist, self-assertive energy of popular culture may be reclaimed in music video's use of lip-synching; viewers may make that voice their own by singing along. Even Jameson, while positing a new relationship between artwork and audience, suggests that euphoria may have expressive qualities we cannot yet judge.

Whatever one's view, the rapid spread of the music video look is motive enough to take the phenomenon seriously. But it is particularly important because it is in the vanguard of reshaping the language of advertising—the dominant vocabulary of commercial culture—in a society that depends on an open flow of information to determine the quality of its political and public life. And so consideration of its form also implies questions about the emerging shape of the democratic and capitalist society that creates and receives it.

Music video was pioneered on television with three-to-seven-minute films or tapes whose visual images were coordinated loosely (or not at all) with a pop song's lyrics. Until recently, almost all music videos on TV were rock songs from the dead center of mainstream pop. With the growing appeal of the form, one sees music videos of country singers, easy-listening musicians, black rock stars, sometimes even rhythm and blues groups. If there are no waltz or tango music videos as yet, they are on their way. When music video has completed its present phase of being either acerbically challenged or heralded by hip pop culture critics (J. Hoberman of the *Village Voice* put a music video on his list of top-ten films of 1984), it will be ready for the easy-listening, easy-viewing audience. Indeed, VH-1, a music video channel aimed at adults aged twenty-five to forty-nine, has launched the process and wobbles toward viability. But long before there is a music video channel for Lawrence Welk tastes, the format will have pervaded nonmusical features of daily life. Indeed, one of the striking features of music video is its mutability.

This analysis of music video circa 1985 performs an unnatural act on the form, by taking a kind of photograph of a process defined by constant mutation. Most examples will have disappeared from viewers' memory; performers will have taken on new personas; and the form may have relocated itself on the social landscape. But its energy in this pioneering stage guarantees its importance in the emerging national pop culture—where the distinctions between public and private, between social standard and individual taste, are eroded to a rock beat.

Music video's roots are in the mass marketing of popular songs, not only as populist entertainment but as talismans of subcultural autonomy and rebellion in successive generations of American youth. Top-40-hits radio programs cemented a pop cultural consciousness in the 1930s. In fact, national mass media were instrumental in shaping a national self-consciousness stratified by generation—unlike regional and folk culture, which unified the generations, transmitting legacies while incorporating the new. As new groups and sounds were created in the image of rebellious self-assertion, they were also pop-ified, which usually meant whitening them as well. (English outsiders could market black rhythm and blues to mainstream white audiences as the R & B masters never could.) The 1960s generation celebrated its uniqueness in rock concerts, wore the badges of rock groups, and never moved to communal farms without stereo equipment.

Putting together the music with pictures was an early innovation. The Max Fleischer cartoons of the 1930s and 1940s were cut precisely to songs sung by the likes of Cab Calloway and Louis Armstrong. As early as 1943, the Panoram Soundies had brief success. These were jukeboxes placed in nightclubs and diners, where viewers could punch up songs and watch performers on the mini-screen atop the jukebox. A European device called Scopitone brought the gimmick back in the 1960s, though it never caught on, some say because it generally featured mainstream European singers without the oppositional appeal of American pop idols. More influential were commercials borrowing a hip edge from rock sounds, and the commercial-fed work of film artists like Richard Lester, who turned the Beatles into a visual experience. In *A Hard Day's Night,* Lester made the Beatles' screen personae and lifestyle, as well as their performances, the subject of film episodes backed by music cuts. Rock videos were shown in the 1970s in European clubs, and some English underground groups rode them to celebrity. This was a moment in English pop music when the performer's persona had become as important as the sound of the music, and so the form nicely fulfilled its function.

The transatlantic success of music video awaited the moment at which cable TV became an option for a substantial number of Americans. Then targeted audiences became commercially attractive. Amid wild talk of whole cable channels devoted to pet care and chess, programmers brainstormed channels that would deliver the same kind of programming—to a big but still targeted audience—around the clock. Movies were a surefire idea, and music seemed an ideal vehicle to attract highly prized consumers: young people. They had value not merely because the young buy records, but because buyable popular culture is central to their lives. Pop culture commodities are now the tools to express personal taste, even talismans of identity and identification with a subculture. No one needs to sell young people on the key role of fad and fashion in designing their identities; indeed, channeling such information to them provides a service welcomed for its news of what's happening.

Still, no one foretold the success of music video. At Warner, which gambled on the format in 1980, the prospect of a cable channel wholly dedicated to rock videos, on air twenty-four hours a day, was received with major reservations. Even though the program time was to be filled with free videos given to the channel as promos by record companies, Warner hesitated before backing the concept. Even its strongest in-house advocates only promised record companies that they would see increased sales in two years.

But when MTV—Music Television—started up in 1981, its success was almost instantaneous. MTV became a hot media item in itself, and record companies were reporting rising sales within months. Music videos have fueled the current boom in the record industry, a fact reflected in music industry awards for videos. The channel took a little longer to start paying out. MTV stayed in the red for two years before Warner was confident enough of its future to spin it off as a separate company. It showed a profit in 1984, claiming access to 24.2 million viewers, with independent services estimating only slightly less, making it the highest-rated music cable service on the air even after ratings leveled off in 1984.

Nielsen ratings for 1985 showed a dramatic 30 percent drop from 1984; the rating was disputed by MTV, which argued with some reason that Nielsen's cable estimates are flawed. But some falloff is indisputable and may reflect the proliferation of similar services in other areas, both nationally and internationally. And so, mutating again, MTV added rock-oriented and nostalgia-laden sitcoms to its nonstop round of para-information, and also changed the faces of its video jockeys. Meanwhile, MTV's signal is being picked up abroad, among other places by TV pirates in Latin America. In Europe, clubs pirate videos on similar services, and in the Soviet Union, illicit music videos are hot tape items.

Other music cable channels quickly imitated and improvised on MTV's example, but no cable channel on the scale of MTV has been able to compete, partly because MTV has aggressively attacked rivals legally and with such marketing practices as signing producers to exclusives and paying contracts. Ted Turner accomplished the most spectacular failure, with a service he billed as a more wholesome, family-oriented version of MTV. After abysmal ratings in early weeks, Turner sold his venture to MTV, where it became VH-1. VH-1 is offered free to MTV subscribers, and all cable channels that carry VH-1 carry both. VH-1's most important role may be to hold down space competitors might otherwise occupy.

Networks and syndicators also attempted to imitate MTV's success. Some, such as the show *Hot,* which expired after only twelve weeks, collapsed. Others, such as *Night Tracks* and *Friday Night Videos,* became mass-audience successes, and the cable program service Black Entertainment Television began producing its own music video shows. Music video has also made inroads into prime time (see the articles by Todd Gitlin and Mark Crispin Miller). Twenty-four-hour-a-day music video channels have proliferated in low-cost and low-reach markets, and at this writing there are currently about eleven such channels on UHF and low-power frequencies. Many broadcasters expect an all-music TV channel to exist in the top hundred markets within the next few years, although 1985 was financially rocky for several of the low-power sources.

However packaged, the music video format always amounts to wall-to-wall commercials for something. The videos tout particular rock groups and albums. The production "credits" usually include only the name of the group and the record. (This is the viewer's first clue that music videos purvey a peculiar amalgam of celebrity and anonymity; from the outset, they are represented as authorless adventures. The exception comes when a video is made by someone with star status, who has "brand name" recognition.) The videos have become products in themselves, sold in compilation or long-form versions in video stores. Cross-plugging, weaving other products into the atmospherics, is ever more common, and cross-financing goes on too. (RC Cola, for instance, financed a Louise Mandrell video, which then, with its appropriate images of RC-sipping, debuted at the National Soft Drink Association convention in 1985.) When a song cut comes from a movie soundtrack, the video is a virtual movie trailer. Between videos on a program, video jockeys (VJs) tout both the service and, through music industry "news," other music products and tickets for performances. And then there are the commercials.

Advertisers have been quick to take a cue from music video's appeal, just as the videos have built in a stylistic base created by commercials. An advertisement for Clairol Heated Rollers, for instance, features close-ups of muscles and aerobically coordinated bodybuilders backed by a strong rock beat. The "bodybuilder" rollers become one of many trigger visuals for a gestalt. A commercial for the Duster car, like the Clairol ad, features the colors black, white, and blue, a color scheme that in its artificiality locates the action within television's alternative universe. On an outsized indoor-outdoor jungle gym, the Duster car becomes an actor among a group of peripatetic dancers.

It is easy to see why commercials imitate music videos, sometimes even mimicking their opening "credits." It is not merely that advertisers like the pleasure-happy attitude that the videos promote, although Okidata computer software appeals directly to that attitude with a commercial featuring a cartoon character who sits at a terminal muttering "Where's the fun?" It is also that music video never delivers a hard sell, never identifies the record or tape or group as a product. Instead, it equates the product with an experience to be shared, part of a wondrous leisure world.

Commercials have always sold the sizzle, not the steak—that is, depended on atmosphere. But they have usually promised consumers that the product will enhance an experience ("adds life," "takes the worry out of being close") or permit one ("don't leave home without it"). But music videos are themselves primary experiences. Music videos give the product a new location on the consumer's landscape, not as messengers of a potential purchase or experience, but as an experience in themselves, a part of living.

Two decades ago, science fiction writers imagined a commercial-mad future, where consumers were perpetually dunned with demands to buy. Even the prescient Philip K. Dick, in *The Simulacrum,* imagined roving electronic commercials that attached themselves to beleaguered consumers. But the reality of permanent and pervasive commercials turns out to be quite different. Once commercial reality becomes primary in daily life, the direct appeal to buy can be submerged. Products come to seem "natural." Any product—a record, tape, videocassette, article of clothing, car, perfume—takes its place as an aspect of the gestalt. The raw material for postmodern pastiche art is everywhere.

With nary a reference to cash or commodities, music videos cross the consumer's gaze as a series of mood states. They trigger moods such as nostalgia, regret, anxiety, confusion, dread, envy, admiration, pity, titillation—attitudes at one remove from primal expression such as passion, ecstasy, and rage. The moods often express a lack, an incompletion, an instability, a searching for location. In music videos, those feelings are carried on flights of whimsy, extended journeys into the arbitrary.

In appealing to and playing on these sensations, music videos have animated and set to music a tension basic to American youth culture. It is that feeling of instability that fuels the search to buy-and-belong, to possess a tangible anchor in a mutable universe while preserving the essence of that universe—its mutability. It allows the viewer to become a piece of the action in a continuous performance.

Music videos did not discover the commercial application of anxiety, of course. The manufacturer of Listerine was selling mouthwash on anxiety sixty years ago. Nor did music videos succeed in making themselves widely appealing by somehow duping passive audiences into an addiction to commercial dreams. Music videos are authentic expressions of a populist industrial society. For young people struggling to find a place in communities dotted with shopping malls but with few community centers, in an economy whose major product is information, music videos play to the adolescent's search for identity and an improvised community.

The success of MTV has been based on understanding that the channel offers not videos but environment, a context that creates mood. The goal of MTV executive Bob Pittman, the man who designed the channel, is simple: his job, he says, is to "amplify the mood and include MTV in the mood." Young Americans, he argues, are "television babies," particularly attracted to appeals to heart rather than head. "If you can get their emotions going," he says, "forget their logic, you've got 'em." Other executives describe

MTV as "pure environment," in which not performers but music is the star of the perpetual show.

MTV's "pure environment" is expertly crafted. The pace is relentless, set by the music videos, which offer, in the words of one producer, "short bursts of sensual energy." But the image of the program service is casual and carefree. The channel's VJs are chosen for their fresh, offhand delivery and look. They are "themselves," celebrities whose only claim to fame is their projection of a friendly image to youthful viewers. The sets are designed to look like a basement hideaway a fifteen-year-old might dream of, with rock memorabilia and videocassettes adorning walls and shelves. Lighting is intentionally "shitty," instead of the classic no-shadow bright lighting of most TV productions. MTV intends to offer viewers not just a room of their own, but a room that is an alternate world.

MTV promotes itself as the populist, even democratic expression of its viewers. Rock stars in promo spots call on viewers to say, "I want my Em Tee Vee!," as if someone were threatening to take it away from them. "Their" MTV, as its own ads portray it, is the insouciant, irreverent rejection of a tedious other world—not the real-life one of work and family, but the world as network news reports it. One commercial spoofs network news promos. Flashing the familiar "Coming at 11" slogan, the ad promises, "MTV provides *reason to live,* despite news of *botched world!*" On a miniature TV set, a logo reads, "Botched World." MTV superimposes its own version of reality on television's historic moments as well. Space flights—which made history not least for television's live coverage of them—are a favorite subject for MTV's own commercials. One shows astronauts planting an MTV flag on the moon. Another asks, "What if time had never been invented!," showing a space launch countdown without numbers. MTV's promise to remove the viewer from history is succinctly put into the slogan "24 hours every day . . . so you'll be able to live forever!"

Viewers are encouraged to play an active role—as consumers, anyway—in MTV's separate world. They can vote for their favorite video by calling a 900 telephone number, which costs fifty cents. They can compete in contests to win visits with rock stars and vacation trips. The contests have a zany spin; as John Sykes, the restless promotion exec at MTV, says, "Our promotions have to reinforce our irreverent image."

Music video programs that aren't round-the-clock reach a total number of viewers that is larger than MTV, in part because more people have access to broadcast than to cable. They have had a lower media profile, in part because of MTV's hype machine, in part because they compete with other programs, and in part because they do not have a built-in advantage in styling their own image that MTV has. Unlike that twenty-four-hour service, which like a water faucet is there when you need it, programs must begin and end. Viewers there cannot "live forever," and time is an inescapable reality. Still, some broadcast programs attempt to immerse viewers in an alternative environment, whether it is a studio set rigged to look like a permanent party or disco, or the basement hideaway feature on *Rock 'n' America*.

Wherever they appear, music videos are distinctive because they imitate dreams rather than the plot or event structure of bounded programs. Even the usually thin narrative threads in song lyrics rarely provide the basis for a video's look and action. ("If you can hear them, the words help a bit," says video producer Zelda Barron wryly; her videos for Culture Club feature the bizarre, supernatural, and exotic, and use hectic montage rather than narrative logic. Her explanation for her style—that the budgets aren't big enough to produce a coherent story—fails to explain why the features have the heady dream elements they do.) In *Film Quarterly*, Marsha Kinder has noted strong parallels between dreams and music videos. She cites five elements: unlimited access (MTV's continuous format and people's ability to both sleep and daydream); structural discontinuity (for instance, abrupt scene shifts); decentering (a loosely connected flow of action around a theme); structural reliance on memory retrieval (both videos and dreams trigger blocks of associations with pungent images); and the omnipresence of the spectator. In *Fabula*, Margaret Morse notes many of the same features, particularly the absence of reliance on narrative; she focuses on the magical quality of the word, as lip-synched by the performer, who can appear anywhere in the video without being linked with the images or events, as if a dreamer who could create a world.

Many videos in fact begin with someone dreaming or daydreaming. For instance, Kool and the Gang's "Misled" begins with a band member in his bedroom, launching into a dream-adventure in which he is both himself and a small Third World boy, threatened by a glamorous white female ghost and engaged in an adventure that imitates *Raiders of the Lost Ark*—significantly, another commercial fantasy. The dream never really ends, since after his band members wake him up, they all turn into ghosts. Thelma Houston's "Heat Medley" shows the performer daydreaming to escape an unpleasant morning conflict with her husband. She daydreams a central role for herself on a *Love Boat*–like episode that turns into a nightmare of disastrous romance.

While the fantasies of music videos are open-ended, they do play on classic story lines, such as boy-meets-loses-wins-girl and child-is-menaced-by-monster-and-conquers-it. Some weave fairy tale themes—in which the protagonist is either a preschooler or is infantilized—into the dream. But performers easily switch identities, magical transportations occur, and sets are expressionistically large or small. In Midnight Star's "Operator," giant telephones dwarf performers, and a telephone booth magically pops up and disappears on highways. In Billy Joel's "Keeping the Faith," a judge's bench becomes a giant jukebox on a set featuring commercial talismans of the 1950s. In ABC's "The Look of Love," Central Park becomes a cartoon set (commercial kiddie culture), and Nolan Thomas' "Yo' Little Brother" looks like a Saturday morning cartoon version of *The Cabinet of Dr. Caligari*.

Kinder believes that manufactured fantasy may have a much more far-reaching effect on people's subconscious attitudes and expectations than we now imagine, perhaps conditioning not only our expectations today but our dreams tomorrow. Her fears are far-reaching—and unprovable—but her careful analysis of parallels between dream structure and music video structure have fascinating implications for the form. Music videos offer a ready-made alternative to social life. With no beginnings or endings—no history—there may be nightmarish instability, even horror, but no tragedy. Tragedy is rooted in the tension between an individual and society. Likewise, there is no comedy, which provokes laughter with sharp, unexpected shifts of context, making solemnity slip on a banana peel. Dreams by contrast create gestalts, in which sensations build and dissolve. And so they nicely match the promise and threat of consumer-constructed identity, endlessly flexible, depending on your income and taste. Obsolescence is built in. Like fashion, identity can change with a switch of scene, with a change in the beat. The good news is: you can be anything, anywhere. That is also the bad news—which whets the appetite for more "news," more dreams.

The makers of music videos, however, scorn sophisticated analysis and charges of conspiracy to shape the dream world of a generation. From their perspective, the production process imposes stringent limits on fantasy. Music videos are typically made as promotion items for albums, funded by record companies. Almost always, this means performers will appear in the video. (Bruce Springsteen's absence from "Atlantic City" caused a major media uproar.) It also pretty well guarantees they will not be shown performing, although sometimes they seem to. No record company volunteers to use live performance footage, because the sales item is the record on which the musical number in the video appears, and it is difficult to synch the cut to performance shots. Lip-synching does allow the performers to appear as pure celebrities—crooning, resting, acting out fantasies, "performing" without being hooked up to instruments. And, as Morse points out, it allows the viewer to "sing along," participating in the celebrity and the dream, perhaps even claiming ownership of the fantasy.

A more abstract constraint on videos is their cost. Until 1984, most videos were made at a loss, for figures on the order of $35,000 to $50,000, as foot-in-the-door opportunities for aspiring filmmakers. Record studios resist expanding their promotional budgets to meet the real production costs, although they have increased budgets as videos have become more popular. The ever present smoke and mirrors in video are, among other things, cost-cutting measures.

Indeed, if you ask a video producer why a certain image, effect, or look was used, the answer is often a list of production problems, rational reasons for arbitrariness. And yet in spite of increasing diversity—more video graphics, less of the thuggish heavy-metal sadism—music videos from different musicians, visual artists, and record companies show disconcerting similarities.

Music videos have no heroes, because they do not feature individuals in the sense that plot-driven entertainment does. Music video offers unadulterated celebrity. The living human beings do not play characters, but bold and connotative icons. Frequently, those icons evoke sex roles (not sexuality). In her hit video "Like a Virgin," Madonna alternately takes on the aspect of a whore—in black bad-girl clothes—and a virgin, in white ballroom and wedding-type dresses. In other videos, movie-mafioso types abound; performers strut in white ties and black shirts, projecting macho images of power and money. A bold image is crucial to video and, now, recording-artist celebrity. Bryan Adams, whose hit video "Cuts Like a Knife" was widely criticized for its sadomasochistic elements, was pleased that the video removed a hint of weakness from his pop-rock image. "The most important thing [the video did] for me was establish my look," he said.

Just as interesting as the importance of look over character is how quickly the look changes. Several major performers depend on constant innovation and recombination as a defining element of their celebrity. Cyndi Lauper recreates herself with each new video and album in ingenious refashionings of cheap clothes. Her image as an artist with integrity is related to her ability to refashion herself uniquely at each new turn of the product wheel. Many performers hold up as a model the career of David Bowie, who pioneered the concept of the disposable image. In England, a foremost image-manipulator is Malcolm McLaren, the former art student who became a fashion designer and marketer, and also a music promoter of punk groups such as the Sex Pistols. As punk became passé, McLaren remade Adam Ant's image from punker to swashbuckler, appropriating imagery of the pirate, the highwayman, and the Indian "brave." "Pirates steal everybody's culture and shove it all on their backs," he said, "so you could have this ramshackle mixture of exotic clothes." For such pop culture celebrities, look is at least as important as sound, and rock videos are a mass medium that platforms their latest version of themselves. In fact, with rock videos, personal "identity" has become a central element of commodity production. Music may be only the beginning of the possibilities, as McLaren explained: "In England we don't listen as much as look," he said. "The day comes when somebody turns off the sound and just watches images, maybe focuses on the socks the singer is wearing, then runs out and finds he can't get those. Does he want to buy the record? It doesn't even occur to him. And the industry is beginning to pick up on that, and I think that you'll find that by the end of this decade, the record industry won't be called the record industry. They'll just be selling anything and everything.''

The synthesis of television and rock has meant commercial success for people who lack even basic technical skills of musical performance. What was once a scandal, the betrayal of an authentic expression of talent—the sound processing of the Monkees, for instance—is now standard practice, with points given for witty execution. Madonna's own reedy voice is heavily processed on her recordings, and her concerts are notable not for her singing but for her crude gyrations—echoing past pop goddesses of earlier screens such as Marilyn Monroe, in a style that mocks its own referents. Her sultry-sullen, innocent-cynical pose is perfect for labile switches of persona on video. Performers in the video "Yo' Little Brother" do not even pretend to sing. A troupe of four prepubescent children mimic the clothing and stage mannerisms of older rockers, including Bruce Springsteen and Cyndi Lauper—who have thus already been recycled as raw material for pastiche art. The video's producer is now creating a stage act for the four, based on their appearance in the video, in which they will lip-synch on stage. (On TV's version of lip-synching, see Michael Sorkin's article in this volume.)

By contrast, galvanizing rock performers may not produce videos that carry the same charge. The requirements of nonstop video stimulation may work against these performers, for a variety of reasons. Consider Bruce Springsteen, a performer who fiercely maintains a direct connection with his working-class audience as an eye-level hero, who eschews not only glamour but the notion that his image can be altered. He insisted on making a video that used live performance footage for "Born in the U.S.A.," and contracted with independent producer John Sayles. Sayles, a neorealist-style filmmaker, intercut concert footage with scenes of unemployment lines, neighborhood playgrounds, and rustbowl landscapes. Although Springsteen liked the results, his own promotion people were jolted by the video's gritty quality, and it encountered difficulty in gaining time in rotation.

Tina Turner is a distinctive singer, famed for her ability to project raw sexual energy. In videos such as "What's Love Got to Do with It?" exotic fantasies are a weaker evocation of her songs' spirit than her own live performances. Turner changes costumes constantly in her videos, but her persona does not change, and her act fits awkwardly into them as a result. Barbra Streisand also has a distinctive performance style and traditional star status. Her image may be too well defined for the new-age sport of video image permutations. In "Emotion," she engages in a string of unlikely lovers during a dream. But the scene shifts merely look like new locales for Barbra to show off, and the look is the fatally glamorous Beverly Hills chic rather than the improvisational street glitz of populist celebrity.

Music video's lack of a clear subject carries into its constant play with the outward trappings of sex roles. Male images include sailors, thugs, gang members, and gangsters. Female images include prostitutes, nightclub performers, goddesses, temptresses, and servants. Most often, these images are drawn not from life or even myth, but from old movies, ads, and other pop culture clichés.

Social critics, especially feminists, have denounced sadomasochistic trappings and stereotypes of exotic women (especially East Asians) in videos. This may indeed be evidence of entrenched prejudice in the culture. For instance, women are often portrayed in videos as outsiders and agents of trouble, which reflects in part the macho traditions of rock. The fetishistic female costumery of many videos probably reflects the role of artifice in shaping feminine sex roles in the culture; there is a fuller cultural grab bag for feminine than for masculine sexual objects.

All these sex role stereotypes function differently, however, than stereotypes do in stories—for instance, in pornographic videos and movies. In pornography, doing is everything; it's the act that counts. In music videos, the very act of image manipulation is the action. The sex role, more than a costume, is an identity fashioned from the outside in. While pornographic films feature sexual encounter, in music videos contact is a comparative rarity. The bolder the stereotyping, the more likely it is to turn out that these images are evanescent.

You might think that, with romance the theme of most popular songs, videos would feature boy-meets-loses-gets-girl ministories. But love-longing is not the same as a love affair. Soft-focus embraces, memory, and menace make for video visuals, but rarely is there more than a hint of a resolution in the search for bliss. And resolution is more often associated with horror than not. For instance, in a Greg Kihn video, the bride turns into a ghoul on the way to the altar, and becomes a person again when bride and groom escape from the ceremony (an event that marks history, the beginning of something that must have an end), pursued by guests who have turned to ghouls (metaphors for the end of the story they are escaping). In Culture Club's "Mistake Number Three," the bride not only wears black but turns into a robot. The action is an endless transformation of selves, not in what anyone does with or to someone else.

Male or female, grotesquerie is the norm. Combine grotesquerie with shifting identities and you get androgyny, as with Culture Club's flamboyant Boy George. Androgyny may be the most daring statement that an entire range of sex roles is fair game for projecting one's own statement of the moment. Gender is no longer fixed; male and female are fractured into a kaleidoscope of images.

Fashion's unstable icons also exist in a spooky universe. The landscape on which transient images take shape participates in the self-dramatizing style of the performer-icons. Ordinary sunlight is uncommon; night colors—especially blue and silver—are typical; and neon light, light that designs itself and comes in brilliantly artificial colors, is everywhere. Natural settings are extreme—desert sands, deep tropical forests, oceans. Weather often becomes an actor, buffeting performers and evoking moods. The settings are hermetic and global at the same time, locked into color schemes in which colors complement each other but no longer refer to a natural universe.

It can be a lonely world, but even the loneliness is hypnotically engrossing. One music video visual cliché that provides continuity in the absence of plot is the shot of the performer simply gazing, often at himself or herself in the previous shot. In Roxy Music's "The Main Thing," Bryan Ferry gazes from an armchair at his own just projected image. In Chicago's "You're the Inspiration," members of the group pretend to practice in a nostalgically lit loft.

Intercut are scenes of couples in wistful moods and shots of performers brooding individually. It is images like these that provoke Marsha Kinder to call videos solipsistic.

Their world, however, is also one of cosmic threat and magical power. The self-transforming figures are menaced by conglomerate figures of authority, which often trigger all-powerful fantasy acts of destruction and salvation. Parents, school principals, teachers, police, and judges provide a cultural iconography of repression. In Heaven's "Rock School," a principal wears a stocking mask, and a school guard menaces students with a Doberman. Bon Jovi's "Runaway" features a girl in miniskirted rebellion against her parents (harking back nostalgically to an era when miniskirts could express rebellion). In retaliation against restrictions, she incinerates them with powers reminiscent of those used in the films *Carrie* and *Firestarter;* we're seeing word magic, the power of dream-song, at work. Sammy Hagar, in "I Can't Drive 55," exercises his "right" to drive as fast as he wants to (desire being asserted as a right); he ends up before a judge whose name is Julius Hangman, from whom he escapes by waking up. Videos often play on the overlapping sexual and political iconography of power in Naziesque sadomasochistic fetishes, with symbols connoting total power without moral or social context. In Billy Idol's "Flesh for Fantasy," as he sings "Face to face and back to back/You see and feel my sex attack," the video shows Idol strutting, preening, performing Nazi-like salutes. Cutting into this one-man parade is a sequence of body parts and geometric forms, some of them drawn from the starkly abstract set. Idol's "sex attack" is not directed; while he sometimes looks directly at the camera, the video's "story" is the construction of a movie-picture portrait of Idol in his stormtrooper/S & M outfit.

The National Coalition on Television Violence, among other groups, has criticized the violence, "especially senseless violence and violence between men and women," in music videos. The criticisms are grounded in a history of objections to violence in TV programs. These violent actions are seen by NCTV analysts (and the middle-class consumers who support the pressure group) as virtual prescriptions to violence in life. But it is hard to assign a prescriptive meaning to random violence that is used not as action but as atmosphere and aestheticizer. Even Central American conflict has been

retailed in videos by Don Henley and Mick Jagger, as a backdrop
for the dislocated performers making a stand amid rubble and military action in which no side stands for anything. George Gerbner,
dean of the Annenberg School of Communications at the University
of Pennsylvania, has reassessed the implications of violence in music
video, saying, "Many videos express a sense of defiance and basic
insensitivity, an unemotional excitement." The sensations evoked
by video imagery are disconnected from the realm of social responsibility altogether.

In this impulse-driven fantasy world, apocalypse is a recurrent
theme. The title of "Purple Rain" refers to nuclear fallout, and
Prince's earlier hit song "1999" ends with a child's voice saying,
"Mommy, what about the bomb?" Prince's response to the anxiety
in the same song is to sing. "If I gotta die I'm gonna listen to my
body tonight," and his performance-rich videos offer that spectacle
to viewers.

Postholocaust landscapes frame nightmarish struggles to survive
—indeed, to create oneself. The Planet P Project's "Pink World" is
an explicit example. A young boy smothered by his mother's attention has a nightmare in which he wakes up in a deserted military
dormitory after a world disaster. Groping his way toward "outside,"
he encounters a desert world inhabited by zombies. Returning to
the dorm, he sets immobilized children free; they are reborn in
white, all looking like each other.

Music videos may be able to give the once-over to the apocalypse,
but facing tomorrow or yesterday is something else. In music videos, history has been abolished along with other real-world con-
straints. In its place is a set of aids to nostalgia. As the Eurogliders,
in "Heaven," sing, "I want to find a better place," sepia-toned
images of rural life are traced in slow motion. The good old days,
the mythic past of music video, is located in the fashion of the
1950s (the early days of pop rock) and in the television and movie
images of that period. This was the innocent youth of postwar
commodity culture seen from a jaded present, and the closet out of
which the recombinant images of celebrity today are drawn. Elton
John's "Sad Songs (Say So Much)," like many videos, subscribes to
a 1950s dress code, and it echoes *West Side Story* choreography.

Ponytails and soda fountains adorn Billy Joel's paean to golden oldies "Keeping the Faith."

The use of black and white is the quickest way to evoke TV's mythic golden age. Barry Gibb's "Fine Line" exploits the black-and-white connotation in a typical way. The performer implicitly strikes a parallel between himself and early rockabilly performers, and also between himself and Beatles-era singers, in a black-and-white video featuring cuts between himself on stage and a screaming crowd of adolescent girls. A mythic past can also double as futuristic, as in Don Henley's "The Boys of Summer," where a boy drummer in a black-and-white 1950s household is also the spectator of scenes that evoke the postnuclear future of *On the Beach*.

Music video programs rarely take the opportunity to show historical footage of rock performance, as J. Hoberman has pointed out. There is always a danger of invidious comparison between a Bo Diddley, say, and the current video artists. More important, reference to history might rupture the regular delivery of music video's eternal now. Instead, there is a cavalcade of historical references. Music videos incorporate them into the self-reflexive game, giving them an easy, wry, even sardonic tone without social comment or real parody. In David Lee Roth's "California Girls," Roth walks a California boardwalk adorned with pasty manikinlike women in bikinis, while his remake of the 1964 Beach Boys' tune plays. This outdoor body-shopping to a golden oldie tune has ironies ricocheting in every direction: the "California girls" look like bored New York models who never see the sun; Roth aggressively confronts the camera in a way that mocks the Beach Boys' aw-shucks image; girl-watching has become girl-purchasing. But the video itself is neither ironic nor satirical. Roth swaggers through the now kitsch landscape with the confidence of a performer who is above it all, the savvy manipulator of an innocent past.

When the past becomes pastiche, no critical distance is possible. As a result, music video's occasional attempts at satire prove feeble. On *Saturday Night Live*, the "Garage Band"'s parody of Michael Jackson's "Beat It" with the chant "Buy It, Buy It, Buy It" looks like a homegrown version of a plausible video. An amateur theatrical group in Washington, D.C., the Public Interest Follies, included in its 1985 Counter-Inaugural Ball a satirical revue, "Republican TV (RTV)," with songs like "Girls Just Want to Stay Home." Even done well, they became as entertaining as the real thing—but no more so. In fact, they became a version of the real thing.

Consider two videos intended to raise social issues—Donna Summers' "She Works Hard for the Money" and David Bowie's "Let's Dance." Trade and gossip magazines report that Summer met a waitress on whom she modeled "She Works Hard." Bowie has been eloquent on the responsibility of music and video to take social positions; he wanted "Let's Dance" to highlight Australian aboriginal rights, and we do see aborigines slipping into an Australian cityscape, but the lyrics give no hint of such an issue. In both cases, any message was lost in the disjunctive images and dreamy fantasy.

Videos have been used effectively to raise funds for causes, appealing directly to the viewer's wish to buy-and-belong. "Do They Know It's Christmas?," the most popular song of 1984 in England, was also a hit rock video made by English artists raising money for African famine relief. The video features studio performers looking dolorous, intercut with pitiful scenes of starving African children, who look no more bizarre than most video fantasy characters. This rock relief effort, like the later one by USA for Africa in the United States, allowed consumers to participate in a cause at a distance—charity, but not a connection.

It was precisely this distinction that troubled Steve Van Zandt (Little Steven) when he was making his "Sun City" antiapartheid video in mid-1985. In the hour-long making-of-the-video video, he noted that although proceeds of the enterprise would go to the Africa Fund, "this is not a benefit," because South Africans "do not ask us for charity," but rather give us the chance to see ourselves and realize that their struggle is ours. The video, directed by Hart Perry and Jonathan Demme (both directors with a history of social consciousness), has an unusual structure. It begins with scenes of the South African resort Sun City, a South African voice-over explaining its location and significance. As the song begins, musicians in a series of cameo spots look directly at the viewer, gesturing with clenched fists and pointing as they sing, that they won't play Sun City. Documentary footage is interspersed, not only of South Africa but also of historic moments in American civil rights history, including Martin Luther King saying "I have a dream" (with image but no sound). Dynamic graphics emphasize action rather than attitude; black silhouetted arms rip the screen to reveal marchers carrying coffins, and at one point chanting musicians are superimposed on footage of a massive South African demonstration. Black-edged obituary graphics flash images of South African martyrs in unabashed delivery of "hard" and historical information. The last musical word is had by South African demonstrators.

The difference between this and other "cause" videos is not accidental. Van Zandt explains in the documentary that its "look" was intended to "reflect anger and commitment without looking . . . aggressive," and that they wanted musicians to show energy without making it "look like too much fun."

Music videos have already had a powerful effect on their context, that of commercial pop culture and its promotion. They are now key to a musical group's success. In 1984, for instance, only three of the top-100 *Billboard* albums did not have a promo video. Groups now write songs with the video in mind, and performers begin careers on tape. Concerts are staged with an eye to expectations raised by the video, as was the case in concerts by the Jacksons and Prince. Rock critic Jon Pareles has noted the change in concert behavior; audiences of performers noted primarily for their videos, he claims, act more passive—as if they were watching TV—than those of a hot performer like Bruce Springsteen.

Some have charged that videos are narrowing the diversity of popular music, whether it's because mass marketing favors blockbusters over the offbeat or because videos "do your dreaming for you." Rocker Joe Jackson, for instance, protested that videos limit the viewer's imagination and devalue musical ability. Certainly, such bland groups as Stray Cats and Men at Work have built success out of their videos. Video is also, however, responsible for creating a lively demand for a band like The Clash in Boise, Idaho. Critic Pareles believes that video could revive flagging energy in rock: "For me, a great rock song is a good tune plus some inspired irritant," he explained. "Rockers are learning to link a radio-smooth audio track to a wild image, an eye irritant." One could just as easily, however, make the opposite argument—the rock videos appropriate shock value into a syncretic stream. The range of sound may not be narrowed as much as the range of meanings.

Social pressure on record companies and producers has affected the look and marketing of rock videos. When MTV first began, black performers almost never appeared. When a video by Rick James was rejected, he went public with figures showing that in eighteen months of MTV programming with some 750 videos, only two dozen had featured black performers. In an interview with an MTV video jockey, David Bowie reinforced the complaint, saying, "I'm distraught by the fact that there are so few black artists featured." At the time, MTV executive Pittman had a simple business response: "Cable is in the suburbs." But then Michael Jackson's album *Thriller* took off—even in the suburbs. The success of Prince and Tina Turner brought more color to programming, and now black-oriented music video programs provide a minimarket for black videos (most of which feature some white performers, showing a careful awareness of a crossover audience). The combination of protest and pop taste has made video programming less overtly racist, but the more black-sounding R & B is still far on the margins.

Music video has affected the movie industry as well as the record business. Music video influenced both the formal style and the marketing of the films *Flashdance* and *Footloose*. *Flashdance*'s director Adrian Lyne studied rock videos to get the right "look," and then promoted the film on music video programs. The resulting demand was enough to make this a regular marketing approach. A recent evening of the midnight *ABC Video* program consisted entirely of videos for current commercial films, some incorporating scenes specially shot for video. The crossover from video to the big screen has also spurred a host of films aimed at the youth market and featuring such video action as break dancing and aerobic dancing. The formula is not foolproof, since most films remain chained to the logic of real time and social relations with story lines. *Electric Boogaloo* and *Heavenly Bodies,* two late-1984 offerings, both bogged down when their iconic characters were taken out of dreamland and made to observe the conventions of ordinary living.

The rush of music video producers to the wide screen may not dramatically affect the look of movies, which are bounded far more than any TV program, and which cater to audiences who (despite what Jean-Luc Godard once claimed) still expect a beginning, a middle, and an end, and in that order. Studios prize music video producers not for their style, but because they have experience making product fast on low budgets.

The film *Purple Rain* is the major exception, a film that delivered at length what music videos do in bits and pieces. It openly exploited the conventions of music video—especially the search for personal identity through fashion-directed celebrity, and the evocation of nostalgia, a sense of loss, and loneliness. Critics panned *Purple Rain,* arguing that the film lacked dramatic structure and was hopelessly sentimental. In fact, the film was not structured around a plot, but a theme—that of Prince battling his insecurities and adolescent passions. The mawkish quality of its sentiment was matched well to the adolescent's struggle with his out-of-control image. The fact that Prince is an electrifying performer and powerful songwriter gave the film an authenticity rare in any popular art. Prince may have become the royalty of music video's alternative world precisely because he can put tremendous sexual energy and performing ability behind the subject of his own perpetual struggle for expression. In *Purple Rain,* Prince lives in an eternal present under neon lights, swathed in smoke. Resolution means a good gig, a moment of unity between his presence and that of his failed musician-father's. Prince is the authentic child of a society of spectacle, meeting it on its own terms.

Narrative television programs have borrowed from music videos as well, most prominently in *Miami Vice.* But music video's fulcrum position may best be revealed in the way it has traveled beyond television, especially in its use by fashion designers. There, the construction of identity through fashion is at the center of the business. Since 1977, when Pierre Cardin began making video recordings of his fashion shows, designers have been incorporating video into their presentations. Videos now run continuously in retail store windows and on floor displays. For many designers, what sells records already sells fashion, and some foresee a fashion channel. The Cooperative Video Network, a television news service, already offers a half-hour program, *Video Fashion News,* with three-minute segments on current designer models. Some designers regard video as a primary mode of expression. Norma Kamali now shows her work only on video, both in stores and on programs. One of her best-known works is a video called "The Shoulder Pad Song." Another designer, Lloyd Allen, makes videos that sensually evoke his own fashion career. Designer Bill Tice demands that his contracts for personal appearances include showings of his fashion videos. Kamali, saying that her tapes allow her to approach customers "without interpretation," also thinks that video adds a dimension to her work, because it "extends my fantasy," which of course is the reality of her business.

The marketing crossover is becoming global, a kind of perpetual feedback system. Michael Jackson has begun to sell fashion licenses for his look, and Christie Brinkley, a supermodel who starred in Billy Joel's "Uptown Girl," recently started her own fashion line. The videos undertaken at Perkins Productions are seen as prospective vehicles for extensive cross-promotion, in which a performer may use a prominently featured soap and a designer fragrance. The video may then circulate freely—in hotel lobbies, stores, and on airplane flights as well as on television programs. Video thrills are moving into all aspects of daily life. McDonald's has installed TV monitors at many cash registers, offering tempting images of food and giving shoppers the sense that fast food is part of a high-tech media world, a piece of the fashion action. "Video wallpaper" is being produced for bars and discos, with commercial products deliberately inserted into the montages in a style called by one producer "bordering on subliminal advertising." In general, the boundary between commercial and noncommercial images is eroding. One Manhattan boutique asked General Electric for a copy of a music videoesque commercial to use in its floor display, "for atmosphere," not for any message but simply for its style.

As media image-making comes to dominate electoral politics, music video has invaded that domain too. Consultants to both the Democratic and Republican parties have used music video to explore the mind-set of younger generations. "You can see the tensions among kids rising in their music," said pollster Patrick Caddell, "as they struggle to figure out what they will become." Or, he might have added, what they are. Republican strategist Lee Atwater decided, "We've got a bunch of very confused kids out there." That hasn't stopped politicians from using music videos as ads; videos were also enlisted (without marked results) in voter registration campaigns in 1984. The collision of music video with traditional political mobilizing brings one world—that of the consumer, concerned with individual choice—smack up against another—that of the citizen, charged with responsibility for public decisions. It is this collision that led fashion analyst Gerri Hirshey, noting the passionate investment of the young in their "look," to write: "If one's strongest commitment is to a pair of red stiletto heel pumps, style has a higher price tag than we'd imagine." In one sense, politics is fully ready for music video, if the success of Ronald Reagan—whose popularity rests on a pleasant media image to which "nothing sticks" while critics search in vain for a corresponding reality—is any guide.

The enormous popularity and rapid evolution of music videos give the lie to conspiracy theorists who think commodity culture is force-fed into the gullets of unwilling spectators being fattened for the cultural kill. But it should also chasten free-market apologists who trust that whatever sells is willy-nilly an instrument of democracy. Music videos are powerful, if playful, postmodern art. Their raw materials are aspects of commercial popular culture; their structures those of dreams; their premise the constant permutation of identity in a world without social relationships. These are fascinating and disturbing elements of a form that becomes not only a way of seeing and of hearing but of being. Music videos invent the world they represent. And people whose "natural" universe is that of shopping malls are eager to participate in the process. Watching music videos may be diverting, but the process that music videos embody, echo, and encourage—the constant re-creation of an unstable self—is a full-time job.

"We Build Excitement"

TODD GITLIN

*T*oo much software, hardware, so on. Technology. There's a neat correlation between the complicity of the hardware and the lack of genuine attachments.
    DON DELILLO, *Running Dog*

The Lone Driver

An electronic throb comes across the screen. Through a blue-black, haze-shrouded night city wanders the solitary figure of a young blond man. He is handsome in a blank way, expressionless, almost robotic. The city is deserted. In this science-fictional future, the man has left the present, society, the clutter of other people behind. Is he liberated? Troubled? The electronic pulse continues. Vapors hover in the street, catching the light. The man stalks through evacuated streets, seeking a sign of life. Suddenly, he spins around as if startled by a sound. Overhead looms a billboard depicting— what posthistoric icon of the age? The new Dodge. The sight fills him with awe. The car slides off the billboard and out into the world. It has a life of its own: indeed, more life than his own. It pursues him, calls him, teases him; the car is the active agent. The two of them are alone in this vacated kingdom; he might be the last man in the world. Now he turns and goes after the Dodge, which gives him the slip. He follows it down a narrow street, but it's gone. And then, with the abruptness of a jump cut, he finds himself in the driver's seat. His blankness fades; it is a satisfied go-getter who now turns to us and grins. Instantly, dystopia segues into utopia. Accepting the challenge of hypernew technology, the driver has earned his place in the proverbial fast lane. The car then accelerates at *Star Wars*-like warp velocity and takes off into ethereal hyperspace. "Dodge," says the closing logo after a breathless thirty seconds, "An American Revolution."

This commercial ran on the networks throughout 1984 and 1985, an unusually long time in the high-turnover world of the TV spot. Stylistically, it was not one of a kind. Ford, Chrysler, General Motors, Toyota, and Renault—to name only the major players— thumped out similar revved-up, high-tech, staccato barrages of images with a whoosh of crisp editing, as if the commercials themselves were being driven at four-on-the-floor, zero-to-sixty acceleration. Typically, there were thirty or more splices, thirty or more distinct images, in a single thirty-second spot, succeeding each other like fragments glimpsed from an urban freeway, or indeed like the shreds of programs that spin past today's TV viewers as they "zap" across the spectrum of channels with the help of remote-control devices. The music was electronically synthesized, pulsating, thumping, thrusting. The cars swooped along diagonal lines in severely foreshortened perspectives. Glinting like gun barrels, they looked unapologetically metallic; sporting their high-gloss reflective paints, they unabashedly resembled surfaces as much as the rich tones of a generation ago simulated depths. The car which was the point of the whole exercise wasn't slipping reassuringly out of the old-fashioned suburban driveway, or decorously proving its compatibility with a European chateau; rather, it was eerily dislocated, brashly declaring its otherness. It might be found swooping through unpopulated nature, showing its stuff, for example, on a snaky mountain road or through the Arctic tundra. In special cases, it traveled in packs over the flat expanse of the desert: "Mercedes-Benz widens the gap." (Even the Dodge Caravan, a bulky transport for groups, went to the desert to prove it had room for a full load of passengers.) Light trucks preferred to careen off-road along rock-strewn hillsides and sandy beaches, braking with a crunch in the dunes. In one of the few variations featuring a woman, the car glided up a building wall—transformed for the occasion into a mountain—to summon her from her closed-in apartment. Other cars succeeded in escaping the gravitational pull of earthly nature altogether and soared into the ultimate postnature: space. Thus, for example: "The '86 Toyotas are blasting off," rocketing into the starry heavens. Such cars were at home anywhere. Whether found in the mountains, in deserts, or on the beach, in space, in the future, or in combinations thereof, the supercar slid free of a car's normal settings. There was no traffic, no rush hour, no parking crunch. Wherever this car went was the fast lane, the driver unaccompanied, sleek, young, white, and usually male.

Altogether, this style of urgent and displaced velocity represented the most striking innovation in the automotive sales pitches of the mid-eighties. All the fancy-free varieties of the high-tech format bore the implication that the car today is the carrier of adrenal energies, a sort of syringe on wheels. "We Build Excitement," in the words of Pontiac's slogan. The form of the commercial built a particular brand of excitement. In the case of the futuristic Dodge, the relentless flickering pace, the high-gloss platinum look, the glacially blue coloration, the dark ice haze, the metallic music innocent of wood and strings—all suggested something otherworldly and ungrounded. Rapid-fire edits broke up the smoothness of the ride; the car seemed at once everywhere and nowhere. What, after all, was specificity of time and place in the face of this miracle of electronically guided machinery? Ordinary distance, actual earth, no longer mattered; there was only velocity, overpowering distance, and time itself. The Revolutionary Dodge cruised not through a more cheerful version of the present, but a radically dislocated future. These spots created a kind of commercial cubism in which space rearranged itself around the car, evoking the fantasy that material space could be transformed utterly through the magic of technique. The aggregate message was not about cars alone, but about the current incarnations of America's perennial dreams: freedom, power, technology.

High-tech styling, displaced from the ordinary, churning over the rapids of montage: this was the startling new image of the mid-eighties car. Sexual allure, a time-honored staple of the car ad, was still present, but in an altered state. Now the appeal to identify with the car was explicit. One billboard suggests: "Alter Your Ego. Celebrity Eurosport." And consider this variation on the super-charged thirty-second utopia, in which the driver is explicitly invited to identify with his mechanical bride: "If you are what you drive, imagine yourself as a Renault Encore. . . ."At one point, the Renault driver, wearing mirror sunglasses, actually metamorphoses into his marvelous vehicle, his sunglasses turning into headlights. He pulls up to a gaggle of admiring young females—women who have nothing better to do, apparently, than await the arrival of Mr. Driven Right. Gazing into his sunglasses, his ensemble of admirers see only themselves; there is no one home, nothing but the reflection of his beholders. This might stand as a chilling image of his nothingness—but in a world composed of surfaces, it is only to be expected that a man is nothing but pure surface either. The transformation proves that he is, after all, what he drives, marking him as the very spirit of his metallic conveyance. The mutation of mirror shades is itself a revealing indication of ideological change: on the motorcycle cop of the late sixties, mirror shades were a sign of the sinister; in the eighties they have become a sign of untouchable knowingness, paralleling the multinational headquarters and bank buildings of Southern California and its imitators. There, the mirror-glass skin of the building throws back all inquiries to the inquirer, suggesting that today's corporation is to be appreciated precisely for its claim to high-tech universality, that the material product is not important—all that matters is the shiny sac of pure capital, the ultimate postmodern abstraction. Surface is all; what you see is what you get. These images are proud of their standing as images. They suggest that the highest destiny of our time is to become cleansed of depth and specificity altogether.

This style of commercial bears a constellation of elements to be found throughout American culture now: the emphasis on surface; the blankness of the protagonist; his striving toward self-sufficiency, to the point of displacement from the recognizable world. The car thus advertised is not only a means of transportation, it is a carrier of popular feeling. Its image of the car shares an emotional and ideological territory with current trends in prime-time television, fiction, painting, architecture, fashion, film, and other cultural forms—and indeed with the entrepreneurial mystique and the grand political and military illusions of the Reagan years. Ostensibly free men staggering around a depopulated world; blank-faced studs hiding behind steel and glass—in these eerie billboards are inadvertently displayed certain truths about this American moment: about the desire to take flight, and a fear that around us everyone else has taken flight too; about the giddiness we feel at having outlasted the old dull traditions, and an insecurity at finding ourselves dangling in free fall beyond tradition; about the longing for open space, innocence, the sense of infinite possibility, and the distance one has to go to recapture the plenitude of the wild frontier. On the surface, these commercials simply manipulate the romance of freedom in order to sell automobiles. If we look closely at what the ads share with the rest of American culture, however, we see a general sleekness, a desire to slip away from the encumbrances of society, the worship of an individual stripped of any features that belong to him or her alone—indeed, we see something of the prevailing American ethos, its promises and evasions and secret fears.

The Car as American Totem

If there were a national vehicle as there is a national bird, it would have to be the automobile. Even in the Jet, Space, or Information Age—take your pick of promotional slogans—the car remains the national carrier of choice. It is the most accessible, the most essential, the most freely used, the most central to the economy; it is both the closest to the ground and the longest attached to the American imagination. Throughout the twentieth century cars have been chariots, wheels, throne rooms, sedan chairs, tickets to the suburbs, homes away from home, couches of sexual initiation, tickets out of the suburbs—and at each stage the car has been a kind of centaur: half conveyance, half fantasy. Without the internal combustion engine, there would be no car; but without the idea of the car—and the infrastructure of assembly, marketing, highways, and finance that have combined to give shape to the idea—there would be only transportation. The car as a marketed commodity is a car we know, love, desire, hate, abide.

Computer-generated graphics and the electronic synthesizer make possible some of the commercials' state-of-the-art moves; indeed, a thick web of implicit cross-references binds together the computer testing of cars, the computers in the cars, and computer graphics, as if to say that the dazzling displays in the commercials rub off on the excellence of the cars. But the potentials of new technology don't by themselves dictate the uses to which they are put. No technological determinism can account for the new images; for copywriters write storyboards, directors direct, and company executives approve the results to a particular end: aligning their product with a going ideological trend. In the process of selling their product, they crystallize a pattern out of a soup of popular moods and predispositions. Thus, the commercial image of the car cannot be understood simply as an automatic reflex of the state of the technical art, or a sales stratagem as inexplicable as it is idiosyncratic; it is the end product of a complex set of marketing decisions, and therefore, in part, a useful searchlight into larger patterns of meaning. The way cars are presented is an amalgam of the way advertising agencies and their clients think, the way they think we think, and the way they want us to think about what a car is. The image of the car soaks up certain ideals in circulation at the moment, and squeezes a version of them back at us. It offers the incarnation of a popular ideal—or rather, the ideas of that ideal held by the marketers. Thus, a commercial is, among other things, a tiny utopia. It conveys what we are supposed to think is the magic of things; these things which, if we buy them, are supposed to work miraculous transformations in our lives: telephones that wire us into community; eyeliner that makes us alluring; beer that consolidates our desire to be sociable, even American. It hopes to piggyback the product's image onto the image of this transformation, and to leave a trace of the two yoked together within those folds of memory where it may eventually trigger a purchase.

It comes as no news that to accomplish this purpose advertising capitalizes on popular fears and desires, then propounds magical solutions. To track advertisements through historical time is thus to track the changing contours of popular fears and desires, knotted together in complex relation with the commodity solutions which marketers have imagined to be acceptable from moment to moment —solutions whose motives the marketers may not be fully aware of themselves. In the late twenties and thirties, as Roland Marchand has shown in *Advertising the American Dream,* the magazine ads for cars emphasized their high styling, luxury, beauty, comfort, and dependability, although there were already appeals to flee the close-in districts for the remote open road. In the fifties, the image of the car split in half, corresponding to the widening gulf between paraded sexuality and domesticated procreation. Some cars were supposed to be sexy, the model draped across the hood transferring her charms onto the metallic object of her affections; other cars served and certified the baby-boom family, happily stuffed together in that chariot of suburban splendor, the station wagon. What virtually all the fifties cars had in common was their incarnation of affluence. Tail fins, bulging chrome, the plump look, two-tone paint jobs all showed off what abundance could accomplish, indeed what it looked like: metal to burn, extras to spare.

In the sixties, the children once crammed into those backseats wanted to get up and go, whether to Surf City or Mississippi. Cars became known, in the vernacular, as "wheels," and the names of the new models were spiffed up to suit. The sportier varieties signified sex and saddles (Mustang) and the wildness of pouncing beasts (Lynx, Cougar). Attempting to trade on Camelot, the Beatles, and rowdy students, the Chrysler Corporation even celebrated "The Dodge Rebellion." In the seventies, however, many younger consumers came to see the car as a burden if, at the same time, a necessity. The vehicle of freedom produced smog. Thanks to Ralph Nader, it was also understood to be a deadly weapon. Thanks to OPEC and the end of the post–World War II economic boom, it was costly. Accordingly, there emerged the small, practical car, marketed for its very smallness and practicality. Enter the Japanese.

Our high-tech car ad of the mid-eighties is a turnabout in style and mood. The car of this moment is unafraid of oil crisis; it doesn't surrender to an era of limits; it knows nothing of scarcity. But it doesn't represent a return to the fat, finned fifties either. After the oil crisis and the Japanese onslaught, who would not be chastened once and for all? The advertising agencies began to conceive of a new generation of ads designed to—in their language—"respond to the Japanese challenge." They spoke of "lifestyle," "image," cars that "forge an identity" and "make a statement." They decided, in other words, to repel the Japanese invaders in a particular way, consonant with a larger ideological mood: thus, the pure thrust of the new ad, offering aggression, liberation, streamlining, and a portentous pseudospirituality all at once. It says, "We're ready for you if you're man enough for us." It is lean and clean; it carries no extra inches of fat; it works out; it sings, once again, a song of the open road.

Most of all, the new-style car commercial reveals something about the new-style man who has been pronounced fit to drive into the future. This fantastical paragon is a pilot who soars through things untouched and unimpeded. Not for him the viscosity of everyday life. He is man on the move, man ready to go anywhere, man whose mobility is literal as well as lateral, carrying him forward, onward, or upward, off the road, if need be, but always advancing. The ideal man of the commercials embodies, in short, the master fantasy of the Reagan era: the fantasy of thrusting, self-sufficient man, cutting loose, free of gravity, free of attachments. (Women are outfitted with a different image, as we shall see.) Here is the contemporary reworking of one of the oldest American archetypes: the hunter, the trapper, the frontiersman *redux,* that mythic solitary reincarnated in the nineteenth century as the cowboy who gallops across the wide open spaces, fused with his horse, responsible to no one and to nothing but virtue, to save the day for weaker and more domestic folk—only to get back to the purple sage as soon as the getting is good. Today's Lone Driver is a substantially updated figure, however: he looks out for Numero Uno, and doesn't care who knows it; yet the frontier is closed, his range is bounded, and he inhabits a transformed world of large organizations. Commercial culture now helps him imagine a freedom he has forfeited in fact.

In fact, the Lone Driver of the commercials embodies a common fantasy: the high-performance manager or professional who succeeds in taking on the persona, the aura, the power, the very body of the boss. He is a cultural self-image. What we are seeing on the small screen is the corporate employee trying to insinuate himself into the role of the official culture hero of the Reagan period: the entrepreneur, that Promethean embodiment of progress who answers the call of the market and creates something from nothing, enriching himself to everyone's good and at no one's expense. The entrepreneur is of course more honored in Washington rhetoric than in actual economic life. National economic policy rewards cozy dealmakers more than risk takers, and conglomerates are more interested in acquiring other companies (which, in turn, are preoccupied either with defending themselves against acquisition or making the most of it) than in developing new products. Moreover, our educational institutions are geared to those who have a conservative idea about how to succeed. As James Fallows has pointed out, the legions of today's young, upwardly mobile aspirants are being trained not to take risks but to minimize them; they go to school to become not entrepreneurs but managers and professionals whose career paths will be amply sheltered from both risk and failure in quite firmly established enterprises. Entrepreneurship is much lauded in afterdinner speeches, but venture capital, as always, prefers tax advantages for its ventures. Freed of the tainted image of Robber Baron or Economic Royalist, Mr. Entrepreneur likes to be known as a high flyer, but in practice he is drastically outnumbered by Supermanager, to whom he leaves most of the work.

In more than one way, the high-tech image of the streamlined car finesses the discrepancy: it perfectly embodies the actual training our business and academic institutions are set up to reward, as well as the actual life of the professional-managerial class. Those who start as distracted robots can get promoted to the status of free men. Those whose identities are elusive can rise to power on the strength of their blank adaptability. Supermanager and his racketball partner, Superpro, step into nearby vehicles to emerge as streamlined go-getters. Driving is the perfect representation for their way of life. Always on the go, they owe no loyalty to merely local, even terrestrial, connections. Cosmopolitans by upbringing and training, they uproot with relative ease when the company or the career track relocates them. Their ambitions are as unbounded, indeed celestial, as they are abstract; the earth and its well-trafficked roads are too mundane to hold them—this is the entrepreneurial part of the fantasy. At the wheel, on the road, they are wild and safe, free and contained all at once—this is the ideal bargain for which managers and top professionals strive, or settle. The car itself is intrinsically a perfect symbol for the simultaneous pleasures of freedom and containment; today's commercials force the combination toward some logical infinity. So the commercials reproduce the worldview of a manager who fancies himself, however inaccurately, in the driver's seat, mastering all the onrushing force technology can provide. Like the rhetoric of "decentralized management," "corporate excellence," or "human relations" at the office, this sort of image helps reconcile the manager to his actual dependency on the big institutions and the real movers and shakers.

For all today's talk about the greater glories of entrepreneurship, of course, very few entrepreneurs succeed. The vast majority of small businesses fail. A large proportion of Americans work for large organizations: private corporations and government agencies, often ponderous, unaccommodating bureaucracies. There they strike their bargains; those networks of intrigue and dependency are the playing fields of their adventures. They work in combinations, in tensions and collaborations, in structures not usually of their own making. Implicitly, then, one appeal of the new-style car commercial may be this: During the day, manage your way through the organization; occupy your niche; compete for status and power; take care of business. Feel lucky to have the chance. In return, you have the opportunity to test yourself; and if that is not enough, you will be rewarded with the wherewithal to break free—after hours, on weekends. (It is, after all, the decade of falling gasoline prices.) Sit still and the Force will come to you, all turbo'd and ultradriven; then, in imagination at least, you can cut loose—even peel off the road altogether and take off into another dimension, into a dream of unbridled freedom.

And so our car commercial manages to reconcile the ideological uplift of the Reagan years with its more downbeat realities. Indeed, the tag "An American Revolution" may remind us—may even be meant to remind us—of the Chrysler Corporation's federally subsidized rags-back-to-riches story. Chrysler's tale, as retold in mythic proportions by Lee Iacocca and assimilated to the romance of his

own career, thus becomes a double story of modern bootstrap success
—a "revolution" for independence against monarchs (Iacocca versus
Henry Ford, Chrysler versus the Japanese) rather than a tale of
government bailout. So another appeal of the commercial is: buy
the car, and you can have a piece of the comeback action; the
purchase of the car is an emblem of promotion. The commercial is
very much of a piece with the spectacular 2.5-million copies of
Iacocca in print, with its astonishing full-year-plus at or near the top
of the *New York Times'* nonfiction bestseller list. Indeed, for the first
time since early in the twentieth century, inspirational tales told by
executives—one hesitates to use the word "autobiography" for these
self-serving stitchings of selected fact and homiletic jottings—are
popular reads in America. Instead of hiding behind committee anonymity, chief executives are now at home on *Time* covers and in
People profiles; Iacocca acts in Chrysler's own commercials. Just as
General Eisenhower was considered a possible Democratic standard-
bearer in 1952 until the party bosses found out he preferred to be a
Republican, Iacocca looms large on lists of Democratic presidential
favorites, for corporate experience is to the politics and folklore of
the eighties as military generalship was to the forties and fifties: a
sign of prowess on the battlefield that really counts. In popular
mythology, entrepreneurial heroes like Lee Iacocca and the Olym-
pics' Peter Ueberroth are played off against corporate takeover artists
like T. Boone Pickens and Carl Icahn, who acquire the popular
love-to-hate-'em aura of *Dallas'* J. R. Ewing. The manager on the
make, the small business in need of uplift, even the foreign competitor (Japanese corporations ordered a half million copies of *Iacocca*)
—all are primed to imagine themselves in that well-upholstered
driver's seat.

The successful executive has become a culture hero of such proportions, he even stars in a commercial which stands as a sort of
footnote to the type we have been discussing. Ingenious copywriters
have discovered how to frame that most collectivized form of transport, the commercial airliner, as a carrier for the contemporary
range rider—in particular, for the business traveler who accounts
for the bulk of air travel. Down a carpeted airport corridor, on
cushioned footsteps, strides a square-jawed, silver-haired, three-
piece-suited hero, accompanied by a black female on one side and a

white male sidekick on the other. The latter briefs him somewhat cryptically on what is apparently the latest stock offer. "Not good enough," says the clearheaded, no-nonsense chief, biting off his words as if they were proverbial bullets. He's on his way to the OK Corral to get the best possible deal for his company (ranch, homestead). The female helpmeet crisply passes him his American Airlines ticket. "Good luck" are her parting, admiring words. The corporate savior as folk hero—this man is so imposing, we're meant to think, it's as if he'll have the whole plane to himself. The airline commercial has come a long way from the time when all it could sell were the few inches' lengths of the stewardesses' skirts or the many inches' distance between rows of seats. The CEO's maneuvers are so masterful, his self-assurance so sublime, his transportation must be supreme to suit. The free-striding hero transfers his imprimatur to—what other airline?—*American.* The corporate gamesman so prominent in the press—a virtual entrepreneur in the public mind—here attains his apotheosis. Today, says American, every seat is potentially the driver's.

And yet there is pathos on top of irony in all these commercials' implicit claims that the Real Man gets to be Real only when he slides into the right driver's seat. For as Dodge's deserted city inadvertently (or brilliantly?) suggests, the car's pilot is all but helpless without his equipment. The blank expression he has displayed up to this point could be read as a self-protective response to the anguish of his uprootedness. He manages a grin only at the moment he finds himself—through no apparent action of his own —behind the wheel. Once again, the promise of freedom conceals the fact of dependency. The dream of soaring to consumer heaven presupposes a too, too solid earth.

Even cultural analysis sooner or later has to come down to earth. It is almost too obvious to bear mentioning that the new-style car commercial represents one tactic for piquing the interest of television's most desired commodity, the young, upscale viewer. There are not so many of the young urban professionals who have made "yuppie" the decade's buzzword—4 million is a reasonable estimate—but they are, of course, heavily overrepresented among advertising copywriters; even more important, they make money, spend a relatively high proportion of it, and are thus heavily over-represented among television's most desirable, most heavily targeted watchers. These are two reasons, therefore, why the preoccupations of the upper reaches of the "baby boomers," those born between 1945 and 1964 and now moving up on the fast track, are so visible over the commercial airwaves. Streamlining, high-tech slickness, displacement to exotic realms—these advertising styles aim to capture (and help shape) some of the baby boomers' mind-set. It is altogether to be expected that the auto companies' appeals to potential buyers at mid-decade will reflect and refine this market's other fantasies.

To the auto marketer, what counts above all is to associate the car with an upscale mentality—the ensemble of tastes that are generally taken to mean "upscaleness." Light trucks can be juxtaposed to bulging muscles and tattoos as they roar onto the dirt, but cars have to establish that they are on their way up. The Dodge Revolution spot with which we began takes the high symbolic road, but this genre's eerie thrusting is by no means the only striking image of the car in the mid-eighties. For one thing, a distinct but growing minority of commercials for sporty cars are aiming at women—who can now, for the first time, imagine themselves free behind the wheel. But it is harder to sell the romance of self-sufficiency to women, schooled as they are in the social ties that bind. Therefore, women are less often seen careening through space or slashing diagonally along mountainsides. When they drive alone, it is more likely to be along city streets; they have not left society behind. Moreover, the female driver frequently has a more domestic relation to her car than a man does to his. Thus, in one spot for the Chevrolet Celebrity Eurosport, the sleek woman driver fondles her car—something none of her male equivalents would be caught dead doing. She reminds us that her streamlined machine is culturally coded as phallus, or pet, or in any event something redolent of the home if not the bedroom.

The high disposer of income beloved by advertisers does not live by getaway fantasies alone. And so there are other spots which toss out associations in more prosaic and "realistic" fashion, dressing the drivers in yuppie garb, showing them doing yuppie things, aiming to convey the associated idea that if people who look and play like this drive a certain car, it's the right car for the right people; if you're not yet right, the right buy can certify that you run with the right crowd. Consider, for example, the Buick Somerset. The name already stamps the model with a certain literary gloss; this is a car with a master's degree. In one spot, we see a happy-go-yuppie female driver, with white blouse and tie. Cut to a boy-meets-girl flirtation. Cut to a man in glasses and a suit, Clark Kent as junior partner, flipping a football to a small boy, presumably his son. Flirtation and family images go by so fast, it's as if the two have fused into the image of the ideal upscale couple who've worked out so well—perhaps gone through the right counseling—they still know how to like sex. All this time, an up-tempo jingle tries to rope the images together with lines like "It drives like you and it feels like you," culminating in the punchline: "An innovative Buick looking for a long-term relationship."

In more ways than one, the word has also gone out to exploit the yuppie's attachment to the rock culture of the fifties and sixties, the time when his or her tastes, however encrusted by subsequent patinas, were first molded. Commercials sport the smoothed-out strains of doo-wop and Beach Boys hits of days gone by. One spot for a streamlined Ford van couples high-tech futurism with sixties mainstream rock nostalgia, spawning a jingle which recycles a tune itself slicked up from the Broadway musical *Hair*: "This is the dawning of the age of the Aerostar."

Finally, no tour of marketing appeals to the under-forty-five would be complete without a free ride on the Bruce Springsteen express. President Reagan tried to cash in on Springsteen's muscular evocation of a gritty, unpretty blue-collar world during a 1984 appearance in New Jersey, and where Reagan trod, could Chrysler be far behind? Dodge in its Revolution ends up rocketing to space, but in its 1986 sales effort Dodge's poor relation Plymouth reminds the young that "the pride is back" and that it was "born in America"—ripping off Springsteen's angry anthem, smoothing it into a Chamber of Commerce ditty as shots of just plain productive-looking folks, black and white (including Lee Iacocca himself, signaling his folksiness with a wave), whiz by in montage-made community.

None of Springsteen's losers need apply—or rather, if only they would roll up their sleeves and see what good company they're in, they wouldn't feel like losers any longer. This fabricated nationalism, an artifact of editing, promotes the theme that what's good for Chrysler is good for America—indeed that Chrysler *is* come-from-behind America writ small. But Chrysler isn't the only beneficiary of the rough-tough mood of national revival; at this writing, a J. Walter Thompson executive anticipates that advertising will soon be swept by what he calls "the Springsteen heartland of America approach." And why not? Springsteen's nationalism waves the flag for big-hearted "fairness," Iacocca's for competitive truculence, but there is a thin slice of overlap and the copywriters are astute to seize on it: they peel away Springsteen's left populism and, like Reagan and Rambo, flatter the crowd (You/America/the fighting man are fine as you are, it's just that you were sold down the river by Them) in order to market their badges of belonging. Even the Japanese companies try in similar ways to detoxify themselves of "Japaneseness" in order to retail their cars as genuinely American.

Loners in Groups

This last spate of car commercials complement the go-getting individualism of the Lone Driver. Through the juxtapositions of editing, they relocate the car in a populated world, the internal-combustion equivalent of two other contemporary television settings treated in this volume: *General Hospital*'s small-scale community (as Ruth Rosen portrays it) and Pepsi's beachside idyll (as analyzed by Mark Crispin Miller). Ramrod individualism and covenant-bound community, Daniel Boone and John Winthrop, are the historical flip sides of American culture, with the former ascendant now; one expects to see them each displayed in comparatively pure form within the half-minute confines of a television commercial. But if television is going to give America's central historical tension its due, it needs the relative amplitude of the episode series. The car commercials match certain moods and tensions present in prime-time mayhem. Here the Lone Driver and the national ensemble can be blended into the elite team. The Lone Driver finds congenial company, breaks through the crust of claustrophobic society, and roars into overdrive action.

Consider two of the most popular shoot-'em-ups of recent years, the NBC series *The A-Team* and *Miami Vice.* There are manifold differences between them. The A-team are freelances, the Vice team are cops. *The A-Team* is done in semislapstick and plays to kids at eight o'clock, *Miami Vice* is done in voguish seriousness and plays to adults at ten. *The A-Team* is conventionally driven by character and plot, *Miami Vice* unconventionally by look and sound. But the conspicuous differences make certain similarities all the more interesting. It is obvious but worth noting, in the first place, that the protagonists are teams of males, relying on each other as in the barroom bonhomie of a Miller Lite commercial. There was a time when television's law enforcers were more likely to be solitaries—*Gunsmoke*'s Matt Dillon, *Have Gun Will Travel*'s Paladin—but more recently it has become television wisdom as well as a larger cultural premise that two or three principals "work" more entertainingly than one. The Lone Driver spirit of the car commercial is therefore not to be found in these shows' character structure.

But it is present nevertheless. Along with the drivers of our high-tech car commercials, the heroes of these series skitter like water-bugs over the surface of a displaced world. The episodes of *The A-Team* are set in a vaguely delineated America whose locales are as poorly differentiated as fast-food outlets along the interstates. Even the apparently specific "Miami" of *Miami Vice,* as John Leonard has pointed out, does not correspond to the Miami in which anyone but cops and criminals actually lives, loves, or works for a living. This postindustrial Miami exists to be seen and seen in; it is a state of being, really, in which everyone is more or less a person of leisure, and cops and criminals maneuver in a barely distinguishable manner —a queasy (and titillating) fact underscored by the way in which the forces of order appropriate the name of their designated target, Vice, as their own private, convenient badge. Theirs is a tourist's Miami, full of hot spots, "sights," flamingos and jai alai, boats and bosoms. It has as much to do with everyday expectations as the electronic muttering and grunting of the opening theme music— one hesitates to call it a song—has to do with melody.

In this wonderland of drugs, sex, and rock 'n' roll, things take place for strictly visual reasons; the throwaway plot is full of holes, and much of the writing is as banal as anything television has seen since *Barnaby Jones*. Everything happens for the sake of display; *Vice* only makes sense if the viewer is willing to regard images as self-sufficient. Just for openers, the viewer has to take for granted that two Miami cops (1985 take-home pay: $429 a week) can blithely afford the latest and flashiest in cars and clothes. That hurdle crossed, the viewer has to agree to suspend narrative disbelief and surrender to the trashy pleasure of sheer look and sound, just as our Dodge driver takes for granted that a car drives off a billboard and into the sky, and we take for granted that such things will happen on television.

Even the obligatory car chases have a special look on *Miami Vice;* the low-slung camera multiplies the sense of vertigo and transcendence—again, the car-commercial look—as pursuer and pursued slide their way scenically through the city. The rat-a-tat pacing, as in MTV and the pulsating car commercials, draw attention away from the narrative, such as it is, diverting it to the "look," which slides by as if on the other side of a tour bus' picture window. Place is backdrop for free-hanging sound and velocity, as in the high-tech car commercials. In *Vice*'s Miami, the players are regularly composed into fashion tableaux, sequences of disconnected stills, as in the music videos which inspired the series, but in *Vice* more artfully arranged—strictly for their pastel colors, the spaces between them, the way they stand framed in an alleyway or deployed against a wall. The hard-edged look echoes the fashion magazine layouts which preceded both MTV and the pulsating car commercial, all meant to "break through the clutter," as the advertisers say—the clutter being the profusion of images themselves, of billboards, commercials, and television shows, the unending cornucopia spilling its promises upon the national attention, the noise finally drowning out each of its poor components. *Vice*'s environments of artifice are intended to arrest the attention; self-consciousness is precisely the point.

The environment sings the songs and virtually speaks the lines. The songs themselves are thick with portent, suffusing the action with a blanket of import draped over the thin characterizations and holes in the plot. Like good fashion models, indeed like the high-tech cars in the commercials, Detectives Crockett and Tubbs seem to embody their surroundings; vacuous themselves, like manikins, they "wear" the show's self-consciously created look and sound. Color-coded like the walls, they exist for the sake of spacial arrangement. Artfully arranged in a long shot on a beach, they are the crosshatch where sound waves meet. There is not much character and not much motive in this mythic Miami—only compositional moments and extraordinary spasms of crime and punishment. Asked what was distinctive about the show, executive producer Michael Mann told NBC's Brandon Tartikoff laconically, "No earth tones." "We Build Excitement," indeed.

Both the Vice team and the A-Team establish their heroism by being ready and willing to buck the top law enforcement command. The A-Team started out as escapees from an Army stockade during the Vietnam War, after all; now, in their freelance crime-fighting days, commanding a fine array of cars and vans, they run up against stupid, heavy-handed, uncomprehending police, even the Army itself. They are thus a good-humored anticipation of Sylvester Stallone's Rambo, who knows the GI was stabbed in the back by chicken politicians and pointy-headed bureaucrats hiding behind their fancy technology, whence the loss of the Vietnam War. Crockett and Tubbs of *Miami Vice,* for their part, also run up against meddling bureaucrats, who prove venal, thickheaded, cruel, manipulative, even crooked. To get their jobs done in the nether world of the drug trade, Crockett and Tubbs have to break the rules of the rule-bound organization; but unlike the conscience-stricken heroes of *Cagney & Lacey* or the earlier years of *Hill Street Blues,* they don't agonize about whether to violate department rules or civil liberties. All efficiency, they put on their shoulder holsters and get the job done. Darting off to Colombia, the Everglades, or New York City when special episodes call, they are the Turbo team of law enforcement.

In short, all these heroes bridle in the face of rules and rule-enforcing bureaucrats, even if in the end they strike their bargains. Teams of enforcers at war with bureaucracies (whether Army or Mafia), they take on the appearance of Lone Drivers. Their penchant for high flying is signaled by traces of outlawry: they've taken a walk or two on the wild side themselves. The A-Team are wanted men, while Crockett's permanent stubble, his love of high living—and actor Don Johnson's well-publicized adventures with drugs and failure—mark him as a man who has followed his own star, however errant. To keep up his rep as a rugged individualist in a managed world, Crockett resorts to fashion: his patented loose white sport jacket over solid-colored T-shirt. Though younger, slicker, and more conventionally attractive, Crockett and Tubbs show an affinity with Hammett's and Bogart's Sam Spade, Polanski's and Nicholson's J. J. Giddes, and Elmore Leonard's still rougher and wiser heroes. When organized society is corrupt, outsiders have to step in to guarantee society's moral values. When off-key heroes are born again into a life of right action, they still sport the stigmata from the old days, just as the police force itself is besmirched by the general social dirt. (In this way, *Miami Vice,* fascinated like *Hill Street Blues* by cops on the take and gone haywire, is truer to the America of the eighties than *Dallas* or *Dynasty.*) If the true blue carry some of a corrupt society's dirt with them—well, if you can't stand the stench, stay out of the stockyards.

This saga of palefaces with redskin blood, outsiders defending insider values, is an old story in American culture, but its contemporary resonance is striking. If the tale sounds familiar—the outsider rides in from the margins, striding front and center to push back corruption, drive the interlopers out of town, take care of business—consider the last two presidents of the United States. Recall Jimmy Carter, part of whose appeal was that he was not a "real politician." Although not without sin (he did, after all, confess that he had known lust in his heart), Carter was untainted by association with Washington—a decided advantage in immediate post-Watergate America. Carter tried to convey the fact that he was both nuclear engineer and peanut farmer, the technocrat and the good ole boy—anything but a politician. And there is of course Ronald Reagan, the sportscaster, actor, TV host, gentleman rancher, and ex-liberal (once fooled, twice wary) who has been carried to high office "to clean up the mess in Washington," and who even succeeded in running against Washington a second time after presiding over the government for four years; who could, for example, miraculously, propose a constitutional amendment requiring a balanced budget while running up the largest budget deficit in history. Among Reagan's winning ways was the fact that, like cool cops and Mr. T, he talked tough and didn't quite seem to mean it. (See Michael Sorkin's article in this volume for more on the slippage in television today between the meant and the unmeant, the serious and the unserious.) Can anyone imagine a presidential candidate running as an insider in the midst of this public mood, in which familiarity with politicians breeds contempt—a Lyndon Johnson, say, whose prowess came from his mastery of the wheeling and dealing of lawmaking? "You know me," said Walter Mondale over and over during the 1984 primaries, never grasping that this was precisely one of his problems. Nothing more devastating can be said about a politician today than that he or she is, in the end, "only a politician."

As an ideological cartoon, then, television's contemporary dispenser of justice shares a niche with the president of the United States. An ideological ensemble, like Reagan, his virtue is the fusion of sheer liberty with sheer loyalty. Again and again, today's defender of the innocent falls back on memories of a time and place in which high-stakes companionship really counted: the Vietnam War. Since *Magnum, P.I.* came to the airwaves in the fall of 1980, virtually every series about law enforcers or freelance protectors-of-the-peace has sooner or later summoned up the blood knot: the veteran's memories of moments when he and his buddies were bound together in absolute mutual reliance. All unpleasant questions of morality and politics are left behind. The war now signifies noble camaraderie. George Wallace's myth of 1968 has belatedly swept the country in the decade of Reagan and Rambo: the war was winnable, and only the politicians kept it from being won. This is exactly the myth enshrined in *The A-Team*: crime could be crushed if only the authorities would get out of the way of lean-and-mean specialists.

The same line of argument leaps from the screen in *Rambo*, of course. As in *Miami Vice, Soldier of Fortune,* or the foreign policy of the Reagan right, it takes a guerrilla to clobber a guerrilla. Freelance technokillers could mop up the gangsters if only the pointy-headed bureaucrats would stand out of their way. The good-guy Rough Rider, half Indian and half German, in the end wreaks his revenge against civilian duplicity. Rambo has learned his lessons from the Viet Cong: all he really needs to slay the Russians, aside from their own helicopter, is his ruthless Germanness and updated Indianness—fancy knife, bow, arrows. Having lost the fancier equipment during his helicopter jump, he can still manage. The point is to have the *right* high tech and not to trust anyone, with the possible exception of a love interest predestined to be mowed down by Commie bullets moments after the hero has mumbled his undying vows. In the world of rough-and-ready counter-counterinsurgency, then, Rambo is the apostle of appropriate technology. Usable technology should be something you can take with you anywhere, like a Turbo. The militarist Rough Rider and the Lone Driver turn out to be kissing cousins.

Blankness Is All

Miami Vice and the high-tech car commercials share yet another feature to be found high and low throughout contemporary culture: their studied blankness of tone. Crockett, Tubbs & Co. often share the frame but stare past each other. Their bodies form part of an arrangement, like models and Japanese flowers. They don't have much to say to each other. They go for long periods without speaking; they play on muted strings. Their boss, Lieutenant Castillo, in one way surpasses them, displaying a constant effort to clamp a mask over suppressed grief and rage as he passes down the higher-ups' stupid commands. (Actually, devotees of the series learned in a double 1984–85 episode that Castillo has even more reason to glower, for he suffered the loss of his wife in—where else?—Southeast Asia, the place where all men lose their innocence. Anyone who missed those episodes has to take Castillo at face value—as a specialist in forced blankness.) Now he lugs private sorrow like a great dog behind him. Growling his few words with supreme reluctance, he also expresses his disdain for the alternatively wimpy, whimsical, and unfathomable law enforcement bureaucracy by straining to discipline his facial muscles.

At least Castillo has a seething character to suppress. By contrast, Crockett and Tubbs seem devoid of biography; they are blank from the outset. For all three, though, feeling is revealed to be difficult and dangerous—as Crockett also discovers whenever he lets himself fall for the *femme fatale;* one way or the other she is setting him up for the bad guy. The safe thing is to stay cool, hang loose, be a pro, wear mirror shades, keep to the surfaces; surrender to the surroundings, indeed *become* them, as the Lone Driver becomes his car and its synthesized music. Given *Vice's* portentous pulsations, in fact, private feeling is dwarfed and superfluous. Whatever mood emerges through the music and color of *Miami Vice* is not so much a property of characters as of the *mise en scène.* Crockett, Tubbs, and the Lone Driver partake of that "waning of affect" which Fredric Jameson rightly identifies as one of the hallmarks of postmodern culture. What began as a mood of the avant-garde has surged into mass culture. The wise course is to look upon things as aesthetic ripples, and feel nothing.

Blank expression and flat appearance come together in a common chord which resounds through contemporary culture like a great dead sound. Everything that exists meets the eye, and the trained eye—the voyeur's eye—refuses to blink. It would take another essay to track this two-dimensional *Zeitgeist* through its manifold incarnations, but a few examples, taken more or less at random, may begin to suggest just how wide is its sway. A deliberate, stylized, even aggressive blankness is evident in the arbitrary, unmeant gestures that became the normal presentational style for fashion models and avant-garde manikins in the seventies, even (or especially) in the presence of stylized violence. It is on display when the young who perform punk and dress punk affect blank expressions at the same time they know they are freaking out passersby; they aim to annihilate the banal "Good heavens" reaction—of course, it is exactly the reaction they are looking for—by rising to a plane of sublime indifference. There is a corresponding blankness in the aggressive irony of new wave fashion. Just what statement *is* being made by a jumpsuit made of Army-style camouflage material? (But how banal to inquire!) Then too there is short hair, simultaneously mocking and aping the conventions of the fifties. The sluggish antidrama, deadpan faces, soft-pedaled feeling of the cult film *Stranger than Paradise* is the cinematic equivalent. (Do they mean it or not? But to be cool is to know the question is passé.) In their own ways, Devo, Blondie, Brian Eno, and Talking Heads have

carried the same spirit into the ever vanishing avant-garde of popular music. (Should Brian Eno's self-consciously "pretty," glazed,
abstracted "Music for Airports" be taken at face value?) The serial
repetitions of Philip Glass and Steve Reich represent a triumph of
Zen minimalism, a rejection of both romantic ideas of progress and
classic ideas of unity; they can also be heard as the printouts of a
tremendous weariness, statements that large feeling, narrative sequence, and individualistic variation are no longer possible or significant, have all been done, or are somehow not worth the effort.
In a similar tenor, the trendy shops on the trendy streets in cities
across the country feature the icy understatement of elegantly thin
neon lettering. The trendy restaurants serve less food with more
style. The habitués of streets and restaurants alike adopt the streamlined look which says "Less is more," as if keeping fit were a matter
of increasing one's personal ratio of surface to depth.

Painting and serious writing were the avant-garde. Blankness
was essential, of course, in the programmatic flatness of much
American painting in the sixties and after; in a high-consumption,
high-turnover world where everything trades on appearance and
every appearance has its price, to insist on depth would be to sink
into pathetic nostalgia for some unmoved mover. Andy Warhol's
self-conscious images called attention to their sheer "imageness,"
reminded the viewer how they were derivative, mechanical, and
concocted; how laughable it would be to seek authentic meaning
while strolling down the long, long aisles of the social supermarket.
Along with Jasper Johns' textured maps, Roy Lichtenstein's cartoon
blowups, Frank Stella's streaks on shaped canvases, or photoreal-
ism's suburban streets, say, Warhol's productions were emblematic
of the postmodern idea that what used to be quaintly considered
"depth" consists of nothing but images all the way down. The same
could be said of the self-conscious "intertextuality" of fiction and
criticism, in which the poker face of Donald Barthelme, and the
aesthetics of Roland Barthes, say, slipped from irony toward indul-
gence, betraying—or, rather, displaying—the sheer ejaculatory
pleasure in the play of surfaces.

Likewise, we see a deliberate cultivation of surface in the so-
called "historicism" of postmodernist architecture, which does not
so much absorb and rework as shuffle and staple together the shards

of distinct historical periods, refuting as absurdly old-fashioned any notion of passionate statement, aesthetic coherence, or historical continuity; for all surfaces are styles, all styles are arbitrary bits in the great data bank of art history. The Disneyland exuberance of some of these recombinant forms coexists with a poker-faced we've-seen-it-all attitude which verges on premature fin-de-millennium exhaustion. Passion and distance are meant to cancel each other out. The urgency of the blasé, the mocking juxtaposition of understatement and bravado, shows up in much of the most interesting and celebrated of recent fiction as well—in Raymond Carver's stories of the emotionally strangulated, for example, and most successfully in the novels of Don DeLillo, who skates confidently along the seam of two attitudes: an apparent rapture for flat, breathless understatement, and a heart-chilling recognition of what is missing in today's burned-out cases. The ability to slide along the razor edge between blank irony and exquisitely masochistic surrender is perhaps the most characteristic feature of this mood—which may deserve the imprecise label "postmodern" only because it laughs at the idea of being pinned down to being anything (including modern) at all; in other words, because it insists on being post-everything.

Are we in the presence of a clear-cut "structure of feeling," Raymond Williams' elusive term for an interlocking cultural complex—"a pattern of impulses, restraints, tones"—that forecasts the common future as it colors the common experience of a society just at or beneath the threshold of awareness? What is especially difficult is to understand what relation there is, if any, between the stylized blankness growing in the culture and the actual state of feeling in American society today. Does the icy quality of an artificial outer space, the self-conscious displacement and blankness of car commercials, MTV, and *Miami Vice*, correspond to a glacial inner space, as, for example, Christopher Lasch would seek to persuade us? What relation is there between the blank look and the therapeutic hug, the denial of tears on the screen and the delight in tears among friends? Are the people who compose the blank look—design the manikins, write the ad copy—the same population as those who speak cloyingly, stereotypically, of what they "feel," the way reporters now routinely ask people how they "feel" about whatever it is they have done or has been done to them? Do the middle-class

populations who make a fetish of feeling in public go in for psychotherapy to teach them how to "express their feelings" precisely
because otherwise they would not know? Is blankness a way of
coping with a surge of tangled feelings kicked up by recent changes
in work and family, or by the undermining of old myths in the
sixties—a way of managing contradictions by pretending we don't
care?

I confess, anticlimactically, but I hope not blankly, that I am
not sure. But my intuition is that there is something revealing and
disturbing in a culture many of whose most serious talents propose
to cast away feeling, to confine themselves to the surface, to beg
questions of purpose and authenticity. Fredric Jameson argues that
the superceding of the problem of authenticity belongs to, is cou-
pled to, corresponds to, expresses—the relation is not altogether
clear—the culture of multinational capitalism, in which capital,
that infinitely transferrable abstraction, has abolished particularity
as such along with the coherent self in whom history, depth, and
subjectivity unite. Surfaces meet surfaces in these postmodern forms
because a new human nature—a human second nature—has formed
to feel at home in a homeless world political economy. I am less
convinced than Jameson that the postmodern gestalt of surfaces and
uprooted juxtaposition is the triumphant, dominant, overarching
form of this epoch, sweeping all else before it. There are popular
trends that reach beneath surfaces and slickness. There are the networks of mutual support beneath the pieties of psychobabble; genuine communities that counterbalance the loneliness of the long-
distance driver. Within popular culture there is, indeed, Bruce
Springsteen, the minstrel of authenticity. The *Zeitgeist* has two
wings, and hasn't taken its last flight.

Leaving these teasing difficulties aside, one conclusion is compelling, Despite the I've-seen-it-all posture of Crockett, Tubbs, and
the Lone Driver, there remains an enormous innocence in the all-
American idea of the loner, the man with no name, the hard-bitten
conqueror of feelings whose hard-won prowess costs him nothing.
The idea of self-sufficiency as such carries a certain nobility. The
sovereign I who stalks through the transcendental verse of Walt
Whitman and the essays of Henry David Thoreau does not think he
has the right to go anywhere and tell anyone where to get off; even

the hard-boiled I of Raymond Chandler's Philip Marlowe or Ross MacDonald's Lew Archer honors the depth and power of social decencies and binding commitments. But the surfer of surfaces is a committed innocent, and his innocence makes him dangerous. To insist on the obvious, Americans are not loners. We traffic with a world society which is more than an empty place into which, American Express cards in hand, we plunge. The Pilgrims who came to these shores came to an inhabited land, not the vacant wilderness they had imagined. The "shining city upon a hill" of which John Winthrop wrote exists only in commerce with other cities upon other hills—not all of them shining, but all of them utterly real. The fantasy of innocent power contributed to the slaughter of hundreds of thousands of Vietnamese as well as fifty-eight thousand Americans in Vietnam—all mutely bearing witness to the impossibility of innocence and the intractable weight of the real world.

Yet the fantasy retains its extraordinary force. Consider how we witness the fantasy of ultimate, self-sufficient innocence in Reagan's "dream" of a "Star Wars" shield which presumably guarantees national security—although the same gentlemen who today call "Star Wars" "the only thing that offers any real hope to the world" have been telling us for forty years that nuclear deterrence was so foolproof as to be, itself, that hope. Indeed, the little thirty-second utopia with which we began carries the same wishful premise as President Reagan's "Strategic Defense Initiative": whatever technology has rendered problematic (including human life itself), technology can save. If the city has become poisonous because of cars, get a car to escape it. If nuclear weapons threaten the prospects of life on earth, instead of rethinking the international system and the politics which has normalized the threat of Armageddon, spend hundreds of billions of dollars on dubious protections—making the world safe, in a sense, for nuclear bombs. Like rocketing cars and sleek cops—indeed, like the pulsating planets and smash-'em-up cartoon figures of which Tom Engelhardt writes elsewhere in this volume—"Star Wars" represents the triumph of absolute, abstract wishfulness. The fantasy of the technological fix, of unbridled power wrapped in a revamped innocence, represents the nation's lingering childhood. But there must be a sliver of the child's mind which knows that childhood has to end.

SIMULATIONS

Faking It

MICHAEL SORKIN

The "Exquisite Corpse" was an entertainment favored by the Paris surrealists. André Breton describes it as a "game of folded paper played by several people, who compose a sentence or drawing without anyone seeing the preceding collaboration or collaborations. The now classic example, which gave the game its name, was drawn from the first sentence obtained this way: "The-exquisite-corpse-will-drink-new-wine." This game was held in considerable esteem. "Finally," writes Breton, "we had at our command an infallible way of holding the critical intellect in abeyance, and of fully liberating the mind's metaphorical activity."

Watching television takes place across folds of time and frequency. Television is not simply an unincisible continuum of "flow and regularity," overcoming any hope of distinguishing its "texts." Rather, it yields a text at any given watching. TV is like the "blind" elaboration of the exquisite corpse: the final figure is at once unpredictable yet always whole enough to be comprehended by aesthetic strategies. Television is to be distinguished from mere broadcasting as the apple, eaten, differs from the orchard.

Like the "Exquisite Corpse," TV is about juxtaposition. TV's formal environment thrives on the multiplier effect of the accidental collaborations among the community of propagators and users. At the simplest level, the form of my Tuesday evening's prime-time pleasure is structured by a dialectic of elision and rift among the various windows (commercial scheduling, programming, "news") through which images enter the broadcast and are combined as television. "Flow" is more of a circumstance than a product. The real output is the quantum, the smallest maneuverable broadcast bit. And, with the spread of cable, VCRs, computer games, and the power to zap, "broadcasters" are accelerating toward the relinquishment—or rather the transcendence—of interest and investment in sequence. Any arrangement of bits will ultimately produce the same effects.

When television pros speak of "production values," they speak precisely about this quantum. Commercials are esteemed, in many cases, because of the disproportionately large number of shots they contain relative to the narrative norm. What's being celebrated here is not simply the minusculization of TV's combinable bits, but also its inevitable distancing from antique realist modes of representation. The obsession of the pointillist painters with the single dot of luminescence is reflected in the latter romance of disintegration, this slouch toward the logic of chaos. *La Grande Jatte* is ultimately just a coincidence of photons, like the miracle of those infinitely typing monkeys finally producing *Hamlet*. The only problem with that system is the implied waste of manuscripts obtained before the Bard could be aped. Television's logic accelerates toward a boldly economic resolution of this difficulty. The system, by definition, cannot make an illegible artifact: every chimp is a Shakespeare. No combination is lost to meaning. In the land of the blind, Cyclops is king.

If any accident produces coherence, all coherence is artificial. Under postmodernism's regime, we celebrate the hegemony of the ersatz, the logic of the supermarket, its shelves lined with "natural" foods compounded of petrochemicals. Quintessence here resides in the invisibility of the simulation, in the perfection of the appropriation, in the food that "tastes just like the real thing." Of course, a system of simulation requires that second term, some memory of the genuine. Simulation can only be artistic as it approaches the line of invisibility: once the crossover is complete, the game is lost. We all know that Reagan is only "acting" president, but he's so damn good that we can't quite be sure. It's scarcely a coincidence that his is the first triumphantly electronic presidency, deploying telegenic fragments in a collusion of coherence.

Saturday morning is TV's laboratory of the simulated. It's the time most caught up with (Jean Baudrillard's words) "substituting signs of the real for the real itself." Let's begin with wrestling. As Roland Barthes has pointed out, wrestling is, by its nature, grandiloquent, fixated on excess, a spectacle of gesture. Wrestlers are hypervisible: renown results from the combination of literal enormity (of muscle, of hairiness, of avoirdupois) with an excessively schematic presentation of personality. Wrestlers never merely speak, they shout. Their selves are compounded from aggressiveness plus a single mediating component which allows the spectator to rapidly apprehend whether theirs is a force for good or ill. This predetermines (wrestling being as Calvinist as the evangelicals who occupy the same morning slot on Sundays) the outcome of the match itself and structures the allegiances of the beholding fans.

Wrestling binarizes the world's horizons into the weightable distinctions which can ethically frame the outcome of the match. Black/White, Russian/American, Moslem/Christian, Good Body/ Bad Body, Gay/Straight, Hairy/Smooth, Urban/Rural: these are the topical centers for the construction of value, weighted with the cartoonish hyperbole that characterizes wrestling generally, yielding a gross and phobic Reagan/Rambo politics of homely hatred and affable intolerance. Like the Reagan Switcheroo of presidentiality for presidency, wrestling's barbarism is shielded by its daffy aura of mirth. Qaddafi may be a terrorist and a barbarian, but he's also . . . a *flake!*

The match, then, is a ritual dance in which accident has been precluded. The very visibility of the faked violence acts as the guarantor of the outcome. Slips in the choreography invariably err on the side of further dissipating the illusion of violence. Blows fail to fall where they should but still elicit the simulated anguish of the recipient who—like the professional he or she is—holds up his or her side of the game plan. Like Sunday morning religion, wrestling is structured as a contest but without actual competition. Wrestling thus locates itself at the very point at which simulation is born. Its pleasures are explicitly associated with the detachment of a form from its received content. Chance always takes the fall at the hands of necessity.

To sustain the simulation, wrestling must construct and maintain a little universe of the simulated. To do this, its discourse refers in its every enunciation to the apparatus used to broadcast conventional sport. Wrestling features the same style of ringside commentary, the same interpolation of interviews, the same mystification of sporting expertise, the same freeze-frame and instant replay formats, the same faintly prurient interest in the wrestlers' private lives (not to mention parts), the same cults of personality, and so on. This system of understanding, however, is marshaled in the service of an event which is a parody of its originating source: "real" sport. The effect of placing this mode of comprehending at the service of the faintly ridiculous is not, however, to dissipate the validity of its structure, but to affirm it. Wrestling's relation to sport (like the relationship of the *Saturday Night Live* News to the *NBC Nightly News*) suggests not the limits but the expansiveness of the mediating mode, its inevitability. It tightens the link between the representation of reality and the comparable validity of its infinite distortion.

This efficiently schematized version of sport is placed in an immediate environment that does not simply sustain the simulation, but begins to generalize it across the broadcast band. The wrestling match sits in an entire culture of wrestling which proposes, in effect, that there's a whole universe out there centered on these matches. There are advertisements for wrestling matches, publications, clubs, souvenirs, and further broadcasts. Real celebrities are juxtaposed with the overdrawn wrestlers, celebrities who speak, alternately, in wrestle-speak and more conventional language. While the entire duration of the Saturday broadcast tends to be wrestle-culture's exclusive domain, fragments detach themselves and crop up elsewhere in the broadcast environment, undeniable *inter pares*. Wrestling "specials" appear in prime time, like any others.

The home slot establishes crucial congruences: Saturday morning is the nominal preserve of kid's programming. What's striking about this environment, however, is not so much its audience but the consistency of its agenda in dislocating realism. Wrestling has often been compared to the cartoons among which it sits, and it certainly has attributes in common with them. Both present reality as constructed rather than depicted. The most current style of cartooning offers animated versions of the immensely popular GoBot and Transformer toys, little machines (generally vehicles) that, when unfolded, reveal hidden identities as humanoid "superheroes." What we have here is an expanding simulated great chain of being along which the mutating continuity of simulation is elaborated.

An exemplary member of this chain gang is Mr. T, an iconic figure whose "real" position vis-à-vis the knowable world is by now impossible to pin down. Consider the natural history of his serial rerepresentation. Mr. T (whose "real" name had decomposed before his initial penetration of general consciousness), began life as one of Muhammad Ali's bodyguards and first came into view in one of the *Rocky* sequels in which he was cast as the larger-than-life opponent of Sylvester Stallone's larger-than-life hero (by now, superhero, if grosses are any measure) boxer, Rocky. He was thus materialized in the wrestling format: heavily symbolized sporting combat, outcome invariable. But, in the world of simulation, nothing succeeds like excess and Mr. T (visibly larger than life than Rocky, even) was set for a rapid program of genre transcendence and simulated evolution. That his beginnings were as a brusque (to put it mildly) talking black man and rigorous primitive (the hair cut! the costume! the discourse!) only fitted him more precisely to his destiny as Darwinian burlesque.

He next emerged as one of the stars of *The A-Team,* a prime-time hit of pathological schematization. Its four (super)heroes (personifications of the superego) are established (in the miniature narrative that precedes the show and fits their relevant prehistory into a space the size of a short commercial) as Vietnam vets "unjustly convicted of a crime they did not commit" who now live in the "underground" from which they weekly emerge to defend weakling victims of gross injustice (an old man, a woman) against their tormentors (some supervillain). The four (one of whom is amusingly portrayed as "insane") are galvanized into competence and sanity by collective enterprise. Mr. T (represented always by his inscrutable initial, clearly a nominalist dodge) portrays the character "B.A." (initials again, but evoking a certain intellectual attainment) who is inevitably called upon to construct in extreme haste some sort of military contraption, generally a tank, from scrap materials. Mr. T is also closely identified with a somewhat sinister black van with opaque windows which he drives. However, Mr. T is traumatized by the prospect of flying, adding a low terrestrialism to his portrait as primitive.

From the A-Team, Mr. T crossed over into wrestling itself, teamed in a much publicized bout with the reigning champ, Hulk Hogan. Hulk (whose name collapses those of two comic book heroes, one a "monster" of towering strength, the other a superhuman GI) and Mr. T wrestled a pair of bad guys in prime time with predictable results. The sanctification via wrestling of Mr. T totemized him by a baptism in television narrative at its most minimalist. More or less concurrently with this, Mr. T was offered to the public in doll form, literally totemized. This is an old mode of adulation of entertainment celebrities—witness, for instance, Michael Jackson and Brooke Shields (or, for that matter, Shirley Temple) dolls. But the doll was merely an intermediate step in Mr. T's movement from autosimulation to a fuller version, if the one that sufficiently unsexed him to allow Nancy Reagan to sit on his lap. Now Mr. T has joined the Saturday morning ranks as a cartoon show, completing the circuit from deanimation to reanimation, swiftly and efficiently. Such are the consequences of reach that persistently exceeds its grasp, a process not without precedent. The Beatles (more popular than Jesus Christ, as Lennon had it) were given their truly sufficient fantastic existence in *Yellow Submarine,* an animation adequate to their aura. No coincidence that the replicant hagiography called Beatlemania (actors *as* the Beatles) forms the linguistic and conceptual prototype of Wrestlemania and Hulkamania. Here, though, there's an efficient short circuit, self-imitation conflating the two terms in a single figure. Hulk Hogan is *sui generis,* more or less.

Concurrent in certain markets with the wrestling broadcasts is another show consecrated to the serial realization of simulation, *Puttin' on the Hits.* Like wrestling, the program is formatted as a contest. And like wrestling, the contest is about the studiousness of a crossover into altered reality. Here, however, the show focuses on the passage of quotidian citizens into the realms of celebritydom by their self-transformation into the figures of rock 'n' roll superstars, about no less than autoroboticism. *Puttin' on the Hits* is a lip-synching competition. The contestants, costumed variously as Tina Turner, Michael Jackson, Cyndi Lauper, Madonna, or Sting mount the stage and simulate a performance, an act of scientific surrogacy, mechanically moving their lips to emulate the oscillations of the recorded star, played over. For this, they are judged by a panel of media business operatives according to the criteria of "appearance," "lip sync," and (*sic*) "originality."

As we shall see, the juridical mode recurs as a device for establishing the authority of TV's various simulations. Here, the circumstances of "judging" (like voice-over expertise at the wrestling match) serve mainly to tag a given position in the great chain. This function is signaled in the first instance by the makeup of the empaneled judges on *Puttin' on the Hits*. Their ranks are dominated not by performers but by a variety of "experts," mainly publicists and record company A & R types. This suggests a special sort of connoisseurship which is expressed statistically (contestant number one earns twenty-seven out of a possible thirty points) and contains an implicit precisionism that vamps science. Unlike originality, replication can be tested exactly. The "originality" scored in the judges' triad of criteria is itself a statistical conceit, an accolade for an unusual retrieval, a hedge against an entire show of Madonna Wanna Be's.

Where does this particular simulation sit? Clearly at the third degreeat least. Interpolated along the chain between performer and simulator is a significant other, the performer's autosimulation. On shows like *Soul Train* or *American Bandstand,* the same stars who are the subjects of imitation on *Puttin' on the Hits* appear, performing "as themselves." But their performances are only conceptually more "live" than the masqueraded versions of their citizen imitators. These actual performers perform by lip-synching their own voices, guaranteeing the clinical perfection of the studio recording. But there's a further link within the boundaries of this autosimulation. To the degree that a recorded "performance" is enabled only by the electronic mixology of studio practice, the live performance being simulated on *American Bandstand* has no literal existence, either in memory or at the moment. Thus, the performer simply simulates the conceit of "live" performance. Memorex is the natural condition of the "sung" artifact: self-synching is the natural mode of rock videos, the seamless soundtrack transcending visual jolts. The question of whether it might be live is entirely moot. Like *Puttin' on the Hits, American Bandstand* is engaged with establishing not simply the primacy but the complexity of the simulated.

Hulk Hogan's Rock 'n' Wrestling! is a new Saturday staple which territorializes an intriguingly long section of the great chain. Basically a cartoon show, the "characters" in *Rock 'n' Wrestling* are all drawn versions of the "live" performers already familiar from wrestling itself, including Hulk Hogan, Andre the Giant, Junkyard Dog, the Iron Sheik, and so on. This hagiographication via cartooning is familiar from, among other examples, the aforementioned Mr. T show. However, *Rock 'n' Wrestling* factors in additional links. First, the periodic presence of the live characters who are cartoonsimulated during the bulk of the broadcast. Hulk himself (often shown parading down city streets accreting enthralled children like the Pied Piper) acts as host for the show (Mr. T does the same for *his* cartoon show), interpolating his "higher" reality between cartoon segments. Other live figures appear in various vaudevillian blackouts.

The rock component of *Rock 'n' Wrestling* figures both in a general esprit de pop, the labored effort to link two categories of manufactured celebritydom, and in a startling segment that habitually appears near the top of the broadcast. It is a studio set—very much like that of *American Bandstand* or *Soul Train*—in which dozens of wrestlers are dancing to the (recorded) strains of some rock classic. There are periodic cuts to close-ups of these figures who—on cue—lip-synch some apt lyric in voices represented as theirs. Clearly, lipsynching is simulation's primal scene and the touchstone of its mobility. The astute inclusion of this moment in *Rock 'n' Wrestling* would seem to be primarily a message about the proprietorship of essence.

The visual device which *Rock 'n' Wrestling* uses to bridge from one degree of simulation to another is a kind of dissolve. The conceit behind the image is of a magnification of pixilation. The bits of the picture/image grow larger until it has been transposed into a field of multicolored squares which await reresolution in order to re-achieve comprehensibility—a nice metaphor for TV as a whole. This dissolve is only used in one direction, however. The image of Hulk as himself dissolves into the image of Hulk as cartoon. Higher "reality" (or lower-degree simulation) dissolves into higher simulation (or lower reality). The implication is of simulation established not as reality's mirror but as its microscope. As the power of resolution is adjusted up and down, the subject becomes, variously, man as cartoon, cartoon as man, man as robot, etc. Hulk is not so much dehumanized as he is conceptualized, rendered isomorphic with his aura.

This working along the great chain of simulation occurs, of course, not merely within each text but between texts as well. Sharing *Rock 'n' Wrestling*'s time slot on a typical Saturday morning are both cartoon shows, purely consecrated, and "live" wrestling shows. The inducement to switch among these is inextricably inter-woven with their segmented character. A typical viewing at that hour, either across the wavelengths or within a single frequency, necessarily exposes the viewer to simulation in varying degrees. In passing, it's to be noted that the character of cartoon shows has shifted dramatically in recent years, away from the humanoid ducks and wabbits of the genre's dawn to the current fixation on GoBots and Transformers. This new paradigm—imported from Japan—is involved with the depiction of entities with the capacity for self-transformation (like the eponymous toys that inspired them) from machine to *Übermensch*.

While this might be seen as merely part of our general fixation with the putatively more advanced industrial culture of the Japa-nese, the rise of the Transformer shows fits with television's more general project of extending the great chain of simulation. One of simulation's key agendas is the psychic extension of the realm of the prosthetic. Most primitively, lip-synching—allowing the acquisi-tion of an electronically perfected substitute voice—captures the idea, a literal and comprehensible vision of the superpowers of the superheroes, here permitting an ordinary citizen to transform him-self or herself into a superstar. One step up the prosthetic ladder is the model of *The Bionic Woman* or *The Six Million Dollar Man*. These early odes to the possibility of biomechanical prosthesis (now retired to reruns) were crucial in bridging the gap between the fantasy discourse of Superman and Wonder Woman and the plausible discourse of the scientific. The Six Million Dollar Man was a superhero for the post–Christiaan Barnard age.

But the Bionic Woman and the Six Million Dollar man were finally too coy, their prostheses concealed, their powers primitive dumb-showy like the emulators of stardom on *Puttin' on the Hits*. New programs are more happily explicit, whether in cartoon form or in the theater of feigned verisimilitude which inspires a show like *Knight Rider*. Here, the hero is rendered super by his relationship to a supercar which not only transforms his physical powers but—by speaking to him—acts as an alter ego as well. While *Knight Rider*'s strategy is essentially conservative, using the car's somewhat fey voice synthesizing R2D2 and Magnum's pal Higgins to establish it as a conventional sidekick, the specifics of the image carry a more advanced content. At the formal level, the GoBotic imperative is unmistakable in the symbiosis of car and man.

While the above examples are rife with a certain ideological refinement, they are technically primitive, retaining a crude anticipatory recognition of the moment of crossover, not yet fully engaged with the representation of seamless equivalence. Not that technology lacks. As a careful watching of any number of current commercials reveals, the craft of computer animation is profoundly advanced and leaping forward. Given the very finite number of phosphors to be activated on the home screen, the difficulties in creating a fully simulated television environment are mainly those of computational time and treasure, awaiting only the next generation or two of mainframes to emerge as fully possible. The computer-generated image of *Remington Steele* need look no different from his conventionally video'd form. At that point (a future amply hinted at both in commercials and such Hollywood production as Disney's *TRON*, the first feature film to insert human actors in a computer graphic environment), the simulated image will emerge as infinitely capable: Mr. T's presence will be fully continuous, spared the segmentation which presently characterizes the states of his transformation.

This analysis, however, runs ahead of itself. The main thrust of television's simulation is not yet directed primarily to the invention of a culture predicated on the prosthetic construction of the human subject. Its simulations serve primarily as an implement for the creation of continuities across the range of broadcast quanta, to further establish the principle of equality among images. Simulation is presently absorbed not with a structure of certainties but with a radical agenda of destabilization. It establishes the tenacious problematic of Memorex (is it real or is it . . .) as a useful, binding constant. Naturally, the raising of such a question is the harbinger of its erasure.

There's a popular show in syndication called *The People's Court*. Superficially, it has the look of any of the familiar "courtroom dramas" that have been TV staples for years. But *The People's Court* is justice pared to its essentials. The courtroom is minimalist austere and the legal apparatus is also held to a minimum: no lawyers, court stenographers, inscriptions, swearings in. Just a bailiff, plaintiff, defendant, and, of course, the snow-haired, black-robed figure of the judge. In this case, the presiding magistrate is one Judge Wapner, the very personification of no-nonsense adjudication. With flawless equanimity, Judge Wapner disposes of two cases per episode, serving justice astutely on a ten-minute schedule.

The points at issue tend to be less than Dostoyevskian in proportion. This after all is small claims court, and small claims court in lotusland at that. But Judge Wapner never loses his cool before the deluge of complaints about imperfectly developed snapshots and neighbor Dobermans doo-dooing on the dahlias. Day after day, he shows infinite patience before infinite foible. Unlike, say, *Divorce Court*, *The People's Court* is not the great arena of affect, the venue of the exceptional (my wife came under the influence of this so-called guru and now she's pregnant!). Rather, it's the stage of small disruptions in the pathology of the normal, an arena for dignifying the emotional claims of the nearly trivial. Its ostensible message (uttered at the end of every show) is the more potent for its relentless accessibility: don't take the law into your own hands, take it to court! The advice is irresistible. Judge Wapner is unfailingly fair.

What distinguishes *The People's Court*, however, is not the swift certainty of its justice (the courtroom format has always been predicated on the Solomonic capacities of the judiciary) but its alleged verisimilitude. As is explained by the voice-over at the top of each episode, "what you're about to see is real." The litigants on the screen are not actors. Rather, they are genuine citizens who, having filed complaints in a real small claims court, have been persuaded to drop their suits there and instead have them heard in the "people's" court. For this, they are offered a treble inducement: first, the fairness of Judge Wapner's decision making (by definition, he does not err, television is in control); second, the chance of a perfect moment of Warholian celebrity on national TV; finally, the prospect of truth without consequences.

Nobody really loses in *The People's Court.* Judge Wapner's awards are paid by the producers of the show; the only punishment is humiliation. This delimiting of penalty engenders an interesting slippage. Justice assumes the character of a game show, a format in which the worst outcome is loss of face and a failure to win. On *The People's Court,* infraction carries no real risk beyond this. By restricting justice to the parameters of entertainment, *The People's Court* becomes a show trial. It's lip-synch justice, however exemplary, because a way has been found to remove risk from uncertainty. The litigants (all of whom receive scale) become no more than actors in an ersatz real-life drama.

It's worth recalling that the seminal incident in the history of the game show was the scandal that erupted in the wake of the discovery that Charles Van Doren had "cheated" on *Twenty-One,* primed in advance with the answers. The fracas broke because a putative civilian had been covertly transformed into an actor, a conspicuously professional simulator. The whole matter then slid into the juridical arena which, naturally, constituted the continuation of the show by other means. Thus, in the larger view, the episode prefigured *The People's Court,* excepting the rearrangement of a few of the terms. In this historic slip from dissimulation to simulation, questions of praise and blame—those wellsprings of the mimetic—remain at the core.

The People's Court is as much a simulation as a wrestling match between Hulk Hogan and the Iron Sheik. Although Judge Wapner's decisions are—the viewer is informed—based on the legal codes of the state of California, that code functions principally as the guarantor of his expertise. Judge Wapner is not so much a servant of justice as vice versa. Judge Wapner is quizmaster Bill Cullen in robes—or, to be more precise, Vin Scully, the learned sportscaster.

In most cases, there's an interruption between the conclusion of argument and the rendering of the judge's decision. During this interval—which is occupied by commercials—the judge repairs to his chambers (where—one presumes—his decisions are vetted for their broadcastability) to make up his mind, invisibly. This concealment of the space of expertise corresponds, generally speaking, to the conceptual space occupied by the computer terminal of the sportscaster which endlessly and invisibly provides complex grist ("That's the nineteenth left-handed batter whose age is a prime number to take a base on balls under the sign of Saturn") for broadcasting's encyclopedic mill.

What *The People's Court* represents is the juridical quantum laid bare. While it may not be the most concise example—which would have to be a commercial—it may be its most explicit. The relatively languid pace of *The People's Court*'s proceedings does, however, render all of the components visible. There's an interesting ambiguity at the outset. While the show opens with an explication of the "reality" of the process, an account of the source of the litigants presented over pulsating music, there's also a strong signifier of the primacy of narrative. Each case is given a title in a form particular to fiction. Thus, one is invited to witness not *Smith* v. *Jones* but "The Case of the Disappearing Dachshund" (pets figure prominently). Then there's an immediate reversion to a format of simultaneity. Each case begins with the voice of the (as yet) unseen announcer, who alerts us to the imminent arrival of the litigants in the courtroom. The trial ensues, its verisimilitude established primarily via the unprepossessing and unactorly appearance and demeanor of the contestants and by the often excruciating banality of the cases at issue. Judge Wapner renders his judgment and the parties leave the courtroom. In the "corridor" outside, they're greeted by the announcer, Doug Llewelyn, now visibly an "announcer" type, clean-cut, wearing a blue blazer, holding a mike. He questions them briefly about the outcome of the case, generally offering a few cautionary remarks to the losing party. The little interview is terminated by the announcer (whose role as commentator at this point is merged with his role as an "official" of the court) telling the party that they have "papers to sign" somewhere offscreen. Those "papers" are *The People's Court*'s authenticating coda.

The juridical quantum is a parable of property. *The People's Court* is like an attenuated commercial with its marshaled narrative putting some stupid issue to the test ("Which is whiter, Mrs. Jones?") under the watchful eye of male expertise. The announcer (Dan Rather, Bryant Gumbel, Doug Llewelyn, Don Pardo) stands both within and without the narrative, performing as its guarantor. "She's right, it's whitest." "I guess you won't let Fido out without a leash again." It's an unusual position, particular to television. Simulation thrives on the migration of categories, in the Memorex manner. The erasure of the difference between broadcasting the news and being the news, between being Mr. T, being B.A., and being a cartoon, between adjudicating and narrating—this is what must be accomplished.

If any show on television is "about" inventing TV's simulated universe, it's the *Today* show. Even its name induces a certain metaphysical problematic. *Today* is a two-hour exercise, broadcast every weekday morning, in the elaboration of the major figure in the rhetoric (and therefore substance) of simulation: the big slur. It's a superb show, thematically consecrated to a relentless effort to demonstrate the homogeneity of bits. *Today* is in a position of particular privilege as the effectively commencing program of the broadcast day. Strategically identical shows—*Good Morning America* on ABC and the *CBS Morning News*—occupy the same slots on the other networks. All three of them constitute a sort of precapitulation of the day's programming, phylogenic mirrors of larger arrangements. They represent TV's daily trajectory in accelerated form, compressing as well as eliding, a daily demonstration of just how small a pin will accommodate the dance of an angel.

Consider a 1985 morning on *Today* which had as its major agenda the naturalizing of that evening's *NBC Movie of the Week,* a film entitled *An Early Frost.* The film itself dealt with a man with AIDS, and especially with the family drama prompted by his revelation of his condition. AIDS, just at the moment, is one of television's special preoccupations, offering as it does the simultaneous opportunity both to pander and to appear to behave responsibly, the favored ethical stance of the networks. At any rate, the imminence of the show afforded *Today* with a fine opportunity to do what it does best, to compact the fictive and the factual, to simulate. From TV's perspective, the agenda is always to assert that any *thing* that can be represented is ultimately comparable to any*thing* else that can be represented. This is the TV transference, the operation of reciprocal ennobling that makes a can of pop as consequential as a murder, that allows the cut from commercial to carnage, from starving babies in Ethiopia to Morris the Finicky Cat.

On the *Today* show, the movie of the week was shown fully metastasized, spread—prior to its actual presence—over the entire woof of the broadcast day. First, the show was formally interpolated in the *Today* format via an interview with its star. This interview occurred in *Today*'s second hour, with the consequence that the hour and a half which preceded the interview itself could be riddled with anticipatory references to the upcoming event (the interview), itself a prelude to the larger upcoming event (the movie). This discourse of anticipation was supported by a series of parallel discourses, nominally independent of *Today*'s internal agenda-setting but dedicated to the same result. During advertising breaks, a series of network spots appeared, promoting the upcoming movie of the week. During breaks for local news broadcasts, there were announcements from local newscasters which incorporated the promotion of the movie in a threefold manner. First, they announced the upcoming interview segment on *Today* (in which broadcast these nominally independent segments were nested). This announcement structurally associated the upcoming event (the interview) with the series of events which preceded it in the segment (the news). Second, the locals announced that the evening news *(Live at Five)* was also to have an interview segment in which one of the cast members of the movie was to appear. This offered the literal presence of the movie as news, establishing its relevance in both national and local contexts, an event and a story of bridging consequence. The third strategy for incorporating the movie into the news broadcast within *Today* was an announcement about an NBC show which was slated to follow the movie immediately, an "NBC News Special Report" entitled *AIDS Fears, AIDS Facts.* Announcements anticipating this broadcast appeared in all the slots in which announcements for the movie itself occurred: the local news broadcast, within and as part of the *Today* show, and as a network commercial within commercial territory tenuously located between "official" segments of the *Today* show. The network ads for its newscast about AIDS featured Tom Brokaw, the anchorperson of the *NBC Nightly News*, the network's preeminent newsperson and its most important spokesperson in matters of "news." To catalog, then, the various modes in which *An Early Frost* materialized itself in the morning's broadcast, the following must be included: as commercial (that is, a self-contained unit appearing among other commercials), as interview, as "news" about the interview, as "news" about a related interview, as commercial for a related broadcast, as "news" about a related broadcast, and as part of the "conversational" agenda of that day's *Today* show. Typically, this conversation was used to situate the film both in internal terms ("a powerful drama") and as a newsworthy item ("for network TV, it's an unusually honest and probing film.") This latter simulation obliged a stance of dissimulation on the part of its formulator, in this case, Bryant Gumbel.

A brief parenthesis. The commercial which featured Tom Brokaw advertising the news program about AIDS typifies the permeation of the broadcast day by the news rubric, one of the most formidable strategies for the invention of the continuous conceptual parity of simulation. The Brokaw commercial is related in form to the "newsbreak" (the word itself a moment in the course of self-transformation into Newspeak), a phenomenon now pandemic on the networks. These newsbreaks (which take various names on the networks) are one- or two-item news broadcasts which occupy exactly the same space as a commercial. Indeed, the newsbreak appears during the commercial break and is primarily designed to fracture it, thereby creating additional salable spots, while promoting the news show itself. The name is obviously intended to suggest the conflation of a "break" in a "program" with the idea of "breaking" news, an urgent story. Newsbreaks are presented with the full apparatus of the nightly news show. They're initiated with the same musical theme and logo, and the newscaster appears sitting at the same "news desk" one sees on the full-blown version of the show. Segmentation within the break is also achieved via familiar means: with a commercial. The only real difference is the mode of termination, here, not the conclusive adieu, but a teasing "details later."

The newsbreak can clearly chalk up a number of accomplishments. Certainly, it plays a major role in validating both the mode and environment of commercials. It is, after all, isomorphic with them, cotenant of the same interstice, identically slipped in. Equally, it contributes to the generalization of newsness. These "breaks" do not derive from events. Rather, they are simply the creatures of schedule, beholden primarily to their slots. They are filled with available news, not available in the occasional event of news: repetition dominates singularity. The "news" thus becomes no more than another category through which any available televised event is capable of migrating. Simple depiction supercedes any issue of depictability. The newsperson's talking head registers authority, represents judgment. The succession of images of this apparatus of preference constitutes TV's minimum, the repetition of the declaration "It is, it is, it is, it is." It's the raw form of TV ontology.

If the news does no more than postulate the existence of the system, there are still refinements, reflexive elaborations. Recently, the *NBC Nightly News* was given a new set of opening and closing images and a new musical tag. The images consist of a set of unpopulated shots of "American" landscapes culminating in a picture of the Statue of Liberty against a lurid purple sunset—or rather, a special effect: a shot of a model of the Statue of Liberty wheelingly represented against a simulated sunset backdrop. The music which accompanies this camera work is also "special." Composed by the film composer John Williams of *Star Wars* fame, it exceeds the familiar genre of news broadcast fanfares. Hitherto, these have largely been confined to the simplest of motifs, either the traditional continuous tone pattern derived from the sound of the clattering teletype machine or the sparest of musical signatures. Now, though, the music is an elaborated composition, rendered movie style, so that it not only brackets the entire broadcast but, in reduced form, signals the end of a segment and the transition into commercials.

The music also—as closing credits inform—has a title: "The

Mission." An interesting name, redolent of space flight and a civilizing missionary endeavor. The music is full-blown, orchestrated, filled with Williams' consequential sci-fi signature. The association is unmistakable, deliberate. What is suggested is not simply that the events underscored are momentous, both national and galactic, but also that they are entertaining—that the news is an artifact not so different from those other visual artifacts that populate the broadcast day, just more important. Of course, the news is narrative, itself orchestrated for impact. News insinuates itself universally, nothing isn't news. But what gives the system its real force is that the operation is commutative. News is narrative, but narrative is also news. The *Today* show interview with, say, Henry Kissinger, is immediately adjacent with, let's imagine, its interview with Linda Evans. Simulation privileges, above all, the increment. These are the cells of its exquisite corpse. What is created by their combination is a universal protoplasm which—like the TV image itself—obscures its ultimate differentiation. The dot transcends the matrix. *E unibus pluram.*

In this constituting matrix, the likes of Henry Kissinger and Linda Evans and Anwar Sadat (struck down by a jihad of preelectronic fanatics) are just dots themselves, little pixels of human luminescence. Their factory is the talk show, that structure of occasions for self-simulation, for the invention of a negotiable persona. The tenancy of an increment of Carson validates according to a code of frequency and repetition, by means of a test of sameness. Joan Rivers is always vulgar. George Carlin is always wacky. Ed McMahon is always amused. On Barbara Walters' show (prolegomena to assasination and miniseries for the hapless Anwar) the currency is a little different: the simulated compulsion to repeat heartfelt stories about oneself in front of millions on the goading of that goddess of the fraudulent. Barbara Walters is surely the Ronald Reagan of interviewers, a parody of the genuine.

Like the *Today* show, "real" sport occupies TV time in long intervals. Formally, sport offers a compelling precedent for the organization of TV space. American television thrives, naturally, on American sports. Much has been written on the symbiosis of sports and sports broadcasting, on such matters as the "invention" of *Monday Night Football* as a hollow commercial expedient. In this view, sports broadcasting is seen as an essential fabrication, a genre basically alien to television which has been artfully naturalized in order to capture a particularly desirable market segment for an especially long duration at a usually difficult hour.

American television's most charismatic events are the World Series and the Super Bowl. These two spectacles generate titanic revenues and near unbelievable commercial prices per minute. They also constitute the main formal precedents for American television's centerpiece genre, the miniseries. These lavish "special events" are predicated on the explicitness of a relationship between seriality and finitude. TV is always signaling an interruption and an ending. Thus, we stumble upon the strategy for televised narrative. A miniseries is distinguished from a series on the basis of duration. Its value is, like a commercial's, the product of its compaction. In consequence, the short form is privileged, the game taking precedence over the season. The most valued game, however, or the most status-laden narrative, is expanded to replicate the entirety of its larger setting, to offer infinity in an afternoon.

American sports are structured around increment. Baseball and football stand out for the extremely episodic character of their play. The affinity between commercial television and a form predicated on interruption is straightforward: the success of broadcast sports is a tribute to this relationship. But, beyond this mechanical fit, sports is important because its armature is perhaps the principal means for television's lexical self-invention. To say that sports is structured like television is both profoundly true and profoundly insufficient. Sports, rather, is television *in excelsis,* its moment of greatest transparency.

The final game of the 1985 World Series will serve as an example. Like any sports broadcast, its major "meaning" lies in its efforts at the conversion of simultaneity into simulation. Game seven of this year's series was a total blowout, its outcome (and that of the series itself) only briefly at issue. This had the effect of throwing special importance on the mechanism of broadcasting, the game itself being relatively free of "normal" sports tensions. Since this was the case, there was a stronger-than-average focus on the primal act of the modern sports broadcaster, the production (which is to say, the mechanical reproduction) of new bits, the deliberated invention of moments. The technical routines for this invention include a number of possibilities from a burgeoning palette, including freeze-frames, instant replays, slow motion, and the introduction of replays taped from previously unbroadcast angles.

The tests applied to invoke these modalities are either aesthetic (a beautiful catch) or juridical. Sports offers a structure (and this is particularly true of the favored American sports) in which "expert" opinion is crucial to the outcome of events. The 1985 World Series was typical. A disputed call in game six (which went against the team that ultimately lost) was repetitively invoked as the crucial turning point in the "history" of the series. Clearly, the network which conveys the series is neutral in relation to any outcome vis-à-vis the individual teams (even if it, and advertisers, do have some stake in the "excitement" generated by a particular game). However, it's clear that ABC had a crucial interest in the duration of the series, both economic (more games, more high-priced commercials) and formal (the field is controlled in terms of routines of extent). This interest established a peculiar condition. As repeated replays of the nettlesome tag revealed, the official had miscalled the play—the man was safe at first. However, the "correct" call was one which would have imperiled the seventh episode of the series—not a desirable outcome.

The broadcast "dealt" with this apparent conflict by placing the call into the great clanking chain of simulation. As the image of the erroneous call is rebroadcast, slowed down, distorted, over and over again, it is drilled into the normal structure of succession. It ceases to be exceptional and recedes into routine. Television's domination of events is always achieved by this thrust to absolute parity. There's no qualitative difference, finally, between the "live" appearance of the baseball player in the game, the instant rebroadcast of his hit or catch, the delayed rebroadcast on the evening news, or the same baseball player's performance in the razor blade commercial which is interpolated at every point in this succession of images. Indeed, it scarcely matters when you turn on the set: the crucial event will certainly recur. The "moment" is constantly relocated by anticipation and recollection. Thus freed for migration, it becomes available to the profligacy of meanings ordered by eternal rejuxtapositioning.

There's a current commercial (one of a category of commercials) that makes the special position of the simulated especially explicit. In advertising the ability of a Canon camera to record life's special moments (in this case the action of a hockey match), the moving image of the skaters is periodically interrupted by freeze-frames, each of which holds, for a moment, some high point of the play. As the action is stopped, one hears the sound of the camera's shutter release, signifying capture, excerption. However, every time this little conceit is rendered and the play frozen, the word "simulation" appears on the screen. The reason is obvious: these images are on videotape, not thirty-five millimeter photographic stock. The "still" camera is incapable of autonomously manifesting the relationship between sequence and moment. Within this system, "simulation" achieves a higher order of depiction than mere recording. Thus does the simulated enter the realm of the ethical, through its superiority to reality. Falsehood is advertised.

The idiosyncrasy of "watching" television (rather than "seeing" it) turns out to be no idiosyncrasy at all. Nothing fashioned from the field of bits is finally any different from any other selection. The uncertainties are merely formal, not substantial. By such deprivations of meaning, the medium renders itself purely aesthetic. Here it touches the fullness of the surrealist ambition, that total suspension of the "critical intellect." Television's narcoleptic joys suffuse the stymied brain, which is left with no recourse other than to sway to its intoxicating rhythms. Pattern after pattern emerges as the synesthetic kaleidoscope twists and twists, endlessly recombining the filtered light of experience. Judgment without judgment, presence without presence, existence without existence, the corpse grows endlessly more exquisite.

Deride and Conquer

MARK CRISPIN MILLER

Nobody could watch it all—
and that's the point. There *is* a *choice*. *Your*
choice. American television and you.
—JIM DUFFY, President of
Communications, ABC, *in one of a series of
ads promoting network television* (1986)

Every evening, TV makes a promise, and seems at once to keep it.
TV's nightly promise is something like the grand old promise of
America herself. Night after night, TV recalls the promise that was
first extended through America's peerless landscape, with its great
mountains, cliffs, and canyons, tumbling falls, gigantic woodlands,
intricate bayous, lakes the size of seas, heavenly valleys, broiling
deserts, and a network of massive rivers hurrying in all directions,
through a north thick with trees, through interminable plains,
through multicolored tropics, through miles and miles of grass or
corn or granite, clay or wheat, until those rushing waters ultimately
cascade into the surrounding ocean. And throughout this astonishing land mass lie a multitude of huge and spreading cities, each
distinctive and yet each itself diverse, bustling with the restless

efforts of a population no less heroically varied than the land itself —white and black and brown and yellow, bespeaking the peculiarities of every creed and culture in the world, and yet all now living here, savoring the many freedoms that distinguish the United States so clearly from those other places where our citizens, or their ancestors, came from.

Here all enjoy the promise of that very opportunity, that very differentiation which they, and this great land mass, represent: the promise of unending *choice*. Here they are not ground down by party rule, church dictate, authoritarian tyranny, or the daily dangers of fanatical vendetta; and in this atmosphere of peace and plenty, they are free to work and play, have families, and contemplate, if not yet actually enjoy, the bounty of our unprecedented system.

Such is the promise of America; and TV, every evening, makes a similar sort of promise. Each night (and every day, all day), TV offers and provides us with an endless range of choices. Indeed, TV can be said to have itself incorporated the American dream of peaceful choice. This development was poignantly invoked by one of the hostages taken, in June of 1985, by the Shiite gunmen who hijacked TWA Flight 847. Back home after his captivity in Lebanon, Clint Suggs observed that "when you go to Beirut, you live war, you hear it, you smell it and it's real. It made me appreciate my freedom, the things we take for granted." In America, such freedom is available to any viewer: "When we sit here in our living room, with the sun setting, the baby sleeping, we can watch television, change channels. We have choices."

TV's promise of eternal choice arises from the whole tempting spectacle that is prime time: the full breasts, the gleaming cars, the glistening peaks of ice cream, mounds of candy, long clean highways, colossal frosted drinks, endless laughter, bands of dedicated friends, majestic houses, and cheeseburgers. The inexhaustible multitude of TV's images, sounds, and rhythms, like the dense catalog on every page of *TV Guide,* reassures us again and again that TV points to everything we might ever want or need. Nor is this promise merely implicit. The commercials, perhaps the quintessential components of TV's nonstop display, not only reconfirm our sense of privilege with millions of alluring images, but refer explicitly and often to this extensive "choice" of ours: AT&T offers us "The Right Choice," electricity, we are told, grants us "The Power of Choice," Wendy's reminds us that "There Is No Better Choice," McDonald's is "America's Choice," Coke is "The Real Choice," "In copiers, the choice is Canon," Taster's Choice is "The Choice for Taste"—all such assurances, and the delicious images that bolster them, combining to enhance even further TV's rich, ongoing paean to its own unimaginable abundances. And yet, consider carefully just one of those innumerable commercials that seem to celebrate "choice."

A white van parks on a hot beach crowded with young people. Unnoticed by these joggers and sunbathers, the driver jumps from the front seat and quickly hoists himself inside the van's rear compartment—a complete broadcasting facility. Seated at the console, with a sly look on his boyish face, he puts on a pair of headphones and flips a switch. Two white speakers rise out of the van's roof. He then picks up a cold bottle of Pepsi-Cola, tilts it toward the microphone before him, and opens it. The enticing *pop* and *whoosh* reverberate across the beach. A young woman, lying as if unconscious on a beach chair, suddenly comes to, turning her face automatically toward the speakers. The hubbub starts to die down.

Grinning now, the driver pours the Pepsi into a tall Styrofoam cup, so that everyone can hear the plash, the fizz, the wet ascending arpeggio of liquid decanted from a bottle. Inside the van, the full cup sighs and sparkles at the microphone. Outside, the air is filled with the dense crackle of carbonation. Intrigued by the sound, a dog—with a white kite draped raffishly across its head—looks to its right, toward the speakers. Intrigued, a young man shifts his gaze in exactly the same way, taking off his glasses as he does so.

Now the driver leans toward his microphone and drinks the Pepsi noisily. At the sound of his parched gulping, the crowd falls completely still. One girl reflexively smacks her lips. His cup emptied, the driver sits back and delivers a long, convincing "aaaaaaahhh!"

The crowd snaps out of its collective daze. There is an atmosphere of stampede. Now ringed by customers, the driver stands behind his van, its rear doors opened wide, revealing a solid wall of fresh six-packs, each bearing the familiar Pepsi logo. He puts on a Pepsi

vendor's cap and chirps, "Okay! Who's first?" Each customer immediately raises one arm high, and all clamor for a Pepsi, as the
camera zooms far back to show that the driver's victory is total. All
those beach-goers have suddenly converged on the white van like
houseflies descending on a fallen Popsicle. Except for that tight
throng of consumers in the distance, the beach is a wide wasteland
of deserted towels. In this depopulated space, a single figure wanders, the only one who has not (yet) succumbed to Pepsi—a man
equipped with a metal detector, presumably searching for loose
change, and so protected, by his earphones, from the driver's irresistible sound effects. Finally, there is this signature, printed over
the final image and solemnly intoned by Martin Sheen: "Pepsi. The
Choice of a New Generation."

Thus, this ad leaves us with the same vague conviction that all
advertising, and TV in general, continually reconfirm: that we are
bold, experienced, fully self-aware, and therefore able to pick out
what's best from the enormous range of new sensations now available. Like most ads, then, this one seems to salute its viewers for
their powers of discrimination, their advanced ability to choose; and
yet, like most ads, this one contradicts its own celebration of
"choice" by making choice itself seem inconceivable.

Within the little beach universe devised for Pepsico by BBDO,
"choice" is nothing but a quaint illusion. The members of this "new
generation" succumb at once to the driver's expert Pavlovian technique, like so many rats responding to any systematic stimulus.
This easy mass surrender is no "choice," nor are these Pepsi drinkers
capable of exercising "choice," since they are the mere tanned par-
ticles of a summer mob—transient, pretty, easygoing and interchangeable. To belong to such a "generation" is not to derive one's
own identity from that multitude of peers, but to give up all identity, to dissolve into a single reactive mass, and become a thing
lightweight and indefinite, like so much flotsam. In such a primal
group, dog and man are indeed equals, the dog trying, just like a
man, to beat the heat by covering its head, the man removing his
glasses, as if to be more like a dog, the two of them responding
identically to the sound of Pepsi streaming from a bottle.

In place of those capacities that might distinguish man from dog,
here it is merely Pepsi that fills up every heart and mind, just as it

fills that Styrofoam cup. No one thus saturated could make choices. Although not, it seems, as malleable as his customers, the driver himself is no less driven by Pepsi, blitzing his territory on behalf of himself and the company combined. And even the sole survivor of the pitch, temporarily deaf to those delicious noises, escapes only by cutting himself off. His solitary project, moreover, does not really distinguish him from all the rest, since there is apparently nothing he can do, having scrounged those dimes and pennies from the sand, but spend his income on a Pepsi.

So it cannot matter, in this beach universe, that there is no one capable of choosing, because there isn't anything to choose. Here there is nothing but Pepsi, and the mass compulsion to absorb it. As soon as the sound of Pepsi fills the air, all the pleasures of the afternoon evaporate, so that this full beach, with its sunny fraternizing, its soporific heat, its quiet surf returning and returning, becomes, in an instant, nothing more than a sandy area where you crave a certain beverage. Despite the ad's salute to "choice," what triumphs over all the free and various possibilities of that summer day is an eternal monad: Pepsi, whose taste, sound, and logo you will always recognize, and always "choose," whether you want to or not.

It is not "choice," then, that this ad is celebrating, but the total negation of choice and choices. Indeed, the product itself is finally incidental to the pitch. The ad does not so much extol Pepsi per se as recommend it by implying that a lot of people have been fooled into buying it. In other words, the point of this successful bit of advertising is that Pepsi has been advertised successfully. The ad's hero is himself an adman, a fictitious downscale version of the dozens of professionals who collaborated to produce him. He, like them, moves fast, works too hard (there are faint dark circles under his eyes), and gets his kicks by manipulating others en masse for the sake of a corporate entity. It is his power—the power of advertising—that is the subject of this powerful advertisement, whose crucial image reveals the driver surrounded by his sudden customers, who face him eagerly, each raising one arm high, as if to hail the salesman who has so skillfully distracted them.

This ad, in short, is perfectly self-referential; and that self-reflection serves to immunize the ad against the sort of easy charges often leveled against advertising. This commercial cannot, for example, be said to tell a lie, since it works precisely by acknowledging the truth about itself: it is a clever ad meant to sell Pepsi, which people buy because it's advertised so cleverly. It would be equally pointless to complain that this ad manipulates its viewers, since the ad wittily exults in its own process of manipulation. To object to the ad at all, in fact, is to sound priggish, because the ad not only admits everything, but also seems to take itself so lightly, offering up its mininarrative of mass capitulation in a spirit of sophisticated humor, as if to say, "Sure, this is what we do. Funny, huh?"

In the purity of its self-reference, this ad is entirely modern. Before the eighties, an ad for Pepsi, or for some comparable item, would have worked differently—by enticing its viewers toward a paradise radiating from the product, thereby offering an illusory escape from the market and its unrelenting pressures. In such an ad, the Pepsi would (presumably) admit its drinker to some pastoral retreat, which would not then—like that beach—lose all of its delightfulness to the product, but would retain its otherworldly charms. In this way, advertising, until fairly recently, proffered some sort of transcendence over the world of work, trying to conceal the hard economic character of its suasive project with various "humane" appeals—to family feeling, hunger, romantic fantasy, patriotism, envy, fear of ostracism, the urge to travel, and dozens of other "noncommercial" longings and anxieties. Of course, there are ads out now that attempt to make this dated offer, but nowhere near as often, or as convincingly, as the advertising of the past. Like this Pepsi commercial, more and more of today's mass advertisements offer no alternative to or respite from the marketplace but the marketplace itself, which (in the world as advertising represents it) appears at last to have permeated every one of the erstwhile havens in its midst. Now products are presented as desirable not because they offer to release you from the daily grind, but because they'll pull you under, take you in.

As advertising has become more self-referential, it has also become harder to distinguish from the various other features of our media culture. This coalescence has resulted in part from the metic-

ulous efforts of the advertising industry, whose aim is to have the
ads each look like an appealing aspect of what they once seemed to
deface or interrupt. In the world of print, this tendency toward
"nonadvertising advertising" (as it has been termed within the industry) has resulted, for example, in the "advertorial," a magazine
ad disguised as editorial content, and in the "magalogue," a direct-
mail catalog as slick and startling in its graphics as any fashion
magazine. The standard items of print advertising reflect the same
aesthetic pretension, the same widespread effort to make advertising
seem the primary and most attractive feature of contemporary journalism. According to one adman, the major advertisers in today's
magazines "are making great impressions on intelligent audiences
that find the ads a bonus—not an intrusion."

But in this society, TV is the main attraction; and so it is on TV
that advertisers strive most inventively, and at the greatest cost, to
merge their messages with the ostensible "nonadvertising." The
agencies, as one executive at Foote, Cone and Belding puts it, "have
a much greater concern to get the viewer to like the advertising."
The real object of this "concern," to put it in the boyish parlance of
the industry, is to prevent the viewer from "zapping," or skipping
past, the commercials, an evasive action now made possible by the
VCR; and those without VCRs can also zap the ads, by turning
down the volume with remote control devices. Aspiring to zap-
proof status, "commercials," says the executive, "are becoming
more like entertaining films," adorned with stunning cinematic
gimmicks. Timex, for instance, entered the 1984 Christmas season
with a two-minute commercial, broadcast in prime time. "Although its ad is all sell," reported the *Wall Street Journal,* "Timex
believes viewers will stay tuned for the special effects that show
giant watches doubling as beach chairs and racketball courts." Alternately, the advertiser will append his message to, or embed it in,
a long, diversionary bit of pseudoprogramming. Such tactics are
especially prevalent on cable TV. Corporations are now using cable
as "a sort of laboratory where they can experiment with long commercials, creative techniques, and 'infomercials,' which are a blend
of advertising and practical advice." If such "experiments" prove
satisfactory to their sponsors, the ads on network TV will rely more
and more on the sort of camouflage now widespread on cable: "The

General Foods subsidiary of Philip Morris shoehorns its ads in the middle of two-minute recipe spots, Campbell Soup Co. recently produced a music video for teens about exercise and nutrition, and Procter & Gamble is running Crest toothpaste infomercials on Nickelodeon, a children's cable channel."

Such efforts are not new. Advertisers have long sought to disguise their messages as news items or feature stories. The current coalescence is significant not because of its novelty, but because such practices have come to represent the ideal type of TV advertising; and this development cannot be wholly explained by pointing to the admen's various ploys. For the conscious tactics of advertisers, however sly, finally matter less than the objective process that has made them possible. In order for TV's ads to seem "a bonus—not an intrusion," the rest of television first had to change in many subtle ways, imperceptibly taking on the quality of the commercials, just as the commercials have had to begin looking "more like entertaining films." This mutual approximation works to the distinct advantage of the advertisers, whose messages are today no longer overshadowed, contradicted, or otherwise threatened by programming that is too noticeably different from the ads.

Two pieces of advertising news, one from TV's early days and one quite recent, illuminate this shift. In 1955, Philip Morris gave up its sponsorship of *I Love Lucy,* then TV's top-rated show, in part because the company's sales had dropped steeply despite the show's popularity. "There are those at PM and its agency (Biow-Biern-Togo) who subscribe to the idea," *Tide* magazine reported, "that an extremely good show might never sell products. Reason: you tend to talk about the program during the commercials." Others at Philip Morris felt that this painful rift between the show and the commercials ought to have been ameliorated by the commercials themselves: "Certainly, little was done [by the agency] to merchandise Philip Morris with Lucy, as Chesterfield, for example, does with Jack Webb and Perry Como."

There are other such stories from the fifties, of programming not bland enough to offset the intermittent sales pitch, stories that suggest a common wisdom, back then, on the need to maintain, for profit's sake, a certain vacuity throughout TV. Some of TV's insiders have confirmed that this imperative did not lose its force after the fifties. "Program makers," wrote an ABC executive in 1976, must "attract mass audiences" without "too deeply moving them emotionally," since such disturbance "will interfere with their ability to receive, recall, and respond to the commercial message. This programming reality is the unwritten, unspoken *Gemeinschaft* of all professional members of the television fraternity." And Todd Gitlin, describing the TV industry of the early 1980s, reports that the TV writers' "product is designed to go down easy. It has to be compatible with commercials. Advertising executives like to say that television shows are the meat in a commercial sandwich."

Whereas *I Love Lucy* was evidently too exciting to complement the ads, some of the latest research now suggests that when the viewer is happily absorbed in some enthralling program, he or she will enjoy the commercials equally, and even trust them all the more. "Television viewers," a consulting outfit claimed to have discovered in 1984, "generally find commercials more memorable, likable, credible, and persuasive when placed in programs they find involving [*sic*]." In order to arrive at this conclusion, its authors first developed a "Program Impact Index," which "measures the degree of intellectual and emotional stimulation a program provides its viewers." Their subsequent researches led them to conclude that the "commercial message" is more memorable, more believable, and more successful when the program that contains it seems especially engrossing.

These recent findings, conveyed with all the drabness of contemporary social science, seem to contradict, even disprove, the casual intuitions of those unnamed executives at Philip Morris. If, however, we regard both TV and its audience as changeable and increasingly commingled, we can recognize the truth of both those intuitions and these findings. For as TV has undergone vast changes since 1955, so has its audience changed with it, and because of it.

It is not enough to conclude, however accurately, that a rousing TV show will always complement its advertising, because that conclusion fails to take into account the historical character of the relationship. What seemed exciting to TV's audience in 1955 differs immeasurably from what might seem "involving" to us nowadays —a subtle shift in taste that has had everything to do with the gradual triumph of advertising, which today is no longer despised as it was in the fifties. Much faster and more gorgeous than ever, the commercials now seem not to interrupt, abrasively, a given TV narrative, but rather to set the pace for it. The experience of televisual "excitement," in fact, has been closely linked in the last decade to advertising's rise in status and its advances in technique. In other words, TV's managers, through their continuing efforts to create a televisual atmosphere hospitable to the commercials, have surely succeeded, after all these years, in altering their public's expectations: *I Love Lucy,* if it were made today, would seem continuous with its ads, and would therefore probably pay off in ways that would have satisfied those executives at Philip Morris.

Whenever the networks' representatives, or their hired consultants, or the advertising experts tell us what "the people" want or like, they assume that they themselves have had no hand in forming, or deforming, those desires. And yet we must confront the possibility that commercial TV has itself created its appropriate audience. As ads and shows continue to converge, our unvoiced collective standards of "intellectual and emotional stimulation" are also changing, which is to say that those vague standards are descending; and this descent makes any reversal or renewal more and more unlikely. "To the bulk of the audience," Grant Tinker recently worried aloud, "bad programming may not be a problem." Thus, when we speak about the decline of TV's programming as inextricable from the ascent of TV's ads, we have necessarily raised the possibility of a concomitant stupefaction of the American audience—a mass regression that is continuous with TV's advanced development as an advertising medium. As Tinker put it: "The audience has changed some—and not for the better. I don't know why. It has something to do with the maturing of the medium."

This uneasy statement offers us a dismal truth: TV has finally come into its own, and yet neither TV nor its audience has been improved by this "maturing of the medium." How, then, has TV "matured"? Certainly, it has fulfilled none of its documentary or dramatic possibilities, a failure that explains the character of TV's recent consummation. For in order to "bring you the world," whether through reportage or drama, TV would have to point beyond itself. Yet "the maturing of the medium" consists precisely in

TV's near-perfect inability to make any such outward gesture. TV tends now to bring us nothing but TV. Like the Pepsi ad, TV today purports to offer us a world of "choices," but refers only to itself.

The commercialization of TV has now reached a new level. Since the mid-fifties, TV's programs have sold consumption openly, insistently, and garishly. Commodities have been promoted through continuous mention, constant presentation in the foreground or as background, and even through the very look of TV's personnel— the attractive "guest" and "host," the game show MC and his slim manikins, the stars and starlets of the soaps, the animated warriors, all of whom have not only helped to push goods outright, but who have themselves been compact and implicit ads for everything it takes to look almost as telegenic as they do: skin cream, sun block, toothpaste, shaving cream, a blow dryer, dandruff shampoo, hair conditioner, hair dye (if not a wig), tweezers, scissors, blushers, mascara, lipstick (if not plastic surgery), lip balm, exercise equipment, aerobics classes, various diet plans, a new wardrobe, Woolite, eye drops, contact lenses, cold cream, and sleeping pills.

However, it is not just by envisioning a universe crammed with new products that TV now demonstrates its maturity. For TV has gone beyond the explicit celebration of commodities to the implicit reinforcement of that spectatorial posture which TV requires of us. Now it is not enough just to proffer an infinitude of goods; TV must also try to get its viewers to prefer the passive, hungry watching of those goods, must lead us to believe that our spectatorial inaction is the only sort of action possible. Appropriately, TV pursues this project through some automatic strategies of modern advertising.

First of all, TV now exalts TV spectatorship by preserving a hermetic vision that is uniformly televisual. Like advertising, which no longer tends to evoke realities at variance with the market, TV today shows almost nothing that might somehow clash with its own busy, monolithic style. This new stylistic near integrity is the product of a long process whereby TV has eliminated or subverted whichever of its older styles have threatened to impede the sale of goods; that is, styles that might once have encouraged some nontelevisual type of spectatorship. Despite the rampant commodity em-

phasis on TV since the mid-fifties, there were still several valuable
rifts in its surface, contrasts that could still enable a critical view of
TV's enterprise.

For instance, there was for years a stark contrast between the
naturalistic gray of TV's "public interest" programming (the news
and "educational television") and the bright, speedy images surrounding it—a contrast that sustained, however vaguely, the recognition of a world beyond the ads and game shows. That difference
is gone now that the news has been turned into a mere extension of
prime time, relying on the same techniques and rhetoric that define
the ads. Similarly, there was once a visible distinction, on TV,
between the televisual and the cinematic, sustained by the frequent
broadcast of "old movies," each a grandiose reminder of the theater,
of "the stars," of narrative—possibilities quite alien to the process
of network TV, which has since obliterated the distinction. Now
The Late Night Movie will turn out to be a rerun of *Barney Miller,*
and the first broadcast of the latest telefilm is called "A World
Premiere."

Through such gradual exclusions, TV has almost purified itself,
aspiring to a spectacle that can remind us of no prior or extrinsic
vision. As a result, the full-time viewer has become more likely to
accept whatever TV sells, since that selling process seems to be the
only process in existence. Yet it would be wrong to argue that TV
treats its audience like a mass of wide-eyed bumpkins, approaching
them as easy marks; for such a claim would underestimate the
subtlety of TV's self-promotion. TV does not solicit our rapt ab-
sorption or hearty agreement, but—like the ads that subsidize it—
actually flatters us for the very boredom and distrust which it inspires in us. TV solicits each viewer's allegiance by reflecting back
his/her own automatic skepticism toward TV. Thus, TV protects
itself from criticism or rejection by incorporating our very animus
against the spectacle into the spectacle itself.

Like the Pepsi ad, with its cool and knowing tone, TV is
pervasively ironic, forever flattering the viewer with a sense of his/
her own enlightenment. Even at its most self-important, TV is also
charged with this seductive irony. On the news, for instance, the

anchorman or correspondent is often simultaneously pompous and smirky, as if to let us know that he, like us, cannot be taken in. When covering politicians or world leaders, newsmen like Chris Wallace, David Brinkley, Harry Reasoner, Roger Mudd, and Sam Donaldson seem to jeer at the very news they report, evincing an iconoclastic savvy that makes them seem like dissidents despite their ever-readiness to fall in line. The object of the telejournalistic smirk is usually an easy target like "Congress" or "the Democrats," or a foreign leader backed by the Soviets, or an allied dictator who is about to lose his grip. Seldom does the newsman raise a serious question about the policies or values of the multinationals, the CIA, the State Department, or the president. Rather, the TV news tends to "raise doubts" about the administration by playing up the PR problems of its members (PR problems which the TV news thereby creates): Can David Stockman be muzzled? Can Pat Buchanan get along with Donald Regan? Can George Bush alter the perception that he doesn't know what he's saying? Through such trivialities, the TV news actually conceals what goes on at the top and in the world, enhancing its own authority while preserving the authority of those in power, their ideology, their institutions.

Nevertheless, the telejournalists' subversive air can often seem like the exertion of a mighty democratic force. Certainly, TV's newsmen like to think that a jaundiced view is somehow expressive of a populist sympathy with all the rest of us; and, of course, if we glance back through TV's history since the sixties, we will recall a number of thrilling confrontations between some potentate and a reporter bold enough to question him: Frank Reynolds putting it to Richard Nixon, Dan Rather talking back to Richard Nixon, Sam Donaldson hectoring Jimmy Carter or Ronald Reagan. Each time Ted Koppel sits before someone like Ferdinand Marcos, each time Mike Wallace interrogates some well-dressed hireling whose desk cannot protect him from that cool scrutiny, we sense a moment of modern heroism, as the newsman, with his level gaze and no-nonsense queries, seems about to topple one more bad authority for the sake of a vast, diverse, and righteous public—or republic, for there is something in this routine televisual agon that seems quintessentially American. We are, the TV news seems always to be telling us, a young and truth-loving nation, founded upon the vigorous rejection of the old European priests and kings, and still distrustful of all pompous father figures; and so those boyish skeptics who face down the aging crook or tyrant thereby act out a venerable ideal of American innocence.

All such moments dramatize a filial animus against the corrupt and presumptuous father. This family agon has become the definitive subtext of the TV news, now that the anchorman has evolved into a lad. Today's anchorman, in other words, is no longer a stolid papa, like Howard K. Smith, John Chancellor, or "Uncle Walter" Cronkite, but a boy forever young and grave, like Peter Pan after a few years of business school. The earnest Brokaw, the bushy-headed Koppel, Rather in his collegiate sweater, look like only slightly weathered members of some student council, making those whom they interrogate—the generals, CEO's, and heads of state—seem automatically as shifty and decrepit as each probing telejournalist seems young and good.

However trivial his questions, then, the newsman, just by virtue of his looks and placement, always comes across as the heroic representative of a rising generation. Once we step back and look at TV whole, however, the newsman's stance seems less impressive. As we shall see, the assault on the bad father figure goes on and on throughout TV today, not out of any conscious moral program, but as a consequence of TV's self-fulfillment. Like the disappearance of TV's documentary gray, or TV's vestiges of cinema, the now routine subversion of the father is an expression of TV's impending unity. Seemingly progressive, the televisual animus against the Dad of old is, in fact, a device that works not to enlighten but to paralyze us. But before we speculate on the effects of TV's antipatriarchalism, we must first trace its rise; for early on, TV was not yet wholly turned against the father, but was revealingly divided into two contradictory biases. We can best begin to grasp the closure of this critical division by recounting the long decline of Dad throughout the history of the sitcom.

At first, Dad seemed to reign supreme in sitcom country—or at least in its better neighborhoods. On the bulk of those shows set in the suburbs, Dad's authority around the house appeared to be the whole point of the spectacle. It was this implied paternalism that made most of those "comedies" so unamusing: Dad's status was, back then, no laughing matter. Despite their laugh tracks and bouncy themes, the real spirit of those shows was expressed in their daunting titles: *Make Room for Daddy* and *Father Knows Best* were simple threats. And those shows featuring Dad's wife or kids were also tellingly named, with half titles that took Dad's point of view, expressing his permanent exasperation at the foibles of his underlings: *Leave It to Beaver* (to Screw Things Up), *My Little Margie* (Needs a Punch in the Mouth), and *I Love Lucy* (in Spite of Everything).

Although the early sitcoms provided, now and then, a memorable moment of wild farce (usually the work of Jackie Gleason or Lucille Ball), they were, it seems, calculated to induce not laughter but anxiety. As the apparent ruler of the world, Dad, pushed around by no one, somehow deflated all of his inferiors—and all were his inferiors. Since we almost never saw him working, we had no sense that there was any class above his own; and he had no competition in the class below him. On those old sitcoms set among the proles, the husband and provider like Riley or Ralph Kramden wasn't competent enough to lord it over anyone, but was himself, in fact, the eternal jerk, a hapless fatso doomed to live in squalor, always trying to rise above it, always ending up worse off, not only just as poor but "in the doghouse" too. Every one of his efforts at transcendence was necessarily ill advised, earning a weary put-down by "the wife," who, ever yearning for new appliances but thoroughly convinced of her husband's hopeless impotence, could do nothing but look disgusted, arms akimbo.

In his well-appointed suburban home, on the other hand, Dad was subject to no such snideness, but was himself the ironic judge of all below him. He kept his underlings in line by setting an impossible example of self-possession, probity, and sound judgment —the virtues of small business. While the TV lawmen of the West enforced the peace with ropes and guns, Dad policed his indoor territory far less obtrusively, armed only with his pipe and elbow patches. And yet, for all the homeliness of Dad's appearance, his authority was far more awesome than that of any quick-shooting sheriff. Confronted with some hint of independence, Dad didn't have to raise a fist, but could restore conformity just by manifesting his supreme Dadhood: the mild frown of disappointment, the bland

and chilling summons to "a little talk." These methods were un-
failing, and oddly terrifying, primarily directed against Dad's son,
who was a permanent victim, like the sitcom prole. As we watched
in dread, we always knew that young Ricky, Rusty, Bud, or Wally
was going to try somehow to prove himself, to accomplish something on his own, and that the effort would backfire disastrously,
leaving the poor schmuck shamed and lectured, "taught a lesson,"
by his serene and ever watchful Dad.

Although the son was Dad's main victim, the early sitcom also
held Dad's other underlings in place. Mrs. Dad, for instance, was
always trim, erect, and loyal, like a well-bred whippet; but even
she sometimes made trouble, and had to be reminded how to roll
over and play dead. And while Dad's daughter was usually a "good
girl," answering when her Daddy called for his "princess" or his
"kitten," sometimes she too got a little fractious, sprinting upstairs
to yelp into her tidy pillow, until Dad snapped her out of it with a
lopsided grin and a little Understanding.

Today, of course, that old Dad-centered universe has become the
biggest and easiest joke on television. Yesterday's paternalistic vision is now a standard object of burlesque on the specials, on *Saturday Night Live,* in the ads, and on the current sitcoms. Mere
mention of "the Beaver" is enough to inspire a gale of aggressive
laughter, expressing the assumption that "we" today are enlightened well past the point of the naive fifties—the days when
everyone (we think) could still adhere to the belief that Dad's in his
haven, all's right with the world. This assumption of superior
worldliness, this ironic view of those authoritarian fantasies, not
only deprecates those dated TV programs, but also belittles the
whole period in which they were produced. It was "a simple time"
(the laughter implies), whereas today, of course, things are complex, and we all know better.

In simply laughing off the early sitcoms, however, we overlook
their true perniciousness, as well as their implicit critical potential.
First of all, the early sitcoms did not serve to bolster any extant
paternal authority within the middle class, but helped to conceal
the fact that by the fifties such authority had all but vanished. Like
the TV Westerns of the fifties, like many contemporary movies, and
like many of the ads (both print and televisual) intended for the

postwar man of the house, these shows negated the actual and increasing powerlessness of white-collar males with images of paternal strength and manly individualism. Yet by the time those first sitcoms were produced, the world of small business had long since been swallowed up, or superseded, by what C. Wright Mills called "the managerial demiurge," and so the virtues of small business, personified by Robert Young's Dad, were in fact passé. It was already necessary then (as it still is) to get by on "personality" rather than through diligence and thrift, to negotiate with charm and savvy the subtle crosscurrents of an immense and impersonal bureaucracy. Dad, well known to his friends and neighbors, his milkman and his mailman, the high school principal and the policeman on the corner, was therefore utterly unlike the real white-collar workers in his audience. And Dad's real counterparts were no less insignificant around the house, now that the wife and kids were out shopping or bopping with their friends, taking their guidance not so much from father (who in real life could rarely be at home) as from the newspapers, the magazines, the movies, other wives and/ or kids—and (more and more) from television, which was, in fact, a force inimical to fatherly authority despite its early, transitory moment of paternalism.

While the flattering images on those old shows concealed the truth about the father's plight, they also contradicted the prevailing bureaucratic trend with an inadvertent and unconscious protest. Dad did not control his little world, but only haunted it, as a specter from the early days of capitalism (as well as a vestige of the postwar propaganda meant to get the American woman out of the factory and back into the kitchen). Dad's impulses were opposed to the consumerist imperatives that now began to overrun our culture. First of all, he kept his precious family in one piece, an inviolate community despite the lures and pressures of the circumventing market. More importantly, he stood for prudence, thrift, sobriety, self-discipline, pennies saved and joys deferred, exemplifying the old ideal of self-denial that had sustained Our Way of Life since the seventeenth century and that now threatened to impede it in the twentieth. That Puritan ethos was a boon as long as workers only had to earn and try to save, laboring to produce commodities for an upper class of buyers. Since World War I, however, the market had

demanded that those same workers also buy and buy, and so advertisers started to malign the ascetic attitude, requiring those lean
saints to gorge themselves, to give up their grim old abstinence in
favor of our grim new self-indulgence. (Hedonism has never been a
possibility within this system.) The ad agencies campaigned, in
short, to turn the uptight Pa into an open maw; and they succeeded,
which explains why Dad was an anomaly throughout his reign, and
why he was deposed so soon.

If, therefore, we take another, truly critical look at those old
shows, we can now see that their intention was absurd: to represent
a sturdy bourgeois Dad between the ads for Wheaties, Skippy,
Bosco, Lucky Strikes, Good'n'Plenty, Jell-O, Winstons, and a
thousand other goodies that aroused the very tots and teens whom
Dad was meant to scare into submission. Thus, TV had most of its
audience in a double bind. It wooed the wife and kids, and generally
stirred its viewers' infantile desires, with all sorts of bright, delicious images; and yet it contravened its own allurements by giving
lots of air time to the Great White Father, who seemed to stand
against the universal splurging that TV constantly promoted.

Clearly, something had to give, and it would soon be Dad, the
personification of an outmoded ideology and now an obvious drag
on consumption. However, if we look at Dad more closely, we
begin to notice that his fictitious power, even in its heyday, had
already begun to slip in every case. It was not just the fat and pop-
eyed Ralph Kramden, ineffectually roaring in his dingy walk-up,
who had lost control, nor only the timid Riley, humiliated every
week by some "revoltin' development" of his own devising, nor only
Mr. Gillis, Dobie's old man, rasping out sarcasms from his store-
front and always wearing an apron. While these lower-class father
figures were overtly impotent, their more successful brothers were,
although a lot more dignified, also the occupants of a precarious
status. A few of the less impoverished Dads were already broad jokes
—Ricky Ricardo, screaming in bad English, and Vern Albright,
Margie's shrill and fruity Dad. But even those most even-tempered
fathers, those men as bland and decorous as manikins at Brooks
Brothers—the men played all but interchangeably by Carl Betz,
John Forsythe, Robert Young, and Hugh Beaumont—were so respectable, their living rooms and neighborhoods so calm and quiet,

their domestic "problems" so slight and easy to resolve, that their rule begins to seem preposterous, even a little eerie, as we perceive that each of them is not the lord and master of his various dependents, but surrounded by them, held captive in his sepulchral home. And, indeed, these Dads too were often "taught a lesson," although they tended not to be disgraced by such enlightenment.

In any case, that paternalistic moment soon passed, as the significance of the demographics became obvious. Long before the rise of Norman Lear, TV began to champion Dad's wife and kids on programs now contrived to please the actual wives and kids who watched the ads. In flattering its most dedicated customers, the sitcom stuck Dad well off in the background so that he might not cast his shadow over TV's dazzling window show. By the mid-sixties, the titanic burgher of the early years was now remarkably reduced, whether a pleasant nullity, like the Dads of Patty Duke and Dennis the Menace, or a mere straight man, incredulous and dim, like Samantha's husband on *Bewitched,* or the boyfriend on *That Girl,* or Larry Hagman, then colorless on *I Dream of Jeannie.* Of course, there were exceptions, like the tense and hostile Rob Petrie played by Dick Van Dyke, by far the most resentful of all TV Dads, forever struggling to regain his vanished potency by undercutting his pathetic wife Laura, who was not yet Mary Tyler Moore. Whenever Laura tried to prove herself, to accomplish something on her own, like trying her hand at writing children's books, or rediscovering her talents as a dancer, the effort would backfire disastrously, leaving her depressed and him meanly contented.

The sixties generally revealed that Dad's prerogatives were threatened—not by any rise in real authority among women, but by the rising influence of TV and its corporate advertisers. In the culture of consumption, a man's home is not his castle but a temporary storage unit for whatever togs, foods, and gadgets the corporations have lately packaged or repackaged. Mom was clearly the foreman of this unit, the supervisor of most domestic purchases, and so, although still housebound, still subservient, still obediently pretty, she now tended to appear as far more powerful than her predecessors. Jeannie was presented as a genie, Samantha as a witch, and yet it was not the supernatural realm that actually empowered these characters, but the commercial promise of household technologies. These figures were mere comedic extensions of the knowing housewife displayed in a million ads—the woman made magically adept by Brillo and Bab-O, vacuum cleaners and carpet sweepers, room fresheners and TV dinners, and who was thereby made to seem far superior to the very husband whom she still served and on whom she still depended.

The new sitcom was an expression of this contradiction, and yet concealed it under lots of desperate laughs. Dad, who in the fifties usually answered to no one, was now presented as an underling, like Jeannie's "master," an Army major pushed around by senior officers, or Samantha's husband, an account executive in an ad agency, or Rob Petrie, a TV writer forever struggling to placate his celebrity boss. Blatantly cowed by those above him in the corporation, Dad now relied on Mom's advanced consumeristic acumen and/or was outwitted and upstaged by his precocious children, who were also his betters by virtue of their expertise as shoppers. In this transitional period, the only Dad who did not come across as a browbeaten hysteric was the wooden Fred MacMurray on *My Three Sons*, and his semidignity was possible only because his TV family was a bizarre, all-male preserve, his "sons" anachronistically subdued, his "wife" no prim and clever female but a dour old man wearing bangs and an apron.

Between Dad's wife and bosses, there was always an implicit understanding: both they and she were eager to see Dad swallow his yearnings and strive for another raise. This complicity carried over into the commercials, wherein the wife, sharing a little secret with the advertiser, would tip a wink, when hubby wasn't looking, into the camera, thereby demonstrating that her heart belonged to Procter & Gamble, General Mills, Johnson & Johnson, and other such suitors. Here was the beginning of TV's pseudofeminism, which now pervades prime time. The series and the telefilms today are invariably calculated to stroke the female viewers in some way, presenting a heroine who is untrammeled, plucky, confident, "assertive," always in the right, and therefore not to be suppressed by any of the lecherous, pig-eyed males who keep trying to pick her up, slobber on her, rape her, or who succeed in raping her. Thus, the female audience today is flattered with the same formulaic and dishonest fantasy that was used to calm male viewers thirty years ago: "You are more powerful than ever." Or, to invoke a more familiar reassurance: "You've come a long way, baby!"

If we compare this postsixties pseudofeminist exhortation with the fifties' pseudopatriarchalist fantasy, we must observe that women are now far more exquisitely oppressed than their fathers used to be—more oppressed by the very mechanism that keeps telling them they are liberated. Whereas the older fantasy was in part transcendent, sustaining a belief in manly independence from the system, the modern fantasy entails no tolerance at all for any of the traits or pursuits that were formerly considered feminine: TV discredits and detests the power to nurture, derides all household talents, represses the possibility of an ardent female sexuality, and otherwise continues to promote the multinationals' assault on individual capacity. What TV does to women in the very act of seeming to exalt them is to turn them into cool young men, energetic and sarcastic, running their own businesses, or working for the corporation, always wearing suits and carrying major credit cards. It is not women who emerge triumphant in this fantasy, but the very system that degrades and underpays them—women are defeminized, and yet, strangely enough, never free from the requirement that they remain impossibly good-looking at all times. On TV, women are free only to conduct themselves with the same aggressiveness that men must also use in order to keep making it; and it makes no difference—is, indeed, more disturbing for the fact— that these TV images of women are, as often as not, devised by women, who regard this fantasy as most progressive. "There are no woman doormats on this series," says Esther Shapiro in defense of *Dynasty*, which she coproduces. "The women are not victims. They can have the same villainy as the men."

In the early seventies, this development was nearing its fulfillment, just as Dad's demotion was complete, and now represented as a stroke of liberation. As usual, the lower-class father figure was presented as a joke, but now his subversion appeared politically correct. Archie Bunker was a butt, not because he was an overreaching loser, like Ralph Kramden, but because he was socially unenlightened—sexist, racist, militaristic, a nexus of reactionary attitudes that allowed his juniors and his viewers to deride him in good conscience. All TV's prole father figures have been thus depicted and subverted throughout the seventies and eighties. Although generally lovable, the raunchy Schneider on *One Day at a Time* is still at heart a sexist pig, given to swaggering, at which the cool Romano women always smirk demurely. Mel on *Alice* is another such male ignoramus, much bossier than Schneider, but no more with-it, giving the waitresses in his employ a good many opportunities to roll their eyes behind his back.

On the postsixties sitcom, however, it is not just the working-class father figure who is thus further deflated, but every would-be patriarch in every class. As we move beyond the level of janitors, short-order cooks, and factory workers, we find that the formula persists unchanged. Within TV's lower middle class, the father figure is an object of amused contempt, if not ill-concealed impatience. Sauntering amid the laid-back detectives on *Barney Miller,* Inspector Luger is a joke precisely because he would be fatherly: older than everyone else, he presumes to offer solace and advice, wears a fedora, holds all the wrong opinions, and so his overtures provoke the usual grimaces of exasperation from all his hipper juniors. And on a slightly higher economic level, Stanley Roper of *Three's Company* and *The Ropers* is another elder butt, cranky and salacious, and given to rash actions that forever reconfirm the damning judgment of his wife, his youthful tenants, and his audience.

The reflexive ridicule of lower-class father figures no longer implies the exaltation of the bourgeois Dad. TV now undercuts all Dads together, in order to unite the other characters in a fleeting and invidious solidarity. On *Soap,* both Dads, one a prole and the other a wealthy businessman, are fools—the one high-strung and goofy, the other pompous and dishonest, their various mistakes and crimes occasioning frequent eye rolling among their subordinates. The prole, however, is always a lovable incompetent, whereas the bourgeois is not even likable, but an ass so vain and selfish that—it is implied—his observers, both actual and fictitious, have a moral right, even an obligation, to despise him.

So it is with all the neo-Dads. Within each sitcom's middle-class milieu, anyone at all reminiscent of the early Dad—and there has always, until very recently, been at least one such scapegoat—becomes the object of the collective sneer. In the postsixties sitcom, there is usually some fastidious jerk, ramrod-straight and buttoned to the neck; and/or some nervous, middle-aged wimp who disapproves of all the "life" around him; and/or some pushy greaseball in outlandish clothes, who keeps trying to pick up all the women, or otherwise belittles them. Each of these butt types repeats, uncannily and in degraded form, some aspect of Dad's now defunct authority —his sense of propriety, his implied connection to the past, his (suppressed) masculinity, all of which recur as patently reactionary qualities. Thus, we have Clayton on *Benson,* Frank on *M*A*S*H,* Colonel Fielding on *Private Benjamin,* Les and Herb and Carlson on *WKRP in Cincinnati,* the boss in *9 to 5,* Dan Fielding on *Night Court,* and many others, regulars as well as supercilious-looking walk-ons. And outside the sitcom proper, the neo-Dad recurs endlessly as a major source of the comic relief, like Howard Hunter on *Hill Street Blues,* Craig on *St. Elsewhere,* Stanley Riverside on *Trapper John, M.D.,* and Higgins on *Magnum, P.I.*

Over the course of the sitcom's history, then, there has been an apparent reversal in the relationship between the master and his slaves. Each of these butts is a neo-Dad surrounded and subverted by his erstwhile inferiors—the wife, the kids, the colored—who now keep Dad in the same disgraced position that the Beaver or Bud Anderson once had to occupy: Dad is now the one whose every move results in his humiliation, Dad is the one who simply cannot meet the standard, which is now set by his previous victims, the sarcastic mass of women, children, employees. The patriarchal butt is nearly always childless, because these subjugated ironists stand for his children, jeering at the myth of his authority rather than upholding it. Although not as contemptuously treated as the outright butt, the Dad with children of his own is often still despised, albeit gently, undercut with tittering affection rather than with half-concealed hostility. Here we have Ted Knight, blustering adorably on *Too Close for Comfort,* or Dolph Sweet as the ever grumbling "Chief" on *Gimme a Break,* or Tony Randall as the gibbering neurotic on *Love, Sidney.*

These butts and Dads are laughable to the extent that they presume to act like fathers. The only father figures who are not ridiculous are those who know enough to downplay their status and thereby blend in with the kids. Such Dads cannot be subverted because there is nothing in them to subvert. Michael Gross on

Family Ties plays an exemplary cool Dad. Slim, glossy, affable, full of gentle wisecracks, this affluent ex-hippie, wearing earth tones and a tasteful beard, seems to be the child of his own children, who are as cynical as he is earnest in the sentimental moralism of "the sixties." Joel Higgins on *Silver Spoons* plays another Dad so boyish that he seems to be the son of his own son. A millionaire, he holds no job, and spends hours playing with elaborate toys.

The good Dad is nonauthoritative even when he isn't thin and blow-dried. The placid Conrad Bain on *Diff'rent Strokes,* while sometimes capable of a pompous lecturette on ethics, is basically as hip and frisky as his two black sons and white daughter, despite his age and status as a superrich patrician. Tom Bosley on *Happy Days* is another easy Dad, a seventies version of the fifties patriarch and therefore just as mild and insignificant as Dad once seemed crucial. Bosley looks like a homemade dumpling, or a nice bear in a cartoon, and therefore confronts us as the total modern opposite to the watchful hawk face of Robert Young. And then there is the cuddliest and most beloved of TV Dads: Bill Cosby, who, as Dr. Heathcliff Huxtable, lives in perfect peace, and in a perfect brownstone, with his big happy family, and never has to raise his hand or fist, but retains the absolute devotion of his wife and kids just by making lots of goofy faces.

TV, then, appears to have become enlightened. Whereas the early sitcom bummed us out with a gray authoritarian fantasy, today's TV comedy, so upbeat and iconoclastic, must represent a comic blow for freedom. Such, at least, is what the shows themselves would have us think. In the world according to Norman Lear and Susan Harris, the air is thick with liberal self-congratulation as the kids—both old and young, the black and yellow, brown and white—all blink and stare and roll their eyes in unison behind the back of some uptight neo-Dad, and every easy put-down touches off a noisy little riot of predictable applause. The mellow style of each successful neo-Dad implies the same rejection of the old paternal rule. Now the power appears to have been transferred downward and dispersed, according to some ideal program of egalitarian revolution. Our laughter at each butt, or with each cool new father, must therefore be the joyous laughter of emancipation from a tyranny that once required our stiff respect.

And yet power in the real world has not changed hands, but remains precisely in the same unseen and collective hands that have gripped it throughout this century. In turning against the early TV Dad, we merely turn against a superannuated figurehead, and only to the benefit of the very forces that invented him and that encourage us to keep on laughing at his memory. Once purified of Dad's stern image, TV was perfectly resolved to carry on the advertisers' long campaign for our absolute surrender, their effort to induce an incapacity far more profound than that of any bullied wife or son. Whereas Dad often had his little viewers feeling weak and childish, TV tempts all its viewers to remain as infants, with itself the electronic teat that gives us everything we need: "We do it all for you."

On TV, the serious father appears only in frightful caricature, as a "child abuser" or provincial brute. There seems to be no middle ground between such nightmarish aggression on the telefilms and the bantering inconsequence of the friendly sitcom fathers. Certainly, today's good Dad will sometimes have a big maudlin reconciliation scene with his son (although seldom with his daughter), hugging the boy with tearful fervor after some estrangement or misunderstanding, but this routine effusion is always represented as a sign of healthy weakness on Dad's part. He's casting off his usual masculine reserve and "getting in touch with his feelings." Even his moments of unrestrained affection, then, demonstrate that Dad is at his best when *giving in.* And this suggestion of a radical capitulation carries over into those commercials where Dad today appears in his true colors: Tom Bosley pitching Glad bags for Union Carbide, Conrad Bain selling Commodore computers, Joel Higgins singing the praises of Prudential-Bache, and Bill Cosby mugging expertly for General Foods, Ford, Texas Instruments, Coca-Cola, E. F. Hutton.

Cosby is today's quintessential TV Dad—at once the nation's best-liked sitcom character and the most successful and ubiquitous of celebrity pitchmen. Indeed, Cosby himself ascribes his huge following to his appearances in the ads: "I think my popularity came from doing solid 30-second commercials. They can cause people to love you and see more of you than in a full 30-minute show." Like its star, *The Cosby Show* must owe much of its immense success to advertising, for this sitcom is especially well attuned to the commercials, offering a full-scale confirmation of their vision. The show has its charms, which seem to set it well apart from TV's usual crudeness; yet even these must be considered in the context of TV's new integrity.

On the face of it, the Huxtables' milieu is as upbeat and well stocked as a window display at Bloomingdale's, or any of those visions of domestic happiness that graced the billboards during the Great Depression. Everything within this spacious brownstone is luminously clean and new, as if it had all been set up by the state to make a good impression on a group of visiting foreign dignitaries. Here are all the right commodities—lots of bright sportswear, plants and paintings, gorgeous bedding, plenty of copperware, portable tape players, thick carpeting, innumerable knickknacks, and, throughout the house, big, burnished dressers, tables, couches, chairs, and cabinets (Early American yet looking factory-new). Each week, the happy Huxtables nearly vanish amid the porcelain, stainless steel, mahogany, and fabric of their lives. In every scene, each character appears in some fresh designer outfit that positively glows with newness, never to be seen a second time. And, like all this pricey clutter, the plots and subplots, the dialogue and even many of the individual shots reflect in some way on consumption as a way of life: Cliff's new juicer is the subject of an entire episode; Cliff does a monologue on his son Theo's costly sweatshirt; Cliff kids daughter Rudy for wearing a dozen wooden necklaces. Each Huxtable, in fact, is hardly more than a mobile display case for his/her momentary possessions. In the show's first year, the credit sequence was a series of vivid stills presenting Cliff alongside a shiny Dodge Caravan, out of which the lesser Huxtables then emerged in shining playclothes, as if the van were their true parent, with Cliff serving as the genial midwife to this antiseptic birth. Each is routinely upstaged by what he/she eats or wears or lugs around: in a billowing blouse imprinted with gigantic blossoms, daughter Denise appears, carrying a tape player as big as a suitcase; Theo enters to get himself a can of Coke from the refrigerator, and we notice that he's wearing both a smart beige belt *and* a pair of lavender suspenders; Rudy munches cutely on a piece of pizza roughly twice the size of her own head.

As in the advertising vision, life among the Huxtables is not only well supplied, but remarkable for its surface harmony. Relations between these five pretty kids and their cute parents are rarely complicated by the slightest serious discord. Here affluence is magically undisturbed by the pressures that ordinarily enable it. Cliff and Clair, although both employed, somehow enjoy the leisure to devote themselves full-time to the trivial and comfortable concerns that loosely determine each episode: a funeral for Rudy's goldfish, a birthday surprise for Cliff, the kids' preparations for their first day of school. And daily life in this bright house is just as easy on the viewer as it is (apparently) for Cliff's dependents: *The Cosby Show* is devoid of any dramatic tension whatsoever. Nothing happens, nothing changes, there is no suspense or ambiguity or disappointment. In one episode, Cliff accepts a challenge to race once more against a runner who, years before, had beaten him at a major track meet. At the end, the race is run, and—it's a tie!

Of course, *The Cosby Show* is by no means the first sitcom to present us with a big, blissful family whose members never collide with one another, or with anything else; *Eight Is Enough, The Brady Bunch,* and *The Partridge Family* are just a few examples of earlier prime-time idylls. There are, however, some crucial differences between those older shows and this one. First of all, *The Cosby Show* is far more popular than any of its predecessors. It is (as of this writing) the top-rated show in the United States and elsewhere, attracting an audience that is not only vast, but often near fanatical in its devotion. Second, and stranger still, this show and its immense success are universally applauded as an exhilarating sign of progress. Newspaper columnists and telejournalists routinely deem *The Cosby Show* a "breakthrough" into an unprecedented *realism* because it uses none of the broad plot devices or rapid-fire gags that define the standard sitcom. Despite its fantastic ambience of calm and plenty, *The Cosby Show* is widely regarded as a rare glimpse of truth, whereas *The Brady Bunch* et al., though just as cheery, were never extolled in this way. And there is a third difference between this show and its predecessors that may help explain the new show's greater popularity and peculiar reputation for progressivism: Cliff Huxtable and his dependents are not only fabulously comfortable and mild, but also noticeably black.

Cliff's blackness serves an affirmative purpose within the ad that is *The Cosby Show*. At the center of this ample tableau, Cliff is himself an ad, implicitly proclaiming the fairness of the American system: "Look!" he shows us. "Even *I* can have all this!" Cliff is clearly meant to stand for Cosby himself, whose name appears in the opening credits as "Dr. William E. Cosby, Jr., Ed.D."—a testament both to Cosby's lifelong effort at self-improvement, and to his sense of brotherhood with Cliff. And, indeed, Dr. Huxtable is merely the latest version of the same statement that Dr. Cosby has been making for years as a talk show guest and stand-up comic: "I got mine!" The comic has always been quick to raise the subject of his own success. "What do I care what some ten-thousand-dollar-a-year writer says about me?" he once asked Dick Cavett. And on *The Tonight Show* a few years ago, Cosby told of how his father, years before, had warned him that he'd never make a dime in show business, "and then he walked slowly back to the projects. . . . Well, I just lent him forty thousand dollars!"

That anecdote got a big hand, just like *The Cosby Show*, but despite the many plaudits for Cosby's continuing tale of self-help, it is not quite convincing. Cliff's brownstone is too crammed, its contents too lustrous, to seem like his—or anyone's—own personal achievement. It suggests instead the corporate showcase which, in fact, it is. *The Cosby Show* attests to the power, not of Dr. Cosby/Huxtable, but of a consumer society that has produced such a tantalizing vision of reality. As Cosby himself admits, it was not his own Algeresque efforts that "caused people to love" him, but those ads put out by Coca-Cola, Ford, and General Foods—those ads in which he looks and acts precisely as he looks and acts in his own show.

Cosby's image is divided in a way that both facilitates the corporate project and conceals its true character. On the face of it, the Cosby style is pure impishness. Forever mugging and cavorting, throwing mock tantrums or beaming hugely to himself or doing funny little dances with his stomach pushed out, Cosby carries on a ceaseless parody of some euphoric eight-year-old. His delivery suggests the same childish spontaneity, for in the high, coy gabble of his harangues and monologues there is a disarming quality of baby talk. And yet all this artful goofiness barely conceals an intimidating hardness—the same uncompromising willfulness that we learn to tolerate in actual children (however cute they may be), but which can seem a little threatening in a grown-up. And Cosby is indeed a most imposing figure, in spite of all his antics: a big man boasting of his wealth, and often handling an immense cigar.

It is a disorienting blend of affects, but it works perfectly whenever he confronts us on behalf of Ford or Coca-Cola. With a massive car or Coke machine behind him, or with a calculator at his fingertips, he hunches toward us, wearing a bright sweater and an insinuating grin, and makes his playful pitch, cajoling us to buy whichever thing he's selling, his face and words, his voice and posture all suggesting this implicit and familiar come-on: "Kitchy-koo!" It is not so much that Cosby makes his mammoth bureaucratic masters seem as nice and cuddly as himself (although such a strategy is typical of corporate advertising); rather, he implicitly assures us that *we* are nice and cuddly, like little children. At once solicitous and overbearing, he personifies the corporate force that owns him. Like it, he comes across as an easygoing parent, and yet, also like it, he cannot help but betray the impulse to coerce. We see that he is bigger than we are, better known, better off, and far more powerfully sponsored. Thus, we find ourselves ambiguously courted, just like those tots who eat up lots of Jell-O pudding under his playful supervision.

Dr. Huxtable controls his family with the same enlightened deviousness. As widely lauded for its "warmth" as for its "realism," *The Cosby Show* has frequently been dubbed "the *Father Knows Best* of the eighties." Here again (the columnists agree) is a good strong Dad maintaining the old "family values." This equation, however, blurs a crucial difference between Cliff and the early fathers. Like them, Cliff always wins; but this modern Dad subverts his kids not by evincing the sort of calm power that once made Jim Anderson so daunting, but by seeming to subvert himself at the same time. His is the executive style, in other words, not of the small businessman as evoked in the fifties, but of the corporate manager, skilled at keeping his subordinates in line while half concealing his authority through various disarming moves: Cliff rules the roost through teasing put-downs, clever mockery, and amiable shows of helpless bafflement. This Dad is no straightforward tyrant, then, but the playful type who strikes his children as a peach, until they realize, years later, and after lots of psychotherapy, what a subtle thug he really was.

An intrusive kidder, Cliff never fails to get his way; and yet there is more to his manipulativeness than simple egomania. Obsessively, Cliff sees to it, through his takes and teasing, that his children always keep things light. As in the corporate culture and on TV generally, so on this show there is no negativity allowed. Cliff's function is therefore to police the corporate playground, always on the lookout for any downbeat tendencies.

In one episode, for instance, Denise sets herself up by reading Cliff some somber verses that she's written for the school choir. The mood is despairing; the refrain, "I walk alone . . . I walk alone." It is clear that the girl does not take the effort very seriously, and yet Cliff merrily overreacts against this slight and artificial plaint as if it were a crime. First, while she recites, he wears a clownish look of deadpan bewilderment, then laughs out loud as soon as she has finished, and finally snidely moos the refrain in outright parody. The studio audience roars, and Denise takes the hint. At the end of the episode, she reappears with a new version, which she reads sweetly, blushingly, while Cliff and Clair, sitting side by side in their high-priced pajamas, beam with tenderness and pride on her act of self-correction:

> My mother and my father are my best friends.
> When I'm all alone, I don't have to be.
> It's because of me that I'm all alone, you see.
> Their love is real. . . .
>
> Never have they lied to me, never connived me,
> talked behind my back.
> Never have they cheated me.
> Their love is real, their love is real.

Clair, choked up, gives the girl a big warm hug, and Cliff then takes her little face between his hands and kisses it, as the studio audience bursts into applause.

Thus, this episode ends with a paean to the show itself (for "their love" is *not* "real," but a feature of the fiction), a moment that, for all its mawkishness, attests to Cliff's managerial adeptness. Yet Cliff is hardly a mere enforcer. He is himself also an underling, even as he seems to run things. This subservient status is manifest in his blackness. Cosby's blackness is indeed a major reason for the show's popularity, despite his frequent claims, and the journalistic consensus, that *The Cosby Show* is somehow "colorblind," simply appealing in some general "human" way. Although whitened by their status and commodities, the Huxtables are still unmistakably black. However, it would be quite inaccurate to hail their popularity as evidence of a new and rising amity between the races in America. On the contrary, *The Cosby Show* is such a hit with whites in part because whites are just as worried about blacks as they have always been— not blacks like Bill Cosby, or Lena Horne, or Eddie Murphy, but poor blacks, and the poor in general, whose existence is a well-kept secret on prime-time TV.

And yet TV betrays the very fears that it denies. In thousands of high-security buildings, and in suburbs reassuringly remote from the cities' "bad neighborhoods," whites may, unconsciously, be further reassured by watching not just Cosby, but a whole set of TV shows that negate the possibility of black violence with lunatic fantasies of containment: *Diff'rent Strokes* and *Webster,* starring Gary Coleman and Emmanuel Lewis, respectively, each an overcute, miniaturized black person, each playing the adopted son of good white parents. Even the oversized and growling Mr. T, complete with Mohawk, bangles, and other primitivizing touches, is a mere comforting joke, the dangerous ex-slave turned comic and therefore innocuous by campy excess; and this behemoth too is kept in line by a casual white father, Hannibal Smith, the commander of the A-Team, who employs Mr. T exclusively for his brawn.

As a willing advertisement for the system that pays him well, Cliff Huxtable also represents a threat contained. Although darkskinned and physically imposing, he ingratiates us with his childlike mien and enviable life-style, a surrender that must offer some deep solace to a white public terrified that one day blacks might come with guns to steal the copperware, the juicer, the microwave, the VCR, even the TV itself. On *The Cosby Show,* it appears as if blacks in general can have, or do have, what many whites enjoy, and that such material equality need not entail a single break-in. And there are no hard feelings, none at all, now that the old injustice has been so easily rectified. Cosby's definitive funny face, flashed at the show's opening credits and reproduced on countless magazine covers, is a strained denial of all animosity. With its little smile, the lips pursed tight, eyes opened wide, eyebrows raised high, that dark face shines toward us like the white flag of surrender—a desperate look that no suburban TV Dad of yesteryear would ever have put on, and one that millions of Americans today find indispensable.

By and large, American whites need such reassurance because they are now further removed than ever, both spatially and psychologically, from the masses of the black poor. And yet the show's appeal cannot be explained merely as a symptom of class and racial uneasiness, because there are, in our consumer culture, anxieties still more complicated and pervasive. Thus, Cliff is not just an image of the dark Other capitulating to the white establishment, but also the reflection of any constant viewer, who, whatever his/her race, must also feel like an outsider, lucky to be tolerated by the distant powers that be. There is no negativity allowed, not anywhere; and so Cliff serves both as our guide and as our double. His look of tense playfulness is more than just a sign that blacks won't hurt us; it is an expression that we too would each be wise to adopt, lest we betray some devastating sign of anger or dissatisfaction. If we stay cool and cheerful, white like him, and learn to get by with his sort of managerial acumen, we too, perhaps, can be protected from the world by a barrier of new appliances, and learn to put down others as each of us has, somehow, been put down.

Such rampant putting-down, the ridicule of all by all, is the very essence of the modern sitcom. Cliff, at once the joker and a joke, infantilizing others and yet infantile himself, is exemplary of everybody's status in the sitcoms, in the ads, and in most other kinds of TV spectacle (as well as in the movies). No one, finally, is immune. That solidarity of underlings enabled by the butt's incursions lasts no longer than whatever takes or gags the others use against him. Once he leaves, disgraced afresh, each performs his function for the others, the status of oaf, jerk, or nerd passing to everyone in turn. Even the one who momentarily plays the put-down artist often seems a bit ridiculous in the very act of putting down the momentary loser. The butt's temporary assailant—the deadpan child, the wry oldster, the sullen maid—may score a hit against the uptight and boorish victim, but then perhaps the attacker him/herself is a bit *too* deadpan, wry, or sullen, and therefore almost as much laughed at as laughed with.

On the sitcom, in fact, one is obliged to undercut oneself along with everybody else. Such routine autosubversion is effected through the sitcom's definitive form of monologue, a device which might be termed the Craven Reversal. For instance, one of the boys is being menaced by some giant thug. Although clearly frightened, the boy (who might be middle-aged) suddenly draws himself up and delivers a brave, indignant speech along these lines: "You can't push me around like this! We're living in a *free country*, and I have *rights!* I'm not going to let some *bully* try to *impose his will* through *sheer physical force!*" and so on, until the bully growls, or flexes his muscles, or stands up from his chair to tower over the idealist, who immediately crumbles, quickly babbling, "On the other hand, there's always room for compromise!" or something similar. Or a girl sees a celebrity, gets all fluttery, but tells herself she's being childish, must have pride, collect herself, until the famous person says "Excuse me . . ." and the girl collapses into fawning self-abasement. However the Reversal is set up, it always represents the same brief, pointless struggle: someone tries to overcome his nature, rise above his circumstances, hold out against whatever TV says cannot be resisted, and that little effort fails predictably, as the would-be hero/ine contains him/herself for the greater glory of TV.

In short, the point of TV comedy is that *there can be no transcendence.* Such is the meaning of Dad's long humiliation since the fifties, and the meaning of every gratuitous and all-inclusive moment of derision. Because he would have stood out as an archaic model of resistance to the regime of advertising, Dad was, through the sixties and the seventies, reduced from a complicated lie to a simple joke. Lately, he has been regressing even further, for his parodic image has begun to disappear entirely from the sitcom's universe. Equal in their foolishness, the community of sitcom characters can now maintain the derisive pace without an overt vestige of the early Dad, for each can play the Dad merely by presuming to stand out for just a moment. Therefore, on *The Facts of Life, Golden*

Girls, Kate & Allie, Who's the Boss? and other Dadless shows, even when no Dad-like visitor intrudes, there is no shortage of contemptuous asides or knowing glances, because one or another of the children, girls, or women will always somehow try too hard, come on too strong, put up some kind of front, or otherwise set herself up for her inevitable comeuppance from the others, each of whom will get hers too, sooner or later.

Through this subversive process, the sitcom betrays the self-destructive tendency of the social Darwinist ideal—that jungle ethic which has always given aid and comfort to the well-fixed champions of laissez-faire, and which is now respectable again, and highly influential, through the mediation of the Reagan mechanism. The aggression that motivates or undercuts each sitcom character in turn reflects the real aggression that pervades the corporate state, wherein every man and woman must "look out for Number One." And yet these apparent struggles for preeminence do not create heroic individuals, or permit any individuality at all. On the sitcom, what seems like a relentless effort on the part of each to triumph over all the rest is an effort not at self-definition or self-promotion, but at self-cancellation. The aim of each is merely to survive as yet another particle of the watchful and ironic mass.

And yet, despite this pervasive irony, the sitcom (like TV generally) is filled with maudlin intervals. Often there will come a sudden Tender Moment, when the ironists collectively break off from their snide gags and sarcastic looks. During this sentimental cease-fire, which is usually inserted just before the final "pod" of commercials, a hush falls, the synthesizer plays some violins, and everybody goes sincere, until two of the combatants merge into a hug and the studio audience heaves a reverent sigh. This routine show of warmth might seem like a departure from the ironic norm; and yet that "warmth" serves exactly the same purpose as the irony which it ostensibly opposes.

Each "warm" climactic moment, first of all, seems intended to make up for the derision that precedes it: "Hey, deep down, we're very *caring!*" the moment shouts at us. We are invited to believe that all the prior nastiness was really motivated by a lot of love, and so the sitcom's barbs and jeering are exempt from criticism. Conversely, the maudlin moment is apparently to be mitigated by the irony surrounding it: as soon as things get heavy, someone usually restores the caustic atmosphere by turning mean or acting like a jerk, so that the mawkishness seems to have been retracted. Alternately cloying and mean-spirited, then, the sitcom is nevertheless preserved against objection to these defects, since it seems too cool to be so corny, and yet too warm to be so cool.

In its tear-jerking phase as through its general irony, the sitcom functions to suppress all critical response. Whether it seeks to sneer along with us or tries to get us all choked up, its aim is to inhibit any independent thought, to preempt any negative reaction. Dad, the figure of our potential waywardness, is therefore the primary victim not only of the sitcom's ironies, but also of the sitcom's sentimental outbursts. When the music rises and the characters get teary-eyed, Dad is either broken down or driven out. If he doesn't give in and "feel" along with everybody else, earning a big hand for his disintegration, he offsets the general bathos by demonstrating that he's much too frigid or obtuse to deal with it. His exclusion makes the others' sensitivity seem all the more acute, and also frequently provides the opportunity for that mean laugh which must immediately follow, and subvert, the ritual of pseudosympathy. Thus are the sitcom's passages of "feeling," although seemingly anomalous, impelled by the same hostility that motivates the wisecracks and the rolling eyes.

Perfectly settled and enclosed, the sitcom world is now even more cloistral than it was back in the fifties, when Dad's kingdom, filmed rather than videotaped, included a front lawn and other antiseptic outdoor areas. Ricky and David, Bud or Wally could at least leave the house at times, to stroll or bicker mildly out on those sepulchral grounds. Today, each set, while far more colorful than Dad's gray neighborhood, is nevertheless more of a prison, excluding nature absolutely. Now there are no more yards or trees, but only the usual bright living room or kitchen, as hermetic, up-to-date, and well equipped as the air-conditioned offices and studios where all these shows and ads are planned and sold. Here the only character who would ever think of opening a window, going for a walk, or contemplating other worlds is the occasional "weirdo," the stereotypic "space cadet," like the Reverend Jim on *Taxi*. Otherwise, no mind leaps up to any heaven. All here are earthbound, housebound, all but chairbound in a world of gratuitous and interminable jeering.

And this evocation of the chair brings us down to the discovery of that new creature who has displaced Dad as the sitcoms' basic hero. By implicitly extolling the fixed posture of ironic looking-on, TV exalts, in place of Dad, Dad's opposite: a figure not at all opposed to TV's sway, but in fact the very object of TV's triumph. It is, in short, TV's own full-time viewer whose "power" TV now reflects and celebrates. Through its "comic" apparatus, the sitcom persistently derides all tension, all uptightness, because such a state contains the possibility of waywardness, resistance, of a self impenetrable by TV; and the sitcom ridicules this state by playing it repeatedly against a spectatorial slackness, the same attitude of passive irony that the viewer exemplifies to the precise extent that he or she laughs along.

So the sitcom's endless round of sarcasms has served to promote TV itself. The ironist appears to see right through whatever pretense or dishonesty, pomposity or inhibition he confronts—exactly like TV itself, whose vision is, at base, so ruthlessly incisive. Moreover, the sitcom ironist comes across as so superior and hip because he imitates the sort of viewer that TV has finally produced for itself—not a credulous and ardent fan, but a jaded devotee, distrustful of those screaming images, yet somehow unable to give up half-watching them.

Of course, it is not only the sitcom that reflects TV's habituated viewer. TV today is almost unified by its self-reflection. The contemptuous underling who rolls her eyes behind the back of her ex-husband, mother, daughter, boss, or closest friend has analogues throughout the other genres. The talk show host, for instance, is a figure of the ideal viewer. As we watch TV's images, so does he sit and look on at his parade of guests, evincing a boyish wryness against which all too-demonstrative behavior seems comic, especially when he glances our way with a look that says, "Can you believe this?" He is a festive version of the anchorman, with an air of detached superiority that is enabled by his permanent youthfulness, and by his middle-American calm and plainness. Johnny Carson of Iowa, like his heir apparent, that supreme ironist, David Letterman of Indiana, always seems somehow above the excesses of either coast, even as he brings them to us. Although ostensibly more highbrow than these stars, Dick Cavett of Nebraska—now on cable—seems another such teenaged ironist from the Great Plains. (The mobile and earnest Phil Donahue, although another plain Midwestern lad, is an incongruous TV star, his show a throwback to the public forum or "progressive" high school course.)

TV's heroics are now also reflective of the viewers who cannot help but watch them. This has been evidenced in a negative way by the extinction of the TV Western, whose heroes were too self-sufficient, its locales too spare and natural, to survive in an ad-saturated atmosphere. TV now permits the Western only in the form of burlesque, whether as sitcoms like *Best of the West* or in parodic commercials. Today, the solemnity of the old TV cowboys has evolved into the spectatorial cool of the new TV cop: Sonny Crockett is at once the descendant and the antithesis of Davy Crockett. An exemplary voyeur, the TV cop demonstrates his righteousness through the hip judgmental stare with which he eyes the many hookers/pimps/drug dealers/hit men/Mafia dons/psychotic killers/oily lawyers who flash and leer so colorfully before him. The history of TV's cops, in fact, is a history of disgusted looks, from the outraged glower of *Dragnet*'s Sergeant Friday to the more laid-back jeering gazes of the cops today—the casual smirk of Detective Hunter, the sarcastic glances that create the sense of solidarity at Hill Street Station, the deadpan looks of incredulity exchanged by Cagney and Lacey. Like us, the TV cop seems to deplore the bad guys even as he keeps on watching them; and TV's latest cop-hero is not only an adept voyeur, but is himself also a slick visual object, derived from the imagery of advertising. Indeed, his "heroism" is entirely (tele)visual and consumeristic. We see him as "the good" because he knows how to shop for clothes. Preeminently with-it in their tropical pastels, Crockett and Tubbs of *Miami Vice* are two observers of an underworld as seamy and repulsive, with its high-strung felons black and brown and yellow, as these two cops are smooth and chic. The eponymous bodyguard of *The Equalizer* is yet another well-armed and contemptuous onlooker, as stately and impassive as the connoisseur in an ad for scotch, and routinely angered by the many scummy types who, ill-dressed and misbehaving, cross his sight.

TV's reflection on the knowing viewer is a cynical appeal not only to the weakest part of each of us, but to the weakest and least experienced among us. It is therefore not surprising that this reflection has transformed the children's shows along with the rest of TV. Today the slow and beaming parent figures of the past—Fran Allison, Captain Kangaroo, Miss Frances, Mr. Wizard—recur to us like lame old jokes; and the only current survivor of the type, the very easygoing Mr. Rogers, has been the object of hip satire by, among others, Eddie Murphy on *Saturday Night Live,* and J. Walter Thompson for Burger King. The old children's shows were hardly free from commercialism; often the parent figure would engage in shameless huckstering, advising his "boys and girls" to "ask" for the sponsor's latest item. Although often disingenuous, however, the parental guise of the early hosts comprised a subtle barrier to the corporate exploitation of the very young, because that guise was based on the assumption that the child should be regarded as an innocent—fanciful and trusting, in need of some protection from the world that would absorb him all too soon. Such a child would, if respected, be off-limits to the market forces. That child's capacity for play and make-believe also might impede the corporate project, since his or her delight in such free pleasures would, if universally indulged, make trouble for Mattel, Hasbro, Coleco Industries, and other giant manufacturers of games and toys.

In order to prevent this hardship, TV now urges its youngest viewers to adopt the same contemptuous and passive attitude that TV recommends to grown-ups. The child who sits awed by He-Man, the GoBots, the Thundercats, or G.I. Joe is not encouraged to pretend or sing or make experiments, but is merely hypnotized by those speedy images; and in this trance he learns only how to jeer. The superheroes wage interminable war, and yet it is not belligerence per se that these shows celebrate, but the particular belligerence that TV incites toward all that seems nontelevisual. The villains are always frenzied and extremely ugly, whereas the good guys are well built, smooth, and faceless, like the computers that are programmed to animate them. Empowered by this contrast, they attack their freaky enemies not just with swords and

guns, but with an endless stream of witless personal insults—
"bonehead," "fur-face," "long-legged creep," and on and on. Like
TV's ads, these shows suggest that nothing could be worse than
seeming different; but TV now teaches the same smug derisiveness
even on those children's shows without commercials. For example,
Sesame Street—despite its long-standing reputation as a pedagogical
triumph—has become, in the eighties, merely one more exhibition
of contagious jeering. The puppets often come across as manic little
fools, while the hosting grown-ups come across as wise and cool—
a marked superiority which they express through the usual bewil-
dered or exasperated looks. Thus, the program's little viewers learn
how to behave themselves—i.e., as viewers only. They are invited
not to share the puppet's crazed exuberance, but only to look down
on it; and so they practice that ironic posture which the show advises
just as unrelentingly as it repeats the primary numbers and the
letters of the alphabet.

As this flattery of the viewer now nearly unifies TV, so has it,
necessarily, all but unified the culture which TV has pervaded. The
movies now repeat the formulaic subversions that have served TV,
debunking the heroics of the past through parodies of the Western,
the Saturday matinee, the spy thriller, and yet preserving and inten-
sifying the most hostile impulses of that defunct heroism: sadism,
xenophobia, misogyny, paranoid anticommunism, each enacted
graphically, and yet with a wink that tells us not to take it too
seriously, however much we might like it. Even the less overtly
bellicose films are, more often than not, merely televisual, despite
the greater cost and scope of their images: *Ghostbusters, Beverly Hills
Cop,* and *Back to the Future,* to pick just a few exemplary blockbusters, are each little more than a series of broadly subversive confrontations between some ludicrous butt and the cool young star(s).
From TV, American film has now absorbed a stream of ironists—
Chevy Chase, Bill Murray, Martin Mull, Michael Keaton, Tom
Hanks, Steve Martin, Michael J. Fox, and others, some brilliant,
some mediocre, but all used to make a smirking audience feel
powerful. This archetype of boyish irony has spread beyond the
silver screen, having become, in the eighties, through TV, the very
paradigm of national leadership. Ronald Reagan, that low-key and
aged lad, deftly quoting movie dialogue, and otherwise half jesting

at his own theatricality, is yet another sly pseudoinsurgent, forever seeming to stand off, on our behalf, against those grand, archaic entities that menace him and all the rest of us—the "evil empire" based in Moscow, "the bureaucrats" and "special interests" here at home.

Throughout TV, these figures recur seductively as our embattled fellow viewers; and yet these seeming dissidents only serve, like Dr. Huxtable, to bolster a corporate system that would make all dissidence impossible. Of course, through their commercials, these corporations too pretend to take our side (while taking sides against us), defusing our rebelliousness by seeming to mimic it: AT&T advises us, through the soft-spoken Cliff Robertson, to reject its big, impersonal competitors, as if AT&T were a plucky little mom-and-pop enterprise; Apple likens IBM to a totalitarian state, as if Apple Computer Inc. were a cell of anarchists; GE depicts a world of regimented silence, its citizens oppressed and robotized, until the place is gloriously liberated by a hip quartet bearing powerful GE tape players, as if that corporation were a hedonistic sect and not a major manufacturer of microwave ovens, refrigerators and—primarily—weapons systems.

TV is suffused with the enlightened irony of the common man, "the little guy," or—to use a less dated epithet—the smart shopper. Thus, TV has absorbed for its own purposes an ancient comic stance that has, throughout the history of the West, hinted at the possibility of freedom. Countless old scenes and stories have assured us that aggressive power cannot withstand the wry gaze and witty comment of the observant ironist, whose very weakness thereby seems the source of a latent revolutionary strength. Through such a stance, Diogenes embarrassed Alexander, Jesus discomfited the Pharisees; and in scores of comedies from Plautus through the Restoration and beyond, in hundreds of satires from Juvenal well into the eighteenth century, the servile fop or lumbering bully seems to be deflated by the sharp asides of an independent-minded onlooker.

Such spectatorial subversion of the powerful, or of those who have clearly given in to power, recurs throughout the European literary canon—but it was in America that this device became especially widespread, as the familiar comic weapon of a nation of iconoclasts. Here the spectatorial irony took on an overtly democratic force through the writings and performances of our most celebrated humorists: Artemus Ward, Josh Billings, Mr. Dooley, "Honest Abe," Mark Twain, Will Rogers. Through mastery of the native idiom, and by otherwise projecting "an uncommon common sense," such ironists were each adept at seeming to see through, on behalf of decent fellows everywhere, all pomp, hypocrisy, convention, and whatever else might seem to stink of tyranny.

The history of this subversive irony has reached its terminus, for now the irony consists in nothing but an easy jeering gaze that TV uses not to question the exalted, but to perpetuate its own hegemony. Over and over, the spectator recurs within the spectacle, which thereby shields itself from his/her boredom, rage, or cynicism. TV deflects these (potentially) critical responses onto its own figments of the unenlightened Other, and therefore seems itself to be enlightened, a force of progress and relentless skepticism. Yet the televisual irony now contravenes the very values which the older irony was once used to defend.

First of all, TV's irony functions, persistently if indirectly, to promote consumption as a way of life. Whereas the native humorists spoke out from an ideology of individualism, TV's cool tots appear to us as well-dressed hostages, branded with the logos of Benetton, Adidas, Calvin Klein. The self is an embarrassment on TV, an odd encumbrance, like a hatbox or a watch fob. TV's irony at once discredits any sign of an incipient selfhood, so that the only possible defense against the threat of ridicule would be to have no self at all. In order not to turn into a joke, then, one must make an inward effort to become like either—or both—of those supernal entities that dominate TV: the commodity and the corporation. These alone are never ironized on TV, because these alone can never lapse into the laughable condition of mortality. The corporation is, by definition, disembodied; the commodity-as-advertised, a sleek and luminous portent of nonhumanity. Both seem to gaze back at us from within the distant future, having evolved far beyond our weaknesses and fear: TV's irony derives from that contemptuous gaze, which threatens even the most blasé actors, the most knowing spectators.

Through its irony, in short, TV advises us not just to buy its products, but to emulate them, so as to vanish into them.

And TV's irony facilitates an atmosphere of endless war. With its fresh egalitarian bias, the early irony was fundamentally humane, as the works of Lincoln and Mark Twain attest. The televisual irony, however, has merely enabled TV to regress into a continuous scene of brutal domination, by seeming to obviate all critical reaction (whether moral or aesthetic) to such modern barbarism.

Even as it flatters us for our powers of discernment, TV struggles to enforce our constant half attention by assaulting us relentlessly with violent distractions. Despite its pose of deference to the audience, TV's assumption is that the viewer is precisely as edgy, fickle, and dim-witted as TV would make everyone, and so the spectacle now comes to us shattered into a sequence of harsh fragments, overcharged and unrelated: gunshots, punches, screams, explosions, crashes, squealing tires, things and bodies hurtling, hurting, every audiovisual contusion further heightened by the efficient bangs and blaring of the synthesizer. The need to keep us half-engrossed has produced a spectacle of easy cruelty. The definitive image of prime time (beyond the sitcoms) is that nightmarish simulation of pursuit which also recurs throughout the so-called "splatter movies": a nervous, tasty-looking woman walks alone down some dark hallway or deserted street, stalked by the hand-held camera.

Yet such overt sadomasochism is only one component of TV's assault, for TV is violent not only in its literal images of carnage and collision, but in its automatic overuse of every possible method of astonishment. Here we might mention the extreme close-ups, high contrasts, flaring colors, rapid cutting, the stark New Wave vistas, simulations of inhuman speed, sudden riots of break dancing. Yet such a catalog of tricks alone would miss the point, because TV's true violence consists not so much in the spectacle's techniques or content, but rather in the very density and speed of TV overall, the very multiplicity and pace of stimuli; for it is by overloading, overdriving both itself and us that TV disables us, making it hard to think about or even feel what TV shows us—making it hard, perhaps, to think or feel at all.

TV's irony inhibits any critical response, or any other strong reaction, to this brutalizing process. It would be uncool to object, or otherwise to take it hard. Thus, the experience of TV today is doubly terroristic. There is, first of all, the outright mayhem and derision—people ridiculed and/or beaten, burned, shot, knifed, raped, drowned, or blown up, cars crashing into cars, houses, plate-glass windows, cars run off the road and blowing up, cars driving over cliffs and blowing up, or just blowing up, or blowing people up, or running people down. And this explicit depiction of destruction also implies, appeals to, and is protected by a cruelty more refined: the cold thrill of feeling ourselves exalted above all concern, all earnestness, all principle, evolved beyond all innocence or credulity, liberated finally out of naive moralisms and into pure modernity. We all know that we see through it all, and therefore can enjoy it as if not fascinated by it. TV's cop shows, telefilms, and wrestling matches are preserved in their debasement by this assurance that we've seen so much that none of this can bother us. Such is the implicit assurance of the images themselves, and such too is the excuse advanced explicitly by TV's employees, who frequently exonerate themselves by claiming irony. "This is basically a comedy," says George Peppard of *The A-Team*. "We're doing send-up." According to Glen A. Larson, executive producer of *Knight Rider,* the show is "tongue-in-cheek," and works only because David Hasselhoff, the show's star, "has that mischievous look in his eye that tells you, 'Of course you're not going to believe this, but lean back and enjoy it anyway.' "

No matter how bad TV gets, it cannot easily be deplored or criticized as long as it manifests its own unseriousness. Yet the worst thing about TV is not its increasing badness. As long as we can still point out that something on TV is "bad," we continue to invoke a number of traditional aesthetic standards. Such criteria are no longer relevant to TV today, which, increasingly self-referential, is less recognizable as something "bad" as it turns more and more exclusively televisual. For all its promises of "choice," TV is nearly perfect in its emptiness, all but exhausted by the very irony that it uses to protect itself from hostile scrutiny.

This explains in part why the early TV genres are now vanishing. Today the phrase "TV genre" seems increasingly oxymoronic, for the TV spectacle has long since broken down or overwhelmed the old dramatic forms that once comprised it. At first, TV was, gener-

ically, as diverse as either of its parent media, radio and film. Shows
like *I Love Lucy* and *The Honeymooners* preserved something of the
mood and structure of the stage farce, and the spirit of vaudeville
persisted in the live routines of Jack Benny, Milton Berle, Sid
Caesar, Red Skelton. TV's many Westerns derived from the larger
Westerns of John Ford and others, and its detective stories related,
through Hollywood, to the novels of Dashiell Hammett and Raymond Chandler. TV's deliberate forays into the uncanny were similarly inspired by literary/cinematic antecedents: *The Twilight Zone*
derived in part from science fiction, *One Step Beyond* and *Thriller*
from the ghost story, and the shows produced (and sometimes directed) by Alfred Hitchcock were clearly reminiscent of his films.
Early on, moreover, TV even included the sort of social realism that
had marked the American stage since the Depression. Series such as
Playhouse 90, Kraft Television Theatre, Philco Television Playhouse, and
Goodyear Television Playhouse presented a number of plays of a type
too topical and sobering to survive the rising influence of the advertisers—a deliberate (and brief) effort to use TV as an extension of
the off-Broadway theater.

Of course, we ought not to exaggerate the aesthetic or social
value of this generic conservatism. The fact that an early TV show
referred to some prior body of novels, plays, or films need not mean
that that show was any good. "The Golden Age of Television" was
hardly as luminous as its later eulogists tend to suggest. Further-
more, for all their obvious generic traits, a good many of those early
shows were little more than cold war propaganda, scarcely veiled by
the obligatory trappings of the Western or crime drama. However,
even if many of its shows were badly done and/or politically loaded,
TV back then was still not as oppressive and monotonous as it is
today, because its range of generic categories sustained the memory
of a pretelevisual moment. TV alluded to the act of reading, and to
the act of joining others in an auditorium. The live pratfall, the
somber Paladin, the haunted mansion, the lawyers fencing in a
packed courtroom, the gray drama of a labor strike, Ralph Kramden
mistakenly convinced that he's about to die, were among the images
that pointed back and away from the very medium that was presenting them.

But TV now points largely to itself, and so genre has been all but superannuated. Throughout the virtual whole of any broadcast day, TV offers us TV and TV only, representing no action that does not somehow refer to, and reinforce, the relationship, or stand-off, between the bored, fixated viewer and his set. Whereas genre demands that both the viewers and the performers abide by its particular conventions for the story's sake, TV today automatically adapts whatever it appropriates to TV's own reflective project—not to mold a narrative, but only both to signal and appeal to the collective knowingness of TV's viewers and performers. The spectacle is an endless advertisement for the posture of inert modernity. Genre, therefore, is nothing but a source of campy touches—or the material for outright parody, the object of that relentless putting-down whereby TV subverts our pleasure in all prior forms of spectacle. Whatever was a source of pleasure in the past is now derided by and for the knowing, whether it's the Busby Berkeley musical affectionately mimicked in some "special," or the silent movies derisively excerpted in the ads for Hershey or Toshiba, or the cowboy pictures lampooned by Philip Morris or Rich Little, or *The Towering Inferno* as parodied on *Saturday Night Live,* or *Dragnet* as parodied to sell the Yellow Pages, or *Mr. Ed* as excerpted to sell tortilla chips, or the Mona Lisa as ridiculed to sell Peter Pan peanut butter. Through such compulsive trashing, the spectacle makes eye contact with the spectator, offering, in exchange for the enjoyment that TV cannot permit, a flattering wink of shared superiority.

Increasingly, TV is nothing but a series of assurances that it can never put one over on us. Those on TV collaborate with those who sit before it, in order to reconfirm forever our collective immunity to TV as it used to be, back when its stars and viewers were not as cool as all of us are now. Pat Sajak, the MC on *Wheel of Fortune,* distinguishes himself from the sort of overheated game show host that was once common on TV: " 'You've just won TEN THOUSAND DOLLARS!' " Sajak jabbers in unctuous parody, then adds, in his own more laid-back manner, "I just can't do that." Ruben Blades, schmoozing with Johnny Carson after a hot salsa number, complains of "the stereotypes" that TV has imposed on Hispanics: "Lootsie! I'm home!" he shouts in mimicry of Desi Arnaz, then pleads suavely, "Hey, gimme a break!", and the audience laughs, breaking into applause. And Susan Saint James, hosting *Friday*

Night Videos with the two teenage girls who perform with her on *Kate & Allie,* has them giggling at her imitation of the heavy-handed acting she used to do on *Name of the Game.*

Such knowingness sustains the widespread illusion that we have all somehow recovered from a bout of vast and paralyzing gullibility; and yet we cannot be confirmed in this illusion unless we keep on watching, or half watching. Thus, the most derisive viewer is also the most dependent: "Students do not take *General Hospital* seriously," writes Mark Harris in *TV Guide.* "They know it's not life; they say it's a 'soporific'; they feel superior to it. But *General Hospital* is also necessary, indispensable." In short, our jeering hurts TV's commercial project not at all. Everybody knows that TV is mostly false and stupid, that almost no one pays that much attention to it —and yet it's on for over seven hours a day in the average household, and it sells innumerable products. In other words, TV manages to do its job even as it only yammers in the background, despised by those who keep it going.

And it certainly is despised. Everybody watches it, but no one really likes it. This is the open secret of TV today. Its only champions are its own executives, the advertisers who exploit it, and a compromised network of academic boosters. Otherwise, TV has no spontaneous defenders, because there is almost nothing in it to defend. In many ways at once, TV negates the very "choices" that it now promotes with rising desperation. It promises an unimpeded vision of the whole known universe, and yet it shows us nothing but the laughable reflection of our own unhappy faces. It seems to offer us a fresh, "irreverent" view of the oppressive past, and yet that very gesture of rebelliousness turns out to be a ploy by those in power. Night after night, TV displays a bright infinitude of goods, employs a multitude of shocks and teases; and the only purpose of that spectacle is to promote the habit of spectatorship. It celebrates unending "choice" while trying to keep a jeering audience all strung out. TV begins by offering us a beautiful hallucination of diversity, but it is finally like a drug whose high is only the conviction that its user is too cool to be addicted.

Notes

INTRODUCTION: *Looking Through the Screen,* BY TODD GITLIN

PAGE

4   **privatized individuals:** Raymond Williams, *Television: Technology and Cultural Form* (New York: Schocken, 1975), pp. 14–41.

   "charm the taste": Alexis de Tocqueville, *Democracy in America,* revised by Francis Bowen, ed. Phillips Bradley (New York: Vintage, 1945), 2: 50–89.

5   **social bloodstream:** This premise could be detected even in some of the excellently gloomy writings of the fifties, notably those gathered in Bernard Rosenberg and David Manning White, eds., *Mass Culture* (New York: Free Press, 1957).

   passed down to them: See Todd Gitlin, "Media Sociology: The Dominant Paradigm," *Theory and Society* 6 (1978): 205–53.

   genre pedigrees: See the many writings published under the aegis of the Popular Culture Association, for example in the *Journal of American Culture.* The best-known book in this vein is Horace Newcomb, *TV: The Most Popular Art* (Garden City, N.Y.: Anchor/Doubleday, 1974).

   "emancipatory" yearnings: The most elegant and ingenious celebration of commercial television's hypothetically subversive potentials—it takes ingenuity to detect significant truth value in *The Beverly Hillbillies*—is David Marc, *Demographic Vistas* (Philadelphia: University of Pennsylvania Press, 1984). Marc takes as his text Kenneth Burke's notion that drama derives from a culture's historical conversation (p. 40). But he forgets that drama also represses what a culture wants suppressed—and may prove highly popular for doing precisely that.

   Reagan's FCC chairman: Mark Fowler, who has said, "The public's interest determines the public interest." Quoted in Peter J. Boyer, "Ethics of Toy-Based TV Shows Are Disputed," *New York Times,* February 3, 1986.

NETWORK NEWS: *We Keep America on Top of the World,* BY DANIEL C. HALLIN

13   **"packages for consciousness":** Todd Gitlin, "Spotlights and Shadows—TV News," *Cultural Correspondence* 4 (Spring 1977): 3–12.

19   **virtually all are officials:** Daniel C. Hallin and Paolo Mancini, "Speaking of the President: Political Structure and Representational Form in U.S.

PAGE

    and Italian Television News," *Theory and Society* 13, no. 6 (November 1984): 829–50.

26   **slide in ratings:** Sally Bedell, "The Upstart and the Big Boys Head for a Showdown," *TV Guide,* February 6, 1982, pp. 5–8.

27   **Lawrence Lichty:** Lawrence Lichty, "Video versus Print," *Wilson Quarterly* 6, no. 5 (Special Issue 1982): 49–57.

28   **experimental study:** Shanto Iyengar, Mark D. Peters, and David Kinder, "Experimental Demonstrations of the 'Not-so-Minimal' Consequences of Television News Programs," *American Political Science Review* 76, no. 4 (December 1982): 848–58.

    sided with police: John P. Robinson, "Public Reaction to Political Protest: Chicago, 1968," *Public Opinion Quarterly* 34, no. 1 (Spring 1970): 1–9.

29   **Progressive era:** Herbert J. Gans, *Deciding What's News* (New York: Pantheon, 1979), chap. 2.

30   **Trilateral Commission:** Michel J. Crozier, Samuel P. Huntington, and Joji Watanuki, *The Crisis of Democracy* (New York: New York University Press, 1975).

    Austin Ranney: Austin Ranney, *Channels of Power: The Impact of Television on American Politics* (New York: Basic Books, 1983).

SOAP OPERAS: *Search for Yesterday,* BY RUTH ROSEN

I wish to thank Zelda Bronstein, Rose Glickman, Joan Levinson, Jack Litewka, and Roland Marchand for their critical reading of this article. Todd Gitlin, who has raised editing to an art, improved it immeasurably by asking tough but constructive questions. I also want to extend my appreciation to ABC Studios in Hollywood, California, for allowing me to intrude upon the set of *General Hospital.* Thanks also to Gloria Monty, as well as the many actors and actresses—especially Norma Connolly—who graciously answered my endless questions.

42   **"I'm worried":** Paul Lazarsfeld and Frank Stanton, eds., *Radio Research* (New York: Arno Reprint 1979 [1944]), p. 3.

    soaps expanded: Extensive bibliographies of both scholarly and popular literature on daytime drama can be found in Mary Cassata and Thomas Skill, eds., *Life on Daytime Television: Tuning in American Serial Drama* (Norwood, N.J.: Ablex Publishing Corp., 1983). The following trace the development of soap operas from radio to television: Manuel Soares, *The Soap Opera Book* (New York: Harmony Books, 1978): Ronald Stedman, "Soap Operas as a Social Force," in *Don't Touch That Dial* (Chicago: Nelson-Hall, 1979).

43   **viewers' feelings:** Dan Wakefield, *All My Children* (New York: Doubleday, 1976), pp. 124, 128.

44   **Stereotypical viewers:** "For Actors, The Soaps Are Serious Business," *New*

PAGE

York Times, July 28, 1985; Muriel G. Cantor and Suzanne Pingree, The Soap Opera (Beverly Hills: Sage Publications, 1983), p. 116; Robert Lindsey, "Men Are Tuning In," New York Times, February 21, 1979; Harold Neuer, "Soaps Lure Male Viewers," Saturday Evening Post, November 1980, pp. 78–81.

chic status: "Sex and Suffering in the Afternoon," Time, January 12, 1976, p. 46.

45   synopses: Soap Opera Digest, March 12, 1985, p. 104; Lucy Birnbach, "Daze of Our Lives (College Students and Soap Opera)," Rolling Stone, October 1, 1981, p. 33. See, for example, the Los Angeles Times, the Oakland Tribune, or the Washington Post.

with their suffering: Herta Herzog, "What Do We Really Know About Daytime Serial Listeners?" in Lazarsfeld and Stanton, eds., Radio Research, pp. 3–34; Rudolf Arnheim, "World of the Daytime Serial," in Lazarsfeld and Stanton, eds., pp. 44ff.; Dan Wakefield, "Why Soaps Are So Popular," Family Circle, July 1976, p. 92. Probably the wittiest and most insightful analysis of the soap genre in general, and the radio soap in particular, is still James Thurber's "Soapland," in his The Beast in Me and Other Animals (New York: Harcourt, Brace & Co., 1948).

live with them: This point is made by Michael James Intintoli, Taking Soaps Seriously: The World of Guiding Light (New York: Praeger, 1984), p. 2.

46   why they watched: "Sex and Suffering," p. 46; Wakefield, All My Children, p. 136.

47   sexually bifurcated: For a discussion of nineteenth-century gender relations and the development of separate spheres, see Mary Ryan, Womanhood in America (New York: New Viewpoints, 1984); Alexis de Tocqueville, Democracy in America, ed. Thomas Bender (New York: Random House, 1981).

Americans mourned: For an extended discussion of the Progressive era's nostalgia for a mythic past, see Ruth Rosen, The Lost Sisterhood: Prostitution in America, 1900–1918 (Baltimore: Johns Hopkins University Press, 1982), pp. 38–51.

48   radio soaps: Warren Susman, Culture as History: The Transformation of American Society in the Twentieth Century (New York: Pantheon, 1984), p. 160.

"world of strangers": Lyn Lofland, A World of Strangers (New York: Basic Books, 1973), p. 178; Susman, Culture as History, passim. These themes are explored at length in Robert Bellah et al., Habits of the Heart: Individualism and Commitment in American Life (Berkeley: University of California Press, 1985).

49   morality play: John Keeler, "Soap: Counterpart to the 18th Century's Quasi-Moral Novel," New York Times, March 16, 1980.

basic story line: Cantor and Pingree, The Soap Opera, p. 44; Wakefield, All My Children, p. 155.

PAGE

50   **essential difference:** Carol Gilligan, *In a Different Voice: Psychological Theory and Women's Development* (Cambridge: Harvard University Press, 1982); Lillian Rubin, *Intimate Strangers* (New York: Harper & Row, 1983).

51   **"suffering of consequences":** Agnes Nixon quoted in "Sex and Suffering," p. 51. Two studies comparing prime-time drama and daytime soaps are: Horace Newcomb, "Soap Opera: Approaching the Real World," in *TV: The Most Popular Art* (New York: Anchor, 1974), and Muriel G. Cantor, "Our Days and Nights on T.V.," *Journal of Communication* 29 (Autumn 1979): 66–74.

     "we never smiled": "Soap Audience Ebbs, but Profits Abound," *Los Angeles Times,* April 1, 1983.

52   **young daytime stars:** Harry Waters, "Television's Hottest Show," *Newsweek,* September 28, 1981, pp. 60–68; Bradley S. Greenberg, Robert Abelman, and Kimberly Neunendorf, "Sex on the Soap Operas: Afternoon Delight," *Journal of Communication* 31 (Spring 1981): 83–89; "How ABC Found Happiness in Daytime TV," *Business Week,* August 24, 1982, pp. 62, 64.

     long-awaited wedding: "General Hospital: Critical Case," *Time,* September 28, 1981, p. 64; D. Gritten, "Liz Taylor Larks on General Hospital as Luke and Laura Finally Tie the Knot," *People,* November 16, 1981, pp. 34–39.

     American popular culture: Waters, "Television's Hottest Show," pp. 60–66.

53   **advertising revenues:** "Soap Audience Ebbs"; "Daytime TV's Rating Drama," *New York Times,* August 18, 1984, Business section.

54   **"Great Lakes":** All quotations from Gloria Monty, producer of *General Hospital,* unless otherwise stated, are from my interview with her, February 11, 1985.

55   **real time:** See Robert Allen, "On Reading Soaps: A Semiotic Primer," in E. Ann Kaplan, ed., *Regarding Television: Critical Approaches* (Los Angeles: American Film Institute, 1983), pp. 97–108, for a detailed and suggestive analysis of the form of the soap opera. Two other readings of the soap opera are: Dennis Porter, "Soap Time: Thoughts on a Commodity Art Form," *College English* 38 (April 1977): 782–88, and Tania Modleski, "The Rhythms of Reception: Daytime Television and Women's Work," *Regarding Television,* pp. 67–75.

     conventions: Much of the scholarship about soap operas focuses on how the soap world differs from actual reality. For demographic comparisons, see Cantor and Pingree, *The Soap Opera,* p. 113. John Seggar and Penny Wheeler deal with ethnic and sexual representation in "World of Work on TV: Ethnic and Sex Representation in TV," *Journal of Broadcasting* 17, no. 2 (Spring 1973): 201–13. The peculiar ways soaps dramatize illness and death have been analyzed in Mary Cassata et al., "In Sickness and In Health," *Journal of Communication* 29 (Autumn 1979): 73–80; George

PAGE

Gerbner et al., "Health and Medicine on Television," *New England Journal of Medicine* 8 (October 1981): 901–04; Intintoli, *Taking Soaps Seriously*, p. 107. Robert Allen offers a provocative interpretation in "Guiding Light: Soap Opera as Economic Product and Cultural Document," in *American History, American Television*, ed. John O'Connor (New York: Ungar, 1984), pp. 306–28.

58   racial minorities: Also see John Keeler, "How Soaps Whitewash Blacks," *American Film*, March 1980, pp. 36–37.

59   comfort, not controversy: Intintoli, *Taking Soaps Seriously*, p. 197. By quoting this particular viewer, I do not mean to suggest that viewers get exactly what they want. The question of audience decoding is quite complicated. But I want to call attention to the provocative thesis offered by Janice A. Radway, in *Reading the Romance: Women, Patriarchy and Popular Literature* (Chapel Hill: University of North Carolina Press, 1984), who suggests that women use romance fiction as a way of transcending their limited roles in society. After interviewing readers, Radway concludes that the meaning of the act of reading—leaving one's responsibilities to enjoy flights of fantasy and romance—differs from the conservative content of the romance itself. It is not clear that Radway's conclusion would apply to soap viewers. Radway's emphasis on the act itself has been emphasized by other students of popular culture, including Warren Susman, who suggested that "the form of the soap may be considered at least as important as or even more important than the content: the daily ritual of repeated programs, the ritual closing, even the ritual placement of the commercial . . . the entire ritual itself might indeed be the message." Susman, *Culture as History*, p. 255.

the community: The importance of the community is discussed in Intintoli, *Taking Soaps Seriously*, p. 53; Marlene G. Fine, "Soap Conversations: The Talk That Binds," *Journal of Communication* 31 (Summer 1981): 97–107.

60   "murderers, whores": *Soap Opera Digest*, February 12, 1985, p. 11.

61   Brazilian soaps: I am grateful to Ondina Fachel Leal for sharing her research on Brazilian soap operas with me. These cross-cultural comparisons emerged from lengthy conversations and from her paper, "Retelling of One Soap Opera: Class Speech and Meaning Constructs," unpublished paper, Department of Anthropology, University of California, Berkeley, 1984. See also "On a Booming Television Network, Brazil Gets a Clearer Picture of Itself," *New York Times*, December 13, 1984.

sexual revolution: How sex is handled on soaps is discussed in Greenberg, "Sex on the Soap Operas"; "Sex and Suffering"; Carol Lopate, "Daytime Television: You'll Never Want to Leave Home," *Radical America* 11 (January 1977): 33–51.

63   version of feminism: Barbara Ehrenreich makes a similar point in "Combat in the Media Zone," *Seven Days*, March 10, 1978. Stereotypes of women

on the soaps are examined in Soares, *The Soap Opera Book*, p. 59. Gaye Tuchman offers an interesting but limited overview of feminism and the media in "The Topic of the Women's Movement," in *Making News: A Study in the Construction of Knowledge* (New York: Free Press, 1978). Norma Connolly, an actress on *General Hospital*, discusses the way older women are ignored or distorted on soap operas in "Women Over 40: Does TV Treat Them Fairly?" *Soap Opera Digest*, August 14, 1984, p. 132.

65 **moral consensus:** How different kinds of moral dilemma are resolved on the soaps is discussed by John Sutherland and Shelly Siniawsky in "The Treatment and Resolution of Moral Violations on Soap Opera," *Journal of Communication* 32 (Spring 1982): 67–74.

issue of peace activism: Agnes Nixon, "Coming of Age in Sudsville," *Television Quarterly* 10 (Fall 1970): 61–70.

66 **optimistic viewpoint:** Gloria Monty, "Interview," *Soap Opera World*, February 1985, pp. 11–14.

"always tomorrow": Nixon, "Coming of Age," p. 63.

CHILDREN'S TELEVISION: *The Shortcake Strategy*, BY TOM ENGELHARDT

Thanks to Leslie Slocum of the Television Information Office and to Peggy Charren of ACT for offering access to so much helpful information, as well as to Kim Hays, editor of ACT's *TV, Science, and Kids*, for orienting me to what's been written in the field. Heartfelt thanks to Jonathan Cobb for responding to all my absurd demands, and especially to Todd for asking me. Finally, a respectful bow to Erik Barnouw, who did it (like so much else) first—see *The Image Empire*, vol. 3 of his *History of Broadcasting in the United States* (New York: Oxford University Press, 1970), pp. 267–68.

68 **General Mills:** On November 1, 1985, Kenner Products was spun off from General Mills and is now known as Kenner Parker Toys Inc. The reader should be warned that both the businesses behind and the shows on children's television are in a similar state of constant identity flux and name change, a fact which accurately reflects the particularly dynamic nature of the children's consumer business.

69 **Care Bears Family:** "A Family of Fun is Waiting for You with the CARE BEARS and CARE BEARS COUSINS," Kenner Products brochure.

70 **multibillion-dollar industry:** The whole 1985 licensed-merchandise business is estimated to service a $50 billion market, with cartoon characters accounting for approximately one-quarter of that, or almost $13 billion (and that only begins to take into account the dollars involved in this new area of the kids' consumer business). "Retailers are Learning to Choose Licenses," Toy & Hobby World's *Toy Fair Report*, February 14, 1986, pp. 42, 52; Joanne Y. Cleaver, "Starring on Marketing Team," *Advertis-*

ing Age, June 6, 1985, p. 16; Robert Krock, "Big Sell on the Small Screen," *PTA Today,* March 1985, p. 36.

71   **no payment required:** Cleaver, "Starring on Marketing Team," p. 15; David Robinson, "A Tramp is Born," *New Republic,* November 4, 1985, p. 44.

"Howdy Doody cutout": Gary Grossman, *Saturday Morning TV* (New York: Dell, 1980), p. 224.

$70 million annually: Ibid., pp. 228–29.

of dollars annually: Taft Merchandising Group, "Kids Are Our Business," ad in *Toy & Hobby World,* February 1985.

71 – 72   **producing the show:** "An Adult's Guide to Kids' TV," *Dial,* June 1983, p. 13.

72   **"aren't interested":** Grossman, *Saturday Morning TV,* p. 218.

various manufacturers: Jan Cherubin, "Toys Are Programs Too," *Channels,* May-June 1984, p. 31.

72 – 73   **appealing:** Cleaver, "Starring on Marketing Team," p. 16.

73   **"learn to count":** Kenner Products ad, "Strawberry Shortcake Will Never Grow Up," *Toy & Hobby World,* November 1982.

74   **treated that way:** Cherubin, "Toys Are Programs Too," p. 32.

video screen to TV screen: It is tempting to compare video games and children's TV as forms—both being, in a sense, authorless and made up of moderately interchangeable loops—but it's an analogy easily pushed too far, since the adrenaline hit the video-game player gets from the ever imminent danger of being exploded, gobbled up, or in some fashion destroyed on screen is absent from children's TV.

75   **"of salability":** Cherubin, "Toys Are Programs Too," p. 32.

"Reagan campaign team": Ronald Brownstein and Nina Easton, *Reagan's Ruling Class* (New York: Pantheon, 1983), p. 686.

76   **"toaster with pictures":** Bernard D. Nossiter, "The F.C.C.'s Big Giveaway Show," *The Nation,* October 26, 1985, p. 402.

prime-time children's specials: "An Exclusive Interview with Peggy Charren: Telling It Like It Is!" *NATPE Programmer,* May-June 1985, p. 20; Harry F. Waters, "Kidvid: A National Disgrace," *Newsweek,* October 17, 1983, p. 81.

network children's series: Dave Zimmerman, "Where Are You, Captain Kangaroo?" *USA Today,* December 22, 1983.

of the U.S. toy market: Stephen J. Sansweet, "It's Business as Usual at Toy Fair: Mattel Is Breaking Seasonal Pattern," *Wall Street Journal,* February 7, 1985.

"versus evil": Ibid.

77   **"money out there":** Morrie Gelman, " 'He-Man' Leads Way for First-run Fare," *Electronic Media,* February 2, 1984, p. 32.

ratings records: Walt Belcher, "Cartoon Wars," *Electronic Media,* January 3, 1985, p. 6.

countries as well: Gelman, p. 32.

"and back again": Sari Horwitz, "Toy Makers Look to '85," *Washington Post,* December 1984.

"the power": Mattel marketing film seen by author at 1985 American International Toy Fair.

78 in 1984–85: Rushworth M. Kidder, "Show-length Ads: Why Johnny Wants a GoBot," *Christian Science Monitor,* May 20, 1985.

"that ever Wuz": Walt Disney/Hasbro ad in *Licensing International,* February-March 1985.

"in the marketplace": Lucasfilm ad in *Licensing Today,* February 1985, pp. 46–47.

under development: John Wilke et al., "Are the Programs Your Kids Watch Simply Commercials?" *Business Week,* March 25, 1985, p. 53: Peggy Charren, ACT statement released on April 11, 1985.

Saturday morning kids' shows: Cherubin, "Toys Are Programs Too," p. 32.

"rich profits": Taft Merchandising Group, "Kids Are Our Business," ad in *Toy & Hobby World,* February 1985.

79 off in 1985: " 'Wuzzles' to 'Insectoids' Come Alive at Toy Fair," *New York Times,* February 11, 1985; Peter Francese, "Santa Will Be Carrying a Big Bag of Toys," *Advertising Age,* December 20, 1984, p. 30.

"as recently as 1978": James P. Forkan, "TV Toy Licensing Picking Up Speed in '85," *Advertising Age,* March 4, 1985, p. 38; Penny Gill, "Licensing Keeps on Selling Through '86," *Toy & Hobby World's Toy Fair Report,* February 10, 1986, p. 54.

toy launch ever: Wilke et al., "Are the Programs Your Kids Watch Simply Commercials?" p. 53.

five years earlier: Susan Craighead, "Cabbage Patch Dolls and Robots Thrive, But Otherwise There's No Joy in Toyland," *Wall Street Journal,* September 17, 1985.

"just for her": Hallmark Cards ad in *Licensing Today,* February 1985, p. 49.

80 start-up backing: Sansweet, "It's Business as Usual."

50 percent in 1985: Craighead, "Cabbage Patch Dolls," p. 4.

TV show were girls: "He-Man, a Princely Hero, Conquers the Toy Market," *New York Times,* December 15, 1984.

81 targeted for Saturday morning: David Rubel, "On Kids' TV, the Show Is the Commercial, the Commercial Is the Show," *Pacific News Service,* January 6, 1984.

in question: Pamela G. Hollie, "Cereal Makers Woo Children," *New York Times,* March 27, 1985.

81 – 82 what else in mind: Joanne V. Cleaver, "Licensed Cereals Turn Soggy," *Advertising Age,* June 6, 1985, p. 24.

82   in-store events a year: "Character Kicks and Property Promos," *Toys, Hobbies & Crafts,* August 1984, p. 48.

"film's release": " 'Bears' to Provide Gloss for Goldwyn," *Variety,* March 6, 1985, p. 164.

83   Care Bear products: James P. Forkan, "LBS Seeking to Channel Kiddievid into VCRs," *Advertising Age,* June 6, 1985, p. 62.

program-length commercials: Aljean Harmetz, " 'Kid Vid,' A Growing Market," *New York Times,* September 30, 1985.

president of Filmation: Aljean Harmetz, "Video Alters Economics of Movie Animation," *New York Times,* May 1, 1985.

rental store as well: Forkan, "LBS," p. 62.

87   "carriers is planned": Steve Weiner and Bob Davis, "It's Business as Usual at Toy Fair: Violence for Boys, Love for Girls," *Wall Street Journal,* February 7, 1985.

"rebels for weapons": James P. Forkan, "Counterterrorists vs. Toy-Counter Terrorists," *Advertising Age,* May 5, 1986, p. 6.

92   "Cataclysm began": "Sectaurs, Warriors of Symbion," a Coleco brochure.

93   critical, parental: Interestingly enough, though, Action for Children's Television, who have been the most effective advocates of children's interests on TV, have never joined in this reaction, which they consider, at best, beside the point.

94   than speculation: George Gerbner in a TV-effects study of real value concludes soberly that "schoolchildren who watch more television are also more likely to exhibit violence-related fears . . . more likely to mistrust people and believe that others 'mostly just look out for themselves.' . . . One correlate of television viewing is a heightened and unequal sense of danger and risk in a mean and selfish world." This study, however, has been contested and is only partially based on a viewing of children's TV as opposed to the prime-time shows children watch. George Gerbner, Catherine J. Ross, and Edward Zigler, eds., *Child Abuse: An Agenda for Action* (New York: Oxford University Press, 1980), pp. 239–48.

95   "rescue their friend": Walt Belcher, "TV Cartoons for Children Are No Longer Just Entertainment," *Chicago Tribune,* November 26, 1984.

96   "better than one": Russell Miller, "Bugs and Hugs," *In These Times,* April 10–16, 1985, p. 24.

"family and friends": Ad in *Licensing Today,* February 1985, between pp. 10–11.

97   "selling emotions": Miller, "Bugs and Hugs," p. 23.

"bring us together": Promo film seen by author at 1985 American International Toy Fair.

100 teenagers do watch: One study of college students at Radford University in Virginia found that 82.1% of a 1,529-student sample spent some portion of at least some Saturday mornings watching TV, while 13.8%

watched the cartoons every Saturday. Lenore Skenazy, "Cartoons on Campus," *Advertising Age*, April 4, 1985, p. 36.

flow of ads: Given the interchangeable nature of the programs, prosocial messages, and ads on the three networks on Saturday morning, it does not matter that, in fact, children seem to be notorious channel flippers— aided and abetted by the coming of remote control channel changers. According to one recent study of fifth- and tenth-grade children, watching parts of two shows in the same time period is a fairly common occurrence —a phenomenon even more common among children with access to cable, which would change the following analysis somewhat. See Sally Bedell Smith, "New TV Technologies Alter Viewing Habits," *New York Times*, October 9, 1985.

103 $60,000: Sandra Salmans, "Why Saturday Morning Is One Big Ghetto," *New York Times*, August 25, 1985.

presweetened: Michael B. Rothenberg, "The Role of Television in Shaping the Attitudes of Children," *Journal of the American Academy of Child Psychiatry* 22, no. 1 (January 1983): 86.

piece of clothing: Rita Weisskoff, "Current Trends in Children's Advertising," *Journal of Advertising Research*, February-March 1985, p. RC-13. I added "fast food" to the list.

period in 1983: Eugene Gilligan, "DuRona Adds Magic Touch to Toy Ads," *Playthings*, February 1985, p. 114.

for the networks: Bennet Minton, "A Market Explodes," *View*, July 1984, pp. 30–31.

104 the shows themselves: Robert M. Liebert, Joyce N. Sprafkin, and Emily S. Davidson, *The Early Window: Effects of Television on Children and Youth* (New York: Pergamon Press, 1982), pp. 142–43.

350,000 ads: Rothenberg, "The Role of Television," p. 86.

108 *Marriott Inn:* Author interview with Peggy Charren.

twenty-seven per week: Geoffrey Tooth, "Why Children's TV Turns Off So Many Parents," *U.S. News & World Report*, February 18, 1985, p. 65.

weekend mornings: Weisskoff, "Current Trends," p. RC-13.

108 – 109 "eat cable": Charren interview.

MUSIC VIDEOS: *The Look of the Sound*, BY PAT AUFDERHEIDE

112 aesthetic-in-formation: Critical work on postmodern aesthetics is rapidly consolidating, and among surveys are Hal Foster, ed., *The Anti-Aesthetic: Essays on Postmodern Culture* (Port Townsend, Wash.: Bay Press, 1983); Dominick LaCapra, *Rethinking Intellectual History: Texts, Contexts, Language* (Ithaca, N.Y.: Cornell University Press, 1983); and Brian Wallis, ed., *Art After Modernism: Essays on Rethinking Representation* (New Museum of Contemporary Art/Godine, 1985). The essay by Fredric Jameson,

"Postmodernism, or the Cultural Logic of Late Capitalism," in *New Left Review* 146 (July–August 1984): 53–92, and Terry Eagleton's response, "Capitalism, Modernism and Postmodernism," *New Left Review* 152 (July–August 1985): 60–73, provide a particularly appropriate context for this discussion.

has suggested: Jameson, "Postmodernism," p. 72.

as it seems: In the unpublished essay "MTV Wants You: A Critique of the Dire Straits Song 'Money for Nothing,' " State University of New York at Buffalo graduate student in literature Bill Brown cites Marcus and builds an argument that the terms of the music video medium conquer the critical elements.

critic Marsha Kinder: Marsha Kinder, "Music Video and the Spectator: Television, Ideology and Dream," *Film Quarterly,* Fall 1984, pp. 2–15.

Margaret Morse: Margaret Morse, "Rock Video: Synchronising Rock Music and Television," in *Fabula,* no. 5 (1985): 13–32.

114 **its function:** The history of music video is described by several authors with an accuracy missing in much reporting on music video in the special section "Midsection: Rock 'n' Video," *Film Comment,* August 1983.

115 **in two years:** This hesitation in the new format was tracked not only in weekly trades such as *Billboard* and *Broadcasting* at the time, but has become part of the lore of MTV, available in its own press kits—e.g., MTV press kit, 1985. A more jaundiced overview of the same history is in Steven Levy, "Ad Nauseam: How MTV Sells Out Rock and Roll," *Rolling Stone,* December 8, 1983, pp. 30ff.

on the air: MTV press kits herald MTV's own figures, and trade publications constantly report the status of the ratings, effects on the record industry, and events including music video awards—e.g., "Warner Takes MTV, Nickelodeon Public," *Broadcasting,* June 25, 1984, p. 58; "MTV Explains Fourth Quarter," *Broadcasting,* February 4, 1985, p. 10; "Nielsen Report," *Broadcasting,* May 6, 1985, p. 97; "Vidclips Pay Off in Record Promotion," *Variety,* March 17, 1985, pp. 83ff.; "Music Video Festival Competition Gets Hot on the French Coast," *Variety,* July 25, 1984; "MTV Rockits Radio City," *On Cable,* October 1984, pp. 15ff.

nationally and internationally: For the ratings dispute, see, for instance, "MTV Questions Nielsen," *Broadcasting,* January 13, 1986, p. 12.

hot tape items: The problem of pirating is also an endemic feature in the trade papers. While on a 1985 tour with "La Otra Cara: The Other Face," an exhibit of American independent feature films, this author found MTV available on broadcast channels in several Latin American countries, including Panama, where a local publicity agency had mounted a contest to produce nationalist music videos in an attempt to counterprogram. TV officials often cheerfully admitted the pirating of signals, saying that until the United States regularized its own copyright arrangements, Latin

American corporations would continue to pirate a highly popular service. On music video's popularity in the Soviet Union, see "Moscow Joins the Video Revolution," *Washington Post,* Janaury 12, 1986.

116 **might otherwise occupy:** The Turner fiasco was trumpeted in daily and trade media, including, e.g., "Music Video: How Much Is Enough?" *Variety,* August 29, 1984; "Ted Turner Takes on MTV," *Rolling Stone,* October 25, 1984, p. 46; "The Music Dies for Turner," *Broadcasting,* December 3, 1984, pp. 41ff.

and Mark Crispin Miller: See, for instance, "Music Video's Not Very 'HOT' as Group W Pulls the Plug," *Variety,* August 1, 1984, p. 44; "The Beat Goes on TV: Music Videos, Sign-on to Sign-off," *Broadcasting,* June 25, 1984, pp. 50ff.

next few years: Estimates change virtually with the weather, and are tracked closely by, among other trade groups, the newly formed Association of Music Video Broadcasters, headed by the former publisher of *Billboard* magazine, Mort Nasitir. Overviews of the phenomenon as it emerged can be found in "Local Stations Moving to 24-Hour Music Video," *New York Times,* September 4, 1984; and "More Indie TV Stations Use Vidclips as Staple; MTV Exclusivity Hurts," *Variety,* March 27, 1985, p. 88.

in video stores: A survey of music videos in video rental and sales stores, and coverage of them in such retail video magazines as *Video Review* and *Video Times,* suggests their importance. See also "Homevid Suppliers Start Looking Seriously at Music Programs: Rising Percentage of Market," *Variety,* March 27, 1985, p. 86.

convention in 1985: "RC Cola Sponsors Mandrell Music Video," *Advertising Age,* November 11, 1985, p. 74; "Media Beat," *In These Times,* February 6–12, 1986, p. 14.

117 **by commercials:** Susan Spillman's "TV Advertisers All Want Their MTV," *On Cable,* May 1985, is a useful overview of a process being tracked weekly in the trades.

wondrous leisure world: Advertisers are self-conscious in their attempt to make contact with young people in their own language; see, for instance, "Honda Rides Music Videos into Advertising," *Advertising Age,* July 19, 1984, p. 46; "Okidata Aims Printer at Music Video Set," *Advertising Age,* December 31, 1984, p 18E; "Honda Commercial Walks on the Wild Side," *Advertising Age,* June 20, 1985, p. 38.

118–19 **perpetual show:** Pittman and MTV promotion executive John Sykes have been extensively interviewed, and precisely the same quotes can be found in a variety of sources. For instance, see Steven Levy, "Ad Nauseam," pp. 30ff.; "Syke-edelic: 'Mr. Excitement' Puttin' on the Hits," *Advertising Age,* January 10, 1985, pp. 1ff.; and MTV press kits.

120 **Rock 'n' America:** TV reviewers now must cover such programs—e.g., John J. O'Connor, "Music Video Is Here, With a Vengeance," *New York*

Times, July 1, 1984, on broadcast programs. Sykes in "Syke-edelic," pp. 1ff., discusses the set styles. In "Rock Video Forecast, Hot But Cloudy," *Village Voice,* October 16, 1984, pp. 82ff., Michael Shore (author of the useful *Rolling Stone Book of Rock Video*) praises *Rock 'n' America* VJ Rick Ducommon, "the fat boy in his rumpus room basement whose Mittyesque telegenic forays are always interrupted by his upstairs mother." *Rock 'n' America* thus tries to keep the world-of-one's-own within the bounds of a program that ends by using mom as the enforcer of real time.

Barron wryly: Barron was addressing an audience at the Women Make Movies festival, held April 1985 at the American Film Institute; the festival sponsored a rock video panel featuring women producers, an event reflecting the importance of the form for emerging filmmakers.

of the spectator: Kinder, "Music Video," pp. 2–15.

a world: Morse, "Rock Video," pp. 13–32.

122   **more popular:** One of the strongest motivations behind the formation of the Association of Music Video Broadcasters was to create contract standards in the industry, as a result of repeated experiences with cost overruns the studios or performers refused to pay.

     connotative icons: For a refresher on the differences among symbols, icons, and signs, one can refer to Jonathan Culler, *Ferdinand de Saussure* (Harmondsworth, Middlesex, England: Penguin, 1976).

123   **"exotic clothes":** McClaren's interview with rock reviewer Richard Harrington of the *Washington Post,* on February 3, 1985, appeared in the "Style" section, devoted to fashion and trends.

124   **in rotation:** In an interview in February 1985, Sayles discussed production style and problems with this author.

127   **in music videos:** The NCTV's charges were, as NCTV's complaints usually are, well reported in entertainment media, and in the mainstream press, including "Measuring Violence in Rock 'n' Roll Videos," *New York Times,* December 15, 1984, and "TV's Violence Grows More Ingenious," *New York Times,* January 13, 1985, Sunday Arts and Leisure section.

128   **"unemotional excitement":** *New York Times,* January 13, 1985, Sunday Arts and Leisure section.

129   **pointed out:** "Video Radio," *Film Comment,* August 1983, pp. 35ff.

131   **Bruce Springsteen:** Jon Pareles, "Work Hard, Play Hard," *Rolling Stone Yearbook,* 1984. Also on the power of music videos to set the pace of music and fashion, see Kenneth Turan, "The Art of Revolution," and Gerri Hirshey, "The Lure of a Look," both in *Rolling Stone Yearbook,* 1984.

     musical ability: "Joe Jackson Puts Down Video, Contending It Has Hurt Music," *Variety,* June 13, 1984, p. 71.

132   **on the margins:** Steven Levy's "Ad Nauseam" reviews the charges of racism, raised among other places in a *San Francisco Examiner* feature titled "Where Are the Blacks on MTV?" Video jockey Donnie Simpson of

Washington, D.C.-produced *Video Soul* (the Black Entertainment Television music video program) also provided background information and perspective in an interview with the author conducted in May 1985.

on video programs: "Currents: Video," *Advertising Age,* January 31, 1985, p. 13.

133   on low budgets: See "Hollywood Goes to the MTV's," *Newsweek,* August 6, 1984, p. 74. Peter Ochiogrosso provided an excellent overview on the pretensions and trends of video-influenced mainstream films in "Video Dreams: MTV Goes to the Movies," *Village Voice,* July 31, 1984, pp. 36ff.

popular art: Jon Lewis provides a careful analysis of the film in "Purple Rain: Music Video Comes of Age," *Jump/Cut* no. 30 (no date), pp. 1ff.

Miami Vice: This television program virtually pulled itself out of the ratings sewer it was in during its first few months with the hype generated by its claims to innovative use of the television form. Emily Benedek, "Inside *Miami Vice:* Sex and Drugs and Rock & Roll Ambush Prime-time TV," *Rolling Stone,* March 28, 1985, pp. 56ff., offers a résumé of the show's hype as well as its manipulations of the form.

134   of her business: Hirshey, "The Lure of a Look," describes this trend at length, and it is tracked by such fashion trades as *Women's Wear Daily. Advertising Age* regularly features video fashion news—e.g., "Videos Fashioned as Stylish Medium," August 13, 1984, p. 3; "Rock Videos Become Designers' New Runways," September 20, 1984; "New York's Rock Fashion Prince," February 28, 1985. It also attracts attention on the business pages of the elite dailies—e.g., "This Man's Cashing in on Wild, Crazy Clothes," Washington Business section, *Washington Post,* June 25, 1984; and "Slick Videos Selling Fashions," *New York Times,* May 4, 1985.

"subliminal advertising": "Ads Against Wall in Video Background," *Advertising Age,* February 28, 1985.

for its style: Noted in Susan Spillman, "TV Advertisers All Want Their MTV."

134–35   in 1984: "Why Are All the Politicians Watching Rock Video?" *New York Times,* April 19, 1985; "Music Videos Gaining Role in Political Races," *New York Times,* May 18, 1985. Organizers of independent voter registration drives in August and September 1984 in New York City at meetings this author attended expressed both hope and frustration in using music videos for public service announcements.

135   any guide: Jay Rosen explores this theme in a fascinating essay, "The President Who Wasn't There," *Channels of Communications* January-February 1986, pp. 13ff. "TV's most potent images are not dreamed up by clever executives but drawn out from a semiconscious world where the audience's awareness of itself and the medium's awareness of the audience mingle and merge," he notes. "The reason 'nothing sticks to the Presi-

dent,' as the press often complains, is that the President is not really there. He is here, with us and our urges."

CAR COMMERCIALS AND *MIAMI VICE: "We Build Excitement,"* BY TODD GITLIN

I wish to thank Warren Belasco, Daniel C. Hallin, Lisa Heilbronn, Mark Crispin Miller, Michael Schudson, and especially Ruth Rosen for comments, and Jerome Karabel for demographic counsel.

136 **"genuine attachments":** Don DeLillo, *Running Dog* (New York: Vintage, 1979), p. 91.

141 **crystallize:** For the concept of popular culture as a selective crystallization of popular moods, see Todd Gitlin, *Inside Prime Time* (New York: Pantheon, 1983), pp. 29–30.

     tiny utopia: For the concept of popular culture as part utopia I am indebted to Fredric Jameson, "Reification and Utopia in Popular Culture," *Social Text*, no. 1 (Winter 1979): 130–48.

142 **Marchand:** See, for example, *Advertising the American Dream* (Berkeley: University of California Press, 1985), pp. 277, 309, 361.

143 **agencies:** I am indebted to Mark Crispin Miller's research on advertising, for his forthcoming book.

     archetypes: See Richard Slotkin, *Regeneration Through Violence* (Middletown, Conn.: Wesleyan University Press, 1973); Will Wright, *Sixguns and Society* (Berkeley: University of California Press, 1975).

144 **Fallows:** James Fallows, "The Case Against Credentialism," *Atlantic Monthly*, December 1985, pp. 49–67.

146 **early in the twentieth century:** Leo Lowenthal, "The Triumph of Mass Idols," in *Literature, Popular Culture, and Society* (Palo Alto, Calif.: Pacific Books, 1968), pp. 109–40.

150 **J. Walter Thompson:** Bill Lane of J. Walter Thompson, quoted in *Rock & Roll Confidential*, December 1985, p. 3.

151 **Leonard:** John Leonard, "State of the Art: The Cool Heat of 'Miami Vice,' " *New York*, February 25, 1985, pp. 39–41.

     $429 a week: Leonard, "State of the Art," p. 41.

153 **Tartikoff:** Michael Pollan, "The 'Vice' Look," *Channels*, July-August 1985, p. 26.

154 ***Hill Street Blues:*** On the ideological loading of *Hill Street Blues*, see Gitlin, *Inside Prime Time*, chap. 14.

155 **virtually every series:** Lisa Heilbronn, "Coming Home a Hero: The Changing Image of the Vietnam Vet on Prime-Time Television," *Journal of Popular Film and Television* 13, no. 1 (Spring 1985): 25–30.

157 **"waning of affect":** Fredric Jameson, "Postmodernism, or The Cultural Logic of Late Capitalism," *New Left Review*, no. 146 (July-August 1984): 61.

PAGE

158 **Warhol:** Ibid., pp. 59–60.

158–59 **great data bank:** See Gitlin, *Inside Prime Time,* pp. 77–81.

159 **"structure of feeling":** Raymond Williams, *Marxism and Literature* (New York: Oxford University Press, 1977), pp. 128–35, and *Politics and Letters* (London: NLB, 1979), pp. 156–66.

   "impulses, restraints": Williams, *Politics and Letters,* p. 159.

   Lasch: See Lasch, *The Culture of Narcissism* (New York: Norton, 1978), and especially his *The Minimal Self* (New York: Norton, 1984).

160 **triumphant:** Even Fred Pfeil, who argues in an interesting response to Jameson ("Making Flippy-Floppy: Postmodernism and the Baby-Boom PMC," in Mike Davis, Fred Pfeil, and Michael Sprinker, eds., *The Year Left* [London: Verso, 1985], pp. 268–95) that postmodernism is specifically the creation of the baby-boom professional-managerial class, takes for granted that postmodernism is the "cultural dominant."

161 **"real hope":** Secretary of State Caspar Weinberger's phrase. *Los Angeles Times,* December 24, 1984.

PRIME TIME: *Deride and Conquer,* BY MARK CRISPIN MILLER

184 **"we take for granted":** Quoted in the *New York Times,* July 7, 1985.

189 **as any fashion magazine:** For some background on the "advertorial," see the "Advertising" column in the *New York Times,* December 7, 1984. A report on the "magalogue" appears in the *Washington Post,* August 14, 1985.

   "a bonus—not an intrusion": "Advertising," *New York Times,* September 18, 1984.

   "to like the advertising": "U.S. Spots Taking on a Foreign Accent," *Advertising Age,* October 11, 1984, p. 60.

   "and racketball courts": "Marketing," *Wall Street Journal,* November 15, 1984.

189–90 **"children's cable channel":** "Cable TV Attracts More Ads, But It Still Needs Fine Tuning," *Wall Street Journal,* February 13, 1986.

190 **"and Perry Como":** "Television," *Tide,* March 26, 1955, p. 56.

   "of the television fraternity": Bob Shanks, *The Cool Fire: How to Make It in Television* (New York: Norton, 1976), p. 98.

191 **"in a commercial sandwich":** Todd Gitlin, *Inside Prime Time* (New York: Pantheon, 1983), p. 92.

   "it seems especially engrossing": "Executive Summary," Television Audience Assessment, Inc. (Boston, 1984).

192 **"the maturing of the medium":** "NBC's Head Says TV Viewers Spurn Quality Shows," *New York Times,* September 30, 1984.

193 **openly, insistently, and garishly:** For an extended discussion of this point, see Erik Barnouw, *The Sponsor: Notes on a Modern Potentate* (New York: Oxford University Press, 1978), p. 115 et passim.

199   **were in fact passé:** C. Wright Mills, *White Collar* (New York: Oxford University Press, 1951), p. 77. This classic study should be read through carefully by anyone interested in finding out just what the fifties sitcom, and much of the decade's mass advertising, were intended—whether consciously or not—to deny.

200   **to slip in every case:** My use of the epithet "Dad" is determined, not by a TV character's paternity, but by his symbolic power as a figure of possible authority. Although childless, Ralph Kramden may still be deemed a Dad because of his relationship to us who watch him.

203   **"same villainy as the men":** " 'Dynasty' Creators Jump to Defend It," *New York Times,* November 26, 1984.

206   **hawk face of Robert Young:** The trajectory of Robert Young's TV career offers some oblique corroboration of the historical argument offered here. Years after his service as TV's most intimidating Dad, Young returned to play the title role in *Marcus Welby, M.D.,* which ran from 1969 to 1975. Through the sixties and seventies, TV often allowed in its hospitals and clinics some of that fatherly authority which was now missing from the sitcom households. In this second paternal incarnation, Young played a father figure considerably more soothing than Jim Anderson had been. So soothing did Young seem, in fact, that he was hired, in 1977, by General Foods to appear as TV's pitchman for Sanka. Now there was very little left, in Young's persona, of that implied steeliness which had made *Father Knows Best* so disquieting. In the Sanka ads, he would usually appear as a sort of chuckling enforcer, keeping everyone mellowed out with plenty of decaffeinated hits. In any case, Young was, despite his tranquilizing function, ultimately still too Dad-like a figure for advertising in the eighties: General Foods dropped him in 1982, claiming to need "less of an authority figure" for the campaign.

207   **praises of Prudential-Bache:** Higgins not only sings the praises of this particular advertiser, but also writes melodies for a number of other corporate clients, as a partner in a three-man jingle-writing company in Hollywood.

       "a full 30-minute show": "Advertising," *New York Times,* November 12, 1985.

217   **excluding nature absolutely:** It is pertinent to mention here the disappearance, since the sixties, of the sitcom pastoral, exemplified by such shows as *Mayberry R.F.D.* and *Green Acres.*

219   **in parodic commercials:** TV's antipatriarchal thrust has not only eliminated the cowboy, but has also darkened the image of the businessman: Dad's original vocation (insofar as one could ascertain it) has been denigrated along with Dad himself. On TV, one study pointed out in 1982, "businessmen are cast as evil and selfish, social parasites." Predictably, such characterization has been lamented publicly by prominent members of the business world. For instance, Herbert Schmertz, Mobil's vice pres-

ident for public affairs, has warned that such depictions can do serious damage to American business interests. In January of 1984, Schmertz "suggested," according to the *Times,* "that exporting American television's 'crazy-crooked-businessman shows' helps fan foreign suspicions 'of American institutions, particularly the multinational corporations.' "

Such warnings are unnecessary, since TV's "crazy-crooked-businessman" has the quieting effect of making the faceless corporate presence seem all the more trustworthy and benign: Dow and Du Pont (for instance) seem perfectly well meaning and legitimate compared to J. R. Ewing. In any case, TV's automatic deprecation of all father figures—the businessman included—works to the ultimate benefit of Mobil and the other multinationals behind TV, for the reasons already given. See "On TV and in Novels, the Bad Guy Sells," *New York Times,* April 15, 1984.

225 " 'and enjoy it anyway' ": George Peppard made this remark on an installment of *Evening Magazine* broadcast in December 1985. Glen A. Larson is quoted in "David Hasselhoff of *Knight Rider,*" *TV Guide,* June 25, 1983, p. 40.

228 "is also necessary, indispensable": "What TV Means to Our College Students," *TV Guide,* January 7, 1984, p. 8.

THE CONTRIBUTORS

PAT AUFDERHEIDE, a critic of popular culture and a social historian, is currently cultural editor of *In These Times*. Her many articles have appeared in *Harper's*, the *Village Voice*, *American Film*, *Film Comment*, and the *Columbia Journalism Review*, among other journals.

TOM ENGELHARDT, an editor at Pantheon Books, is the author of *Beyond Our Control: America in the Mid-Seventies*, and has written for *Harper's*, *Mother Jones*, *New West*, and other magazines. He spent many hours, while researching this piece, hiding his tapes of children's television from his daughter.

TODD GITLIN is associate professor of sociology and director of the mass communications program at the University of California, Berkeley. He is a co-author of *Uptown: Poor Whites in Chicago*, and the author of *The Whole World Is Watching*, *Inside Prime Time*, and a forthcoming book on the New Left of the 1960s. His first attempts to puzzle out television were parodies of *Perry Mason* and *Have Gun, Will Travel*, written at the Bronx High School of Science.

DANIEL C. HALLIN teaches communication and political science at the University of California, San Diego. He is the author of *The "Uncensored War": The Media and Vietnam*, and many articles on the politics of news. He is currently writing a book on news coverage of Central America, and collaborating with European researchers on a study of television coverage of the Reagan-Gorbachev summit in the United States, Italy, Britain, and Sweden. Professor Hallin received his Ph.D. in political science in 1980 from the University of California, Berkeley.

MARK CRISPIN MILLER is an assistant professor in the writing seminars at the Johns Hopkins University and director of the Film

Studies Program in the department. He has written on television and other aspects of mass culture for the *New Republic,* the *New York Review of Books,* the *Atlantic,* the *Nation,* and other publications. He is now completing a book on American advertising.

RUTH ROSEN, associate professor of history at the University of California, Davis, is the editor of *The Maimie Papers* and the author of *The Lost Sisterhood: Prostitution in America: 1900–1918.* She is currently working on a history of contemporary feminism in the United States.

MICHAEL SORKIN is a writer and architect who lives in New York. He has written about television for (to cite only those periodicals beginning with V) *Vanity Fair, Vogue,* and the *Village Voice* (for which he is also architecture critic). Currently visiting professor at Cooper Union, he has also taught at Yale, Columbia, and the universities of Pennsylvania, Texas, and Illinois, among others. He awaits the call to Hollywood.